# RAPE INCEST BATTERY

## Women Writing Out the Pain

# Rape, Incest, Battery: Women Writing Out the Pain

Miriam Kalman Harris • Editor

TCU Press • Fort Worth, Texas

Library of Congress Cataloging-in-Publication Data

Rape, Incest, Battery! Women Writing Out the Pain/ edited by Miriam K. Harris
p. cm.
ISBN 0-87565-230-1 (pbk. : alk. paper)
1. Sexual abuse victims' writings, American. 2. Sexual abuse victims—Literary collections. 3. American literature—Women authors. 4. Abused women—Literary collections. 5. American literature—20th century. I. Harris, Miriam K.
PS508.S48 R37 2000
810.8"0355—dc21 00-023462

Drawings by Shereen Ramprashad. These drawings are a visual diary of the artist's psychological journey from "tense fragmentation to relaxed healing" as she confronted the painful memories of her past. Ramprashad, a Canadian artist, was inspired by *The Courage to Heal: A Guide for Women Survivors of Child Sexual Abuse* (Ellen Bass and Laura Davis, editors, 3rd ed., New York, NY: Harper, 1994). Used by permission of the artist.

Permissions
Patti Tana: "A Name and a Face," *Matrix: Women's Newsmagazine;* also, *What's a Nice Girl Like You Doing in a Relationship Like This?* Kay Marie Porterfield, editor. "Beware of Lovers," *Ask the Dreamer Where the Night Begins.* "Dark Pages," *How Odd This Ritual of Harmony.* "Gifts," *Wetlands.*
Carolyn Page: "The Judge," *Life on the Line: Selections on Words and Healing.*
Janet Jonathon: "A Bar Scene," *He Hits: Hope for Battered Women.*
Lynne Conroy: "Zone Documents," *Zone Magazine* . "Slings," *Athena.*
"Jane": "Take your Toy Cars and . . . ." *Athena.*
Victoria McCabe: "What the Bride Saw," *The Louisville Review.*
Pat Falk: "To Eros," *Long Island Quarterly.*
Miriam Kalman Harris: "Silent Woman Speaks," *The Beltane Papers: A Journal of Women's Mysteries.*
Margaret Atwood: "Two-Headed Poems," *Selected Poems II.*
Ann Ruth Ediger Baehr: "The School is Gone," *Long Island Quarterly*
Joannie Whitebird: "Breakfast with Father," *Buffalo Press.*

*Book and cover design/ Margie Adkins Graphic Design*

This book is dedicated to future generations
that they may learn to live with one another
non-violently, and to my children

Pepi H. and James R. Wucher
Deborah M. and Earl K. Harris

*the next generation*

The minute you leave, I will raise every blind,
Part every curtain, lift every window.
The house will seem immense.
It may become an orchestra.

From "Take Your Toy Cars and . . . ."
Jane (author of "Alive: A Diary")

# Contents

## Acknowledgments

This anthology owes a great debt to my training in interdisciplinary thinking at the University of Texas at Dallas with Professors Dennis Kratz, Ronald Tobias, Rainer Schulte, Robert Romanyshyn, and the late Nancy Cluck. I especially thank Professor Nancy Tuana, for her guidance into the complexities of feminist theory and Professor Robert Nelsen, for his astute insights on autobiography and on an early draft of this manuscript. Professor Timothy Redman's advice in life studies refines and elevates my work. Dr. Mary Jane Colpi believed in this manuscript and even referred to it in her dissertation—an endorsement of confidence at a time when publishers turned deaf ears.

My gratitude to friends and colleagues for their insight and support extends to the following professors: Dale Spender for her seminars at the University of London on women's life stories; Kenneth Ring for his input during the early stages of collecting; Diana Scully for her expertise on the dynamics of rape; Margaret Moore for her comments during the formative stages of this project and for her friendship; and Peggy Brown for her spirit, friendship, and support.

I thank Dr. Larry Campbell for his invaluable expertise in psychiatry, and Linda Comess for hours discussing this and other writings. Their friendship makes my work more meaningful. Phyllis Prager, Sandra Schwarcz, and Saundra Snyder sustain me in times of self-doubt. Professors Janet Freedman and Mary Davidson set a model for feminist commitment to the enhancement of women's personal and professional freedom. I commemorate this same courage in the late Janet Romanyshyn. Professor Joan Weimer helped me cut the main introduction in half—profoundly improving the focus of this current version. My writing group, the MOSTs (Members of the Square Table) invigorates current projects. Thanks to Peggy Brown, Linda Steele, Kathy Williams, and Paula Grinnell.

Lynne Conroy and Patti Tana are contributors who have become friends because of our work on this project. Patti commented on many contributions, welcoming me as a guest in her home for a three-day work session. Edith Riley's expertise in art history inspired the poem that opens this anthology. Ellen Snow-Brown's prayers and continued belief that these stories "must be told" have been an inspiration through the years. Numerous journals and newsletters published my call for papers and helped locate contributors. I especially want to acknowledge the assistance of Ronald K. Jones, editor of Athena Press, Anna Belle Burleson, former editor of *Heartened* and the editors of *Poets and Writers*.

Volunteers and staff associated with the crisis intervention program all deserve kudos, especially Fay O'Boyle, Yolanda Pusey, Carol Solomon, and Lisa Little. Members of the Dallas Family Violence community gave me a crash course in networking and client services unavailable in books: Susan Bragg, Sherry Lundberg, Donna Pope, Shayla Freeman Simmons, and Lt. Bill Walsh. To my daughter Pepi Harris Wucher who transcribed the interview with Penny Freedman (Section One) I give my heartfelt thanks.

James Lee, acquisitions editor for Texas Christian University Press, embraced this book with great enthusiasm from the first moment I described it to him. Judy Alter, director, nurtured the manuscript and brought it to print with wisdom and taste. Working with them is an honor and privilege.

To thank family seems rhetorical in a volume such as this. I am grateful for my relationship with my children, Pepi and Earl and their spouses, James and Debbie, to whom I dedicate this book. The answer to the end of violence and oppression lies in future generations' responses to our revelations. Many of the insights I have into other peoples' life stories I draw from my experiences growing up in large family with five brothers. I salute my mother Frances Levy Kalman Rose for her perseverance in seeing us all into adulthood, and for the myriad stories of family she has kept alive through the years. I thank all family members who expressed continued support throughout the duration of this project, including Rhonda Harris Polishuk, Janet Harris Rice, and especially Jill Bowers Kalman, now embarking on a career in counseling.

Perhaps the most profound insights, however, I draw from the ups and downs of a long marriage. I am deeply indebted to my husband Stanley for his unquestioning support in all my professional and personal endeavors.

**A Word about the Writing Cure**

My belief in writing as a healing tool informs my choice in every selection and guides my hand in the arrangement of this wide assortment of events and life patterns with its complex network of images and themes into a unified collection. In the introduction, I expand on my ideas concerning "the writing/talking cure." I close with a story of my own, a personal experience of how writing cured one of my obsessions concerning a painful trauma leftover from childhood. Though it is not about violence, there are parallels to be found in all kinds of grieving, and in the process of recovering from unresolved pain.

My father died shortly before my tenth birthday. I have long understood his death to be the most significant event in my life and the source of crucial turning points. During my "growing-up" years following his death, I was to endure hardships and unhappiness that I would not have faced had he lived. Nevertheless, as I lived each day in the present, I had little awareness of how the trauma I suffered infused itself into my worldview and my response to obstacles I faced in young adulthood.

Finding myself married with two children in my late twenties and early thirties many of the conflicts of my earlier years returned to haunt me. Nights when I couldn't sleep, visions of worries and fears seemed to manifest as entities—not human, certainly not divine, but practically palpable—living metaphors, which would, apparition-like, dance around my bed. Voices would chant and I, hyper-alert at two or three A.M. after a full day, would climb out of bed and snuggle myself onto the L-shaped couch in our den where I would curl up in a corner to tell and retell the story of my father's death.

From beginning to end it was always the same. Images floated forth, and I would describe them; dialogues conversed, and I would enter them. I am not sure who my audience was or if they enjoyed my tale, but once it was told I would take myself back to bed. Checking on the children along the way, I would slip quietly beneath the covers careful not to wake my husband (who would have declared me insane) and sleep in peace.

In the summer of 1979, I enrolled in Ronald Tobias' fiction writing class at UTD. I found great pleasure writing short stories and signed up again in the fall. The fourth story I wrote, "And His Name Was Kalman,

Too" is the story of my father's death.[1] I knew it by heart; like liquid gold it flowed off my fingers and onto the page. The class read it; someone cried. After several revisions I considered it finished and put it away.

Though occasionally I would pull it out and submit it for publication, until recently it was consistently rejected. But that didn't matter. Writing it cured me: I never told the story again. And I rarely suffer from insomnia. ■

# Introduction

This book emerges at the intersection of three paths my life has taken: in literature, in counseling, and in health care. As an adult with a young family, I enrolled at the University of Texas at Dallas where I developed an interest in modern literature, experimental writing, and first-person narratives, which soon merged with an awakening passion for feminism and women's studies. After I finished my M.A. I taught English and humanities, wrote essays and book reviews focusing on women's literature, started a novel and a biographical project, but I felt frustrated by a need to work actively in an area concerned with women's issues. To fill that gap in my life, I volunteered in the Battered Woman's Emergency Intervention Project at Parkland Hospital in Dallas. After six months, I was hired as the project coordinator.

My decision to turn my experience at Parkland into a book reflects my commitment to women's issues and literature and brings my life full circle. In my youth, when I went to college the first time around, I became a dental hygienist. Because of my training and practice in this health-care field, I felt comfortable in a hospital setting and in one-on-one dialogues with patients who accessed our service and with clients in the counseling programs and shelters where I conducted workshops on journal writing.

The women who worked as volunteers and the staff who supported our efforts were some of the most courageous and remarkable people I have ever known. Consequently, my activities with the program provided some of the richest and most rewarding experiences in my professional career. Although the program closed because of inadequate funding, this book celebrates the lives that touched mine and ignited the creative spark that resulted in this anthology. The voices of the women who told their stories in the emergency room echo in these pages. As we intervened in their lives, they intervened in ours. Their memory inspires this book.

Although the germination of this anthology centered on battered women and family violence, I enlarged its concept to include contributions that describe the myriad violences affecting women and to explore the idea of a continuum linking categories of public and private crime. Because of my literary background, I recognized a need to record and to preserve these stories for posterity as part of the body of twentieth-century women's literature. Working with abused women through the hospital program, I came to believe that all women are battered by a world that endorses sexism; all women suffer from feelings of marginalization; all women struggle to unlock their silences; all women must fight to reclaim their most precious birthright: Self-Power.

Therefore, I put out a call to professional writers, to women in shelters, and to women in academe; I advertised in literary journals and newsletters as well as those with a social science focus, asking for autobiographical writings by women surviving any kind of violence and abuse. This anthology is the result of that call—and a long process of collecting, selecting, and editing.

These autobiographical narratives and poems relate stories of battering, incest, rape, and imprisonment for murder in self-defense. Contributors range from professionals with advanced degrees to the uneducated, across a wide span of race, class, age, and ethnicity. Recognizing similarities across differences reveals a sense of the universal condition of women's experience, for that which is private and personal speaks most poignantly to others. As Anaïs Nin puts it, "The personal life, deeply lived, takes you beyond the personal" (Hinz 1975, 162).

Working with such intimate details builds deep levels of trust; as a result of consulting on these manuscripts, many of the contributors have become part of my life. Some manuscripts went through lengthy processes of revision, just to break the barriers that silenced the writer even as she struggled to speak. Other manuscripts are published with few revisions. Each woman is represented here by her best effort. Writing is a healing tool. You, the reader, will witness the process of women writing their way from oppression to autonomy in their struggle to transcend the violence in their lives.

**Beginnings**

In a tiny cubicle in the psychiatry department of the emergency room, a woman lies on the floor on a mat, facing the wall. A flimsy hospital gown is slightly open down her back. She is passive, vulnerable, lethargic. The psychiatry resident on duty called me in to consult because she heard my lecture about battered women and she thinks "this woman may be one."

The psychiatrist, who has been trained to lock this "hysterical" woman in a padded cell and leave her there to "dry out," is searching beyond the traditional, institutional solutions for a new way to deal with this problem.

"This woman" has taken an overdose of sleeping pills, but she has "dried out" and is awake if still groggy. She will not speak to me, will not show me her face. I talk anyway, ask standard questions from the case history form.

The room is a padded cell, stripped of all pretenses of comfort, warmth, care. The woman is stripped bare too. I wonder why she has been deprived of her clothing. There was a time when I would have wondered what could have brought her to this condition. But the stories I have heard since I began working in this crisis intervention program have taught me the truth about women's private lives.

Night after night and day after day women enter emergency rooms all over the country, all over the world—ripped apart by knives, shattered by gunshot, beaten and broken from head to foot with fists, chairs, lead pipes, burned with cigarettes, raped by husbands, lovers, strangers, fathers, even mothers.

Most of them want to talk. Some shout with anger, others whisper in shame. Some are in excruciating pain; others are paralyzed by fear of the man who has put them there. Will he return and finish her off? Where should she hide?

All of these women have stories to tell: stories that reverberate with images of the grotesque, as in a horror story or a Gothic novel. But these stories are true, and they have been silenced.

"This woman," whose wounds are not visible lesions, refuses to respond to my questions:

> What is your relationship to the abuser? How long have you been in this relationship? Describe the most recent incident. How did you get to the hospital? How have you been hurt in the past? Physically, verbally, sexually? What forms of abuse? Hit, Slap, Kick, Punch, Burn, Rape, Choke? Are your children safe now?

We ask these questions in a matter-of-fact tone, as if they were ordinary parts of peoples' lives—*because they are*. Women respond to the familiarity the questions evoke. Once a woman can admit such violent incidents have been happening for a long time, she feels better, she feels heard. The questions elicit frightening details.

> What types of injuries have you suffered? What forms of treatment have they required? (Surgery? Hospitalization?) What types of weapons have been used? (Guns, Knives, TV sets?) How often? Have you been deprived of Sleep, Food, Clothing, Family, Friends? Is the abuser violent toward Children, Relatives, Strangers, Animals, Furniture? What kinds of threats does he make?

Eventually, "this woman" turns over, looks up at me. Her face! For the flash of an instant, I sense she has heard something new, something she's never been asked before. Then her eyes go dull. I sense the anger behind her blank stare and feel a chill pass through me.

"She despises me," I think, "she despises my type." I understand why. She's been here before and not received the help she needed. She's had it with hospitals, nurses, doctors, social workers, and other "authorities" asking questions that have no known solutions.

I know that our program is different, that we are finding ways to help women like her. But I can't seem to reach her. She looks away, rolls over to face the wall.

Defeated, I turn to leave; but I feel something change behind me. She stands up, her face haunted, twisted in pain. In halting utterances she speaks, "Doesn't . . . matter . . . nothing ever changes." I take her hand and lead her into a different, more comfortable room with a couch, a desk, a phone. Side by side, we sit and address the questions on the questionnaire, and though she doesn't look at me again she answers each of them.

During this moment, the book you now hold was born: listening, I began to recognize that "this woman's" life is more than a case history. Her life tells a story with characters, a setting, and a plot. This is not her first visit to the emergency room, but it is the first time she has been asked direct questions about her family life framed to invite a new interpretation. She has never discussed the chain of events that repeatedly causes her to overdose. Now she moves from telling what happened to asking what she can do and how we can help. Specifically we talk about the way her husband's behavior affects her life and the lives of her children.

When the resident psychiatrist joins us, we work together to explore new possibilities. We tell her about programs designed for people in her situation; we call shelters and counseling centers. We plan what to tell her husband when he comes to pick her up. To foster change, we must make *him* understand that his wife is not "crazy"; when she overdoses on sleeping pills, it is because she is desperate. He must be taught to see how his anger, violence, and oppressive behavior erase his wife as a human being and leave her in a state of despair. As a result of our intervention, she decides to postpone shelters but to seek counseling. Tomorrow she will return home with a sense of hope and an appointment with a family violence non-residential program.

Weeks later as I walk through the outpatient area of the hospital, someone grabs my arm. I turn to see a woman in her mid-thirties. She wears blue jeans and a red T-shirt; her hair is in a ponytail, her face is scrubbed and glowing. She begins talking excitedly as if we were old friends, but both her hands grip my arm like a water skier holding onto a rope:

> Oh you made a difference things are so much better now we go places together we have fun and we even have a dog we went with the children and bought a dog he doesn't yell any more . . .

As she speaks I gradually realize she is the woman I met weeks earlier in the psychiatry department. I could not have recognized her face, animated and happy now, blank and distorted by suffering then. Indeed, I had no memory of her actual features. Invisible to herself and to her abusive husband, she had been invisible to me, unidentifiable as an individual. Now, with her life validated, her anonymity has disappeared, and the qualities that made her an individual assert themselves on her face. *Recognizing her self, she became recognizable as a self.*

Often I was privileged to witness the transformation that occurs when an interior identity becomes manifest. Nevertheless, I do not kid myself into believing that any woman's problems can end with one crisis-intervention interview. Patterns of the abuse cycle that operate in violent families are difficult to break. Most of the time, breaking the cycle means breaking free: leaving the abusive situation, for, as Lenore Walker found after years of research, "the cycle of violence, once begun, is nearly impossible to stop" (Walker 1989, 7).[1]

### Crimes Against Women

Movements to end family violence and crimes against women are rooted in the women's movement and the consciousness-raising activities of the late sixties and early seventies. As women told the truth about their lives, they began to feel less isolated. Female bonding across social circumstances revealed connections among women, and one of those connections was the violence women had experienced throughout history—and kept hidden. What began as political activism proliferated; women's voices echoed in research and scholarship across disciplines in colleges and universities throughout the country. Women's studies classrooms, rape crisis programs, women's shelters, job counseling and training, transitional housing for women on the run from abusive husbands, and programs for abused children all resulted from these studies. Today, legal advocates continue to work for changes in outmoded laws that fail to punish perpetrators or that consider the history of abuse to be inadmissible evidence in divorce and self-defense trials.

### The Way It Is Now

Nevertheless in the family and on the street, violence perpetrated by loved ones or by strangers infects our culture in epidemic proportions. A woman is raped every three minutes; a woman is beaten in her home every fifteen seconds; one of four women who seek treatment for their injuries in hospital emergency rooms is a "battered" woman. "Upward of four million American women are beaten annually by current and former male partners, and between 2,000 to 4,000 women are murdered (Department of Justice, 1994). According to a Department of Justice press release in March 1995, "more than two-thirds of violent crimes against women are committed by husbands, boyfriends, or someone known to the women. One third of all women killed in the U. S. die at the hands of a husband or boyfriend.[2]

On average each year from 1992 through 1996, about 8 in 1,000 women and 1 in 1,000 men twelve years old or over experienced a violent victimization by a current or former spouse, girlfriend, or boyfriend. Females are five to eight times more likely than males to be victimized by an intimate.[3] Women are seven times more likely to kill in self-defense than are men; however, many more women die each year at the hands of their partners than kill their abusers (Walker 1989, 46; see also Browne and Jones). On the other hand, crimes committed by women against men have declined in recent years by twelve percent. Women who murder their abusers do not act out of premeditation. These murders usually happen in the midst of a beating to fend off attacks. In fact, most of the women tell officials that they still love their abusers and meant them no harm.

The Violence Against Women Act became law on November 20, 1993, requiring state and local officials to deal more efficiently with domestic violence. Two years later, effective October 1995, the Family Protection and Domestic Violence Intervention Act brought further improvements in local policies. With these changes, police must arrest perpetrators for violence against their families, even if the victims refuse to press charges. Thus, victims fearing retaliation from their abusers no longer can be asked whether or not they want the abuser arrested (http://www.divorcesource.com/NY/DS/vanzon.html).

As the movement to identify and shelter victims of violence progressed, a paradox evolved. Women came to be seen as helplessly dependent on men or on social programs and in need of "recovery" from their fear of further violence and/or rape. "Learned helplessness" was the term coined to describe the complex response women received from social agencies, clergy, doctors and nurses, police and lawyers in the early years when too little help was available and laws failed to protect abused women. With time the term, originally intended to "blame" the agencies, became twisted in ways that "blamed the victims" as if they, rather than society, were inadequate to protect themselves.

This book seeks to set the record straight. Women who decide to make the journey from victim to survivor and beyond should not be greeted with condescending attitudes or derogatory labels. Labels that create an aura of weakness shadow the important message of strength their lives reflect. Women who rescue themselves from the effects of abuse and trauma and transcend their painful pasts should be celebrated as heroines of their own life stories.

**The Point Is . . .**

This book celebrates the images of heroic women fighting for their rights, risking their lives, rescuing their children from a violent family life, testifying, speaking out, seeking justice when they are beaten, raped, or otherwise violated.[4] The message is clear and strong: this is not a recovery book because it is not by or about sick women. Neither is this a self-help book. This collection of survival stories intends to inspire a sense of dignity, not in suffering but in the refusal to continue a life of helplessness and pain. These are courageous women who have survived the violence threatening their lives and have found their voices—voices fierce with the reality of self-insight.

**Transcendence and the Writing Cure**

Writing functions not only as catharsis of the soul but as a record of the heroic enterprise of regaining self-power. Transcendence becomes possible when, having told the story as it occurred, we begin to imagine a shift into a story of new possibilities. Transcendence proceeds through remembering, connecting, owning, and letting go, moving a violent event or pattern from inner to outer and then to inner again. Transcendence represents a turning point, a pivot in the healing process that shifts the life pattern so that a woman can move forward and away from the debilitating effects of her abuse. Ideally, then, telling these stories makes it possible to imagine other endings, alternative ways to live.

Healing through words, a writing/talking cure, is a primary focus of this book. The name Sara O. ("Baths," Section Three) recalls Anna O., the fictional name of Josef Breuer's patient, Bertha Pappenheim, the first case history in *Studies on Hysteria* (Breuer and Freud, 1895). Anna O. has come to be known as the originator of the "talking cure" which is in fact a precursor to the "writing cure" effected later in life by this same woman. Exploring the connection between the writing/telling of autobiography as a source for discovering the self, we observe how language, telling, and healing operate as part of an interrelated system.

New possibilities emerge as the woman discovers a new identity by becoming the "subject who writes" rather than the victim who waits in silence. The writing, or story, becomes her "visible representation in the world" wherein she "inscribes herself in the text" (Herndl 1988, 53). Thus, the writer moves the inner reality outside of herself where she can objectify the pain and become the activator, or subject, of her own healing because she is in charge of defining her own reality.

For Beverly Hirsch, telling her story (Section Five) moved present painful issues into the past. Writing from her cell in a Colorado women's prison, she evaluates her process:

> I think doing this has been the best therapy I could have done. I had to re-evaluate my goals and the whys. Look hard at my actions and see what was there . . . I just know that it's over, and now, you have all the emotions I have bottled up for eight years on nothing more than pieces of paper . . . so do as you choose, *I am free, at last* [editor's emphasis].

Her freedom rests on her willingness to claim responsibility for her actions. Owning the past, we move beyond its pull, not to forget but to incorporate its lessons while escaping the prison that locks us in the loop between pain and recovery, victim and survivor. We transcend. But the past informs the present and therefore molds and empowers our character. We dare not allow it to fester in silence. Nor dare we allow the past to become a blueprint for the future. The victim survives the imprint of the past, but the heroine *transcends* it and moves forward into a new life fueled by the energy it takes to own one's autobiography.

"Writing down our lives, not as lives but as stories of lives," permits us to gain possession, to claim ownership, of our pain and joy, trauma, and victory" (Jelinek 1980, 132). "All writers discover nothing has really happened until it has been written down" (Heilbrun 1990, 30).[5] But there are no miracles. In a letter accompanying her short story, "Halloween Flashback," Myrna Sharp (Section Two) conveys her clear understanding of the balm of such writing—and its limitations.

> *I would like to tell you that writing the story was cathartic and now I'm not upset anymore, but I can't. I think the process of getting it out there on the page* did *help* detoxify *the memory and alleviate some of the pain but it didn't make it go away. Unfortunately, these things never go away, [they] just get thrown in with the rest of one's experiences and life history. One just has to* get beyond *them.* (My emphasis on "detoxify" and "get beyond." Quote is from private correspondence.)

Detoxification and transcendence: healing through self-expression and communication is not an ending, but a beginning; not a closure, but a disclosure; not a recovery, but a discovery of the power of language and the power of self, the power to name the conditions of our reality and thereby take charge of our own destiny.

As Dale Spender puts it: "In order to live in this world, we must name it. Names are essential for the construction of reality, for without a name it is difficult to accept the existence of an object, an event, a feeling" (Spender 1980, 163). Breaking the silence not only releases the pain, as Patti Tana's essay demonstrates, it gives the pain "a name and a face" (Section Two). Verbalizing the activities of our past, we create our own reality that reflects our lived experience rather than the cultural one that too often denies our own perceptions.

But healing is tempered by the stigma of the language we must use to heal. To reclaim the vision of woman as hero we must, as Mary Daly suggests, "reverse the reversals" that negate our lives (Daly 1979, 47). By reclaiming our life stories, we rebel against the discrimination that labels victims and survivors as sick or helpless. We thus acknowledge the strength necessary to overcome adversity and to write our life histories in terms of success.

**Structure**

This book is divided into seven sections, arranged according to predominating themes and in the pattern a journey might take: When "Silent Woman Speaks" (Section One), she redefines the events of the past and generates a language that expresses our perceptions. Free of constrictions, "Thoughts after Rape" (Section Two) explores the continuum of sexual violence fostered by a social system that privileges male over female. Challenging that system gives rape "a name and a face" and frees us to light the "Dark Pages" (Section Three) of childhood, which all too often reveal abuse and incest. The language of metaphor shapes memories: "Grinding Axes" (Section Four) wages word battles to call attention to the price women pay for accepting society's definitions of gender. "Behind His Walls" (Section Five) explores imprisonment, both actual and metaphorical, to unlock the bars of social discrimination and prepare us for rebirth. The "strength and fragility of the rose," a symbol of "Regeneration" (Section Six) captures the moments of rebirth. "She Said NO!" (Section Seven) creates a paradoxical *affirmation* of female strength. The closing hymn, "My Name is Gloria," celebrates a "New Gloria" whose dreams of autonomy and self-definition are fulfilled.

In the following pages, life meets art; reality meets fiction; case history meets autobiography. These are women's stories as they have lived them and as they understand them to be true. These are their histories as we record them, their narratives as they dramatize them, their words as they speak them. ■

# Section One

## *Silent Woman Speaks*

Your voice unlocks my lips
parched from long years silent
Behind this mask breathes
passion
to experience a world that lives
in my imagination

I've birthed too many children
baked too many loaves of bread
I've traveled fifteen miles by foot
beyond this village
to garner strength from the Forbidden
Waters    and still I hunger
still        thirst
My reflection in the water
a mirage    I choke
on dusty roads of repetition

I know there are more worlds
to be tasted
I breathe these words
into your heart
that you my child may fly
beyond horizons

I have only
dreamed about.

Miriam Kalman Harris

Silent Woman spoke to me from a nineteenth-century Levy-Dhurmer painting: face like a mask, shrouded by a black hood and cape, against a starlit sky and shimmering ocean, two fingers frozen in a "V" against her lips. Eternal stillness. Quiet. Even her name was *Silence.* If she could speak to us across the years and miles,.what would she say? If she had a voice, what stories would she tell?

Male artists have painted women in silence, painted women into silence, for centuries. We recognize the analogy even before our conscious minds begin to interpret it. For we find these women not only in art and literary history; we have met them in restaurants, in churches and synagogues, in hospital emergency rooms. They are our mothers, our grandmothers, our aunts, sisters, friends. They are the young woman sitting next to us in class, or the professor, the secretary at the bank, the lawyer who draws your will, the doctor who draws your blood. Silent Woman is any woman who has not told the truth about her life. Silent Woman is Everywoman waiting to be heard.

James Hillman writes, "worlds are made by words" (Hillman 1983, 46). The stories in this first section capture the process of dismantling a world so as to construct a new one. Subjects and themes concentrate on the plight of battered women claiming self-determination. Several important themes surface that will resurface in subsequent sections:

- Power and control
- Institutionalized religion
- The criminal justice system
- Threat of violence
- Familial patterns
- Child abuse
- The need for political action
- The tedious process of leaving

Lenore Walker's early study of battered women identified the Battered Woman Syndrome as a "cycle of violence" reinforced by the condition of "learned helplessness," which explains "why women find it difficult to escape. . . ." (Walker 1984, 86). The three-phase cycle consists of (1) tension building, (2) explosion or battering incident, and (3) loving contrition or the "honeymoon phase."

Women describe living with the buildup of tension like "walking on eggshells" and take extreme, but futile, measures to keep the peace. Eventually, the explosion occurs. Violence can range from verbal and emotional abuse, psychological torture, and threats of physical harm all the way to beatings, rape, and murder. One woman describes a television set hurtling through the air to land at her feet (See Section Five). The honeymoon phase seals the couple's bonds. Without it there can be no long-term relationship; however, with time the periods of peace shrink or fade away altogether, while the brutality of the violence escalates. The honeymoon pretends to be real life, the good part, but after a while the women know better.

Learned helplessness becomes part of the victim's response for several reasons: First, no matter what she does, she cannot prevent or predict the violent explosion. Second, often the victim's search for help from family and friends meets with advice to "go back, try again." Third, in the recent past, social agencies were ill equipped to recognize or advise battered women. Currently, shelters and safe homes are often over-crowded, as Ellen Snow-Brown discovers when she tries to hide from her abuser (Section One).

Despite the many advances in domestic violence litigation and law enforcement, police departments in some communities are still without a domestic violence policy in place. Further complications arise when lawyers advise women to wait until the abuse becomes "more severe" so they will have "a stronger case," or when doctors accept flimsy excuses for injuries and send their patients back into the "war zone," or when clergy consider marital vows as sacred, and insist women return to their subservient roles as helpmates. Figures of authority who issue such ill-conceived, traditionally grounded advice reinforce messages of helplessness.

This section answers the common question: "Why don't they leave?" Contributors explore the complexities of escaping violent situations, which include facing financial constraints, familial patterns, community expectations, threats of murder, kidnapping, or loss of child custody. Many of these women still love their men even though they realize it is time to leave. Others have forgotten how love feels. Some leave only to be tracked down, stalked, harassed, and threatened. And these are no idle threats: one-third of women killed by violent crime were killed by husbands or boyfriends, usually *"just after declaring independence by filing for divorce and leaving home"* (Faludi 1991, xvii; author's emphasis).

Rather than asking why battered women do not leave, Section One reveals the enormous courage it takes to survive until they can leave. With these stories we celebrate the heroism of escape. As these Silent Women speak the unspeakable their voices carry us out of the void of despair into dominion of choice. ■

## Young Night

Sheryl St. Germain

1

They are standing in shadows,
he reaches under her shirt
to stroke her breast.
It is the beginning,
the young night, his small
hands that feel cool
on her breasts, her nipples
that ache like pennies
wanting to be spent.

2

Years later she will look at herself
in the mirror, hold her breasts
in her hands like gifts.
Now he says they are too large,

they do not fit my hands.
She lets them fall, and touches
her face, which he says he cannot
look at. She can't remember if
she is ugly or pretty.
There is a weight in her
like a stone moon. Mirrors
can no longer be trusted.
She cooks breakfast,
little sausages, fried in fat.

3

A closet is not such a bad place
to be. It is true there is nothing
to read, but since the light burned
out there has been nothing to read by.
There is a pile of clothes on the floor
that she sits on. The smell of it
is like a perfume of family:
the smell of greasy old slippers,
the pepper of vacuum cleaner dust,
wool and cedar, mildew, old magazine
smell, brittle as fire.

She takes her ring off
and puts it in her mouth.
Metal and soap, it is something.
She can hear the children asking

their father again where she is.
Their voices seep like razors
Under the door.

4
She forgives him and sleeps with him
again. After all, there is the rent,
the groceries, the children,
her face—what kind of job
could she get with this face.
But most of all there is his
regular presence, like a light
bulb, there is his cologne,
which she loves, on his cotton
shirts.

                    She likes to sit up
at night after everyone is asleep
and breathe in his scent on the shirt
he has worn that day. First under the arms,
then the back. She buries her
face in it.

                              A fist,
a kiss, one always follows
the other if she waits long
enough. They are the same.

5

Her friends don't understand
why she doesn't leave him.
She would point to his kindnesses,
which are many. She knows
the world is not black and white.
It is a bruise of splendid and various
blues, purples and blacks that stretches
as far as she can see. ■

**From *Open Hand/Clenched Fist***
Eliza Monroe

*Excerpts from Chapter One*

I didn't have a key of my own. I tried the front door. It was unlocked. I pushed against its heavy bulk and walked in. The forced, cold air was a welcome relief, drying my sweat and what was left of my tears. I never knew if Kip was going to greet me with affection, a lecture, a tantrum, a beating, or an eight-course meal.

The living room was dark. The burgundy velvet couch Kip was sitting on seemed to bleed into the plush, almond-colored carpet. Wearing a cotton caftan and the drawstring pants I had made for him, Kip's dark hair and eyes gleamed in the shadows. I could see the curve of his jaw highlighted behind the single spotlight that flooded the coffee table in front of him. He was leaning forward, staring at something.

I stood in the tiled foyer, thinking of how unnatural my explanation would seem. The longer I waited, the more I imagined a high-pitched, phony tone coming out of my mouth.

"You're late," Kip said loudly and firmly without looking up.

"I missed my bus." I walked close enough to the coffee table to see what it was that Kip had placed so neatly on its antique glass top: six black-and-white eight-by-tens of me half naked. Last night's photo session came back to me. My skin was extremely fair and my eyes very dark, so I had presented a difficult exercise in lighting. I remembered how frustrated Kip became when I started to get creative more quickly than he could adjust the aperture.

I took a close look at my image in the photos. I'd always thought Kip would use bustier models. I was wearing a kimono slightly off my shoulders. My head bowed, my eyes looked up at an angle. Was I somehow escaping the camera in a defiant way? In another, I was starting to pull my T-shirt over my breasts so that my arms were crossed just below my chin. I was shocked. I actually looked sexy. Kip had been my only man and for the first time I thought I could be desirable to other men. I thought of Drew, a boy I had snubbed when I was nineteen. Would Drew find me attractive after all this time?

"Why didn't you call if you were going to be late, Sweetie?" Kip asked, still looking down.

"The phone was out of order." It was the first time I'd ever lied to Kip and I felt chilled all over. But I knew better than to tell the truth. "The enlargements turned out pretty good," I said. "I've been dying to see them."

I couldn't be sure, but I thought I heard Kip say something like, "I'm losing you, Tina." Then I heard him say, "Maybe you're a woman now." I didn't know what to think. His voice was sad and quiet. His face looked cool and smooth, so I thought I should be glad. Would his house-husband demeanor stick all evening? Would it be an easy night after all?

I walked down the hall and slipped into the bathroom. I reached for the toothpaste and my toothbrush. I squeezed enough of the green gel from the tube to cover all the bristles. I looked into the mirror. I wanted to brush my teeth quickly, but I heard the bathroom door creak open in back of me. I felt like I was being photographed in slow motion. Kip's stark, brown reflection outlined me in the mirror.

"What are you doing, Tina?"

"Brushing my teeth."

"Before dinner, with a whole glob of toothpaste? You never use that much toothpaste. Come here."

"What?" I asked, filling up with panic.

"Put down that toothbrush and come here."

He held me by the wrist and took me down the hall to the bedroom. There was no force in his hold. I went willingly because I knew I had to. Then he grasped my shoulders and threw me onto the bed. My body bounced a couple of times, feeling like it was shrinking. Then he was heavy on top of me. He pushed his tongue deep inside my mouth and all around the outside of my teeth. His tongue recoiled and stayed behind his clenched teeth as he pushed himself off the bed. "How'd wine get on your breath, Tina?"

He left the room as if his question were rhetorical. I sat up, watching him pace the hall, wondering if he really wanted me to answer.

He came back and stood in the doorway. "Why'd you try to get the wine off your breath, Tina?" He headed for the living room. I stayed on the bed. I could hear him breathing hard. He came back again, his olive-skinned face pointed down at me as he answered his own question. "Because you knew you'd done something wrong."

"Kip, I missed my bus, so I asked Eric if he could give me a ride."

"Who's Eric?"

"He's in Sales. I've been processing his orders for three years now."

"You used your own judgment, accepting a ride from this Eric dude?"

"Honey, Eric and his girlfriend, Maggie, are real nice people. They want to have us over for dinner sometime."

"No, Tina."

"What?"

"I don't know Eric and don't care to meet him. I don't feel comfortable going to strangers' homes. Seven years, Tina, and you still don't know that?"

"I'm sorry. I won't ask you anymore."

"You're sorry?" He leaned back on the open door frame of the bedroom and tilted his face up for a moment. As if involuntarily, his hands clenched and clicked like magnets to his hips. His powerful upper back jutted forward as he tucked in his chin like a fighter facing his opponent. I could feel the tension extend through his muscles. I thought of The Hulk and his clothes ripping open and falling off his back.

"You went with Eric in his car to his girlfriend's house and drank her wine. They could've drugged your wine and had group sex with you, then killed you. If your body were found and it were suspected you'd gotten in the car willingly, I would take your body and cut it up in little pieces. No telling what could have happened to you tonight. You could have waited for the next bus, but you, you" he sneered, his voice intoning ridicule, "probably wanted to hurry up and get home so you could see the enlargements. You've done a lot of stupid things, Tina, but this is too much."

I let him believe I hadn't been thinking, that I'd just missed a bus, hoping he wouldn't think I had deliberately disobeyed.

"I'm going to hurt you a little bit more than usual tonight because it's the first time you've done anything serious. I should break your bones." He was screaming. "If you do something close to this again, I'll put you in the hospital for a month. If you do it a third time, I'll kill you."

It was the first time Kip had admitted ahead of time that he intended to batter me. All the other times had seemed like spontaneous outbursts. I didn't believe he would really plan and carry out a battering. I thought he was just threatening me. His scream was artificially loud, as if he were trying to scare the evil out of himself. I could feel my gaze unfocus like I wasn't listening. Inside I tried not to feel scared.

I wanted out so badly. It had all gone too far. I stayed in the bedroom, hearing words yelled and things thrown. The sentences and objects were unidentifiable. Their sounds just went through me like the first time I had heard him break something of mine. It was a blue ceramic butter dish with a dome lid, the same blue as Maggie's china. I had been so angry. Gradually, each of my possessions were broken or given away or stolen or abandoned, and things that were replaceable lost value to me. I just had my life left and that had become much more important to me, except when I wanted to die. Now things were happening but I wasn't aware of details. I preferred listening to things breaking than to nothing at all because then I could judge how far away he was. The silences were what scared me. How many hours went by? It was summer and the sun set after nine o'clock. All I knew was that there was no light coming through our heavy drapes and it was dark inside.

There was a knock on the front door. Who was it? A concerned neighbor? The cops? Kip was always calling the cops on the neighbors even though this was a nice middle-class suburb. Kip hated the cops, but he called them if people played their stereos too loud, drank too much, or parked in our parking place even though we didn't have a car. People were usually too scared to call the cops on Kip, but maybe they had tonight. I heard the skinny blinds on our front window squeak open and closed. Whoever it was knocked again. There was nothing I could do. The knocking stopped.

More time went by in silence. My stomach was in knots. There had been another part left out of my story, not just the wine. I hadn't told Kip about Maggie's spaghetti. I wanted to throw it up, but then he'd know and I'd have more explaining to do.

It must have been midnight. I still didn't know what to think. There was something different about this tantrum. He usually exploded by now, but this time he seemed to have simmered down. He was still separate and mad, but quiet.

If he'd already gotten his anger out, then we could have talked about what was really bothering him. Even after he'd been so violent that I thought it should be safe to approach him, I was still scared. He expected me to go to him and explain what had made him mad, and I had to be right. I couldn't make things up just to get the right answer, or make things too complicated or over-simplified. Out of fright, I always waited too long to go to him, which only prolonged his anger. But tonight, the timing was even further off. I'd waited much too long. I didn't want to go in there. I don't know how long I wrestled with the idea of walking into the living room, but all of a sudden I found myself there, like in a dream.

I couldn't pick up any signals from Kip. Was everything going to be all right? Maybe he was tired. Then in the darkness Kip, alert and full of energy, dug the callused fingers of his right hand into my neck. He squeezed my throat and lifted me up until my head reached the ceiling, knocking off some of the sparkles in the plaster. He threw me on the floor. He did it again. I don't know how many times.

Kip grabbed the front part of my short hairstyle that he had designed, and pulled way back with the force he was capable of, so that as he slammed my head into the carpet, it seemed almost gentle, and I thought he was scared to really hurt me. Was he just a bad actor? I was okay for the first few slams, but I could feel the cement slab just under the carpet and my head started to hurt. Gradually, the pain turned to warmth. The room became a dark tunnel with light at the end. Around the tunnel I saw a kaleidoscope of colorful designs. I felt my ghost escaping me in protest. *No*, she said. *This is wrong. She shouldn't be dying yet.*

Suddenly, Kip stopped. He turned on the light, took off his clothes and put them in a pile by his feet. He sat on the couch and looked down at the pile of torn, black-and-white, glossy paper that used to be the enlargements. I was scared to move, but I didn't want to stay where I was. I finally got up off the floor and felt my way to bed. I lay on my back, staring at the fireworks in slow motion. I could tell I was close to releasing into a concussion, but I wouldn't let myself go to sleep. I didn't want to die. What would happen next? Would I be alive for it?

I heard the refrigerator door open and the sound of Kip pouring himself a glass of wine. I expected to hear bottles of ketchup and salad dressing break, but he didn't slam the door. He just closed it. After about an hour, he came to bed. The alcohol had done nothing. He had not yet forgiven me. It didn't occur to me whether to forgive him. All I knew was that he was still tight, still untouchable. I hated the time between the end of a tantrum and the beginning of making up. We had usually made up before now. "Never go to bed mad," he'd say. I think he learned that on *The Donna Reed Show*.

Around three in the morning, he drifted off into a light sleep beside me. I kept my consciousness. By five, I started to feel a strange tinge of courage lighting the inside of my body. Hoping that my skin would not glow and warn Kip, I struggled to make myself blend in with the gray of dawn. The whole idea of leaving had to remain abstract within my brain. If it formed into words, I was sure he would read my mind and stop me. I just knew I was going to leave, or die trying.

I got up at six as usual. My spine and hips were badly bruised. My throat was sore all the way through. My head ached. I tried to cover up my limp, but he woke up and noticed.

"Honey, you want to call in sick today? I won't mind if you don't get your perfect attendance award this year."

"Thanks for offering, Kip, but I can't." I tried not to let my sore throat affect the sound of my voice. "Um—they're really cracking down on me lately and I want to get a good evaluation."

I got ready for work. I painfully put on blue jeans, a T-shirt and running shoes, grateful that my normal work clothes did not yet include high heels. I went to the bathroom and filled my purse with all my makeup. Then I put two lipsticks back. I made sure I had my I.D. and my bus pass. I thought about the twelve crisp hundred dollar bills Kip had saved in the air conditioner by the bed. I wanted that money. I went to the kitchen, buttered some bread and popped it into the microwave. Could I get away with it? I wondered if I should dare be greedy at a time like this, my chance to get away, or should I just be glad to get out alive?

I started back down the hall toward the air conditioner. I saw Kip getting up. He walked over to the air conditioner. The microwave buzzed. Was he awake enough to wonder what I was trying to do?

"It's going to be a hot one," he said as he flipped on the air.

I turned around and went back to the kitchen. I opened the microwave door, slid the hot bread out and bit into it. I opened up my lunch money drawer and took out enough for soup and sandwich. I turned away and opened the front door. The bread went halfway down my throat and seemed to stay there. I squinted as the bright rays of early morning sunlight hit my eyes.

"I'm sorry, Luv Bug," Kip called from the bedroom.

"That's okay, Honey," I said. "I want you to know there's a pot luck today and I don't even want to go." Would that fool him?

"Good girl," he said, yawning.

"Bye, bye," I called, out the door. I couldn't believe I was actually leaving. I kept going, past our tennis courts to the bus stop. I stood at peace in the not-yet-scorching Sacramento sun. I heard footsteps behind me. I didn't care if it was Kip. I had left. I was ready to die now. But it wasn't Kip after all. Kip is still in bed asleep, I thought. I'm actually pulling this off. Could I start a new life without him, or was that too much to ask? ■

## Letter to Carlos

Yolanda Molina

February 1989

Dear Carlos:

I never thought I'd have the opportunity to communicate with you again. Perhaps I never thought I'd want to. This has been one of the most difficult tasks in my life. It's been over twenty years, but unfortunately your memory still haunts me.

I don't know where to begin, or what to say. It's very painful for me to remember that part of my life. I very cleverly managed to suppress those memories not knowing that if they were not dealt with openly, they would not go away, but would fester like a boil waiting to be opened.

A lot has happened to me and the children since we left. It took the kids a long time to understand why it happened. And although I felt very hurt that they didn't share my bitterness toward you, when Debra finally told me as an adult, "I now know why you left him," instead of feeling victorious, I felt so sorry for her because I knew that she finally shared my pain. And as parents, we always want out children to be spared any misery.

I don't think I ever asked you why you abused me. I was probably too scared to ask. I have tried to remember, difficult as it is, to figure out how I might have provoked you into hitting me the way you did. I do recall wondering how it was possible for someone you share a life with to treat you so violently. But I still can't come up with an answer.

Do you have any notion of what it's like to live in fear of being beaten senseless? To lie in bed with the covers over your head, pretending to be asleep, listening to your heart beating rapidly, waiting to be cursed and abused for no apparent reason? And do you have any idea how long it takes a human being to regain her self-worth and dignity after six years of living in terror?

I can still remember the first time you hit me. I was expecting Debra and I was feeling down and homesick. You were so offended and jealous by this that you thought you'd show me how to be more appreciative. This was just the beginning. I never told anyone because I was too embarrassed that my husband would have such a low regard for my condition.

I can't recall all the brutal, senseless beatings, but I can recall the most violent ones. Like the time you took a two-by-four and hit me with it, until it broke on my back. I was expecting Tony then. Or the time that you hit me several times on the face with your fist and broke my nose and damaged an eardrum. And then there were the black eyes that I had to lie about at work to cover up for my embarrassment and your violent behavior.

I always wondered why it was so easy for you to inflict pain on me. I couldn't fight back. Even when you were drunk and unstable, I couldn't take advantage of your condition—instead I felt sorry for you. But you have never shown any remorse.

I have experienced many different emotions since I left you. First I was hurt: Why does he treat me this way? He must hate me. I'd think, "I'm the mother of his children he claims to love so much."

The only times you would come close to an apology was if I'd threaten to leave. You knew you had my mother on your side. Perhaps if I had been more honest with her about our relationship, she might have been more supportive of me. But then it really doesn't matter, because when I divorced you I alienated myself from my church, my culture, and my mother as well. To this day my relationship with my mother is somewhat strained. I've blamed her for a lot of my unhappiness. But as I've grown older I've learned to accept responsibility. Yes, she was wrong to insist that I remain in a miserable marriage for the children's sake. And perhaps she had no right to make me feel selfish placing my own happiness before the children's. But she wasn't completely aware of my insufferable existence.

I suppose it's always convenient to be able to blame someone else. The truth of the matter is that I didn't have the strength or the confidence to do anything about my situation. I felt trapped, and was afraid that I wouldn't be able to manage on my own. We all have our limits.

The breaking point was your last act of violence against me: when you became so enraged by the eye makeup I was wearing. You called me a whore and said that you would not allow your children to be raised by a tramp. So you tried to burn my eyes out with a cigar. What were you thinking? How would it have helped you or the children if you had made me blind? For the first time, I realized how much danger I was in. I knew then that if I really cared for my children, I had to leave.

I can't remember the exact day that I left. I can only remember the children's ages. Tony was not quite two. Poochie was about four and Debra had to be six. They were so young. I don't recall them asking where we were going. I wouldn't have had an answer for them. Can you imagine being that young and leaving your home in the middle of the night without being told why or where you are going? I took a lot for granted. I was alone and frightened and had no idea of the consequences.

I had left you several times before but the separations only lasted a few weeks, one month at the most. But this time I was certain there would be no turning back. I looked around the flat, trying to decide what, if anything, I should take with me. Apparently, I didn't think anything was as important to me as my children and my safety. All I took was a shopping bag stuffed with all the clean diapers I could find, along with a few baby bottles filled with milk and juice. The only clothes we took were what we were wearing.

By my way of thinking now I was acting irrationally, but I had reached my limit. I couldn't take it anymore. I didn't have a plan. I wasn't thinking about the future. The only thing on my mind was to get away as far as I could from you—in order to make it hard for you to find us. Well, it wasn't long before you called my mother crying and asking her to convince me to go back for the children's sake. Only this time it didn't work. I finally had to tell her just how violent your outbursts were.

When I wrote you the "Dear John" letter, I knew you couldn't change. So it was written more to relieve me of any guilt I felt for taking your children away from you. I had no intention of ever returning. Maybe it was unfair of me to be dishonest to you, but I was beginning to feel bitter.

It was that bitterness that hardened me and gave me strength to get on with my life, to try to raise the children by myself the best I could. It was very hard raising three children without any financial support from you. But when you made it clear you would not help me, I didn't beg. It was easier for me to work two jobs than to deal with you. I became a very focused and determined young woman, and in the process of reshaping myself, exploring new values and setting goals for myself, I became distant from virtually everything I had known.

Well, Carlos, as I said, it has been a long time since the night the children and I got on that Greyhound bus. The children are grown and have lives of their own. My only regret is not having had the maturity or experience to see how the kids would later be affected by all the violence they heard and saw before we left. It must have frightened them to see their mother getting beaten up by their father. To this day, Debra and Poochie still recall crawling under the bed or hiding in the closets. And to think that you, my mother, and I thought holding the marriage together was for the sake of the children. What fools.

But after twenty years, I am no longer as bitter. I know you have suffered throughout your own life and probably never intended to be part of the suffering of others. But your violence did have its consequences. You have had to pay. When your sons graduated from high school, when your daughter was married, you were not there and you had no right to be. When your own children told you they no longer considered you their father, you must have realized that something was wrong.

It would probably please you to know that I still remember you. It would not please you to know how. You are still in my nightmares, lurking in the darkness, giving me pain in odd moments when I suddenly break down and cry.

Sometimes I wonder if that's the way you wanted to be remembered. I wonder if you even remember how brutal you were. And I wonder if ever you think about what you've lost, if you ever, ever feel remorse.

Sincerely,

*Yolanda* ■

**This Isn't About Me**

Jolene A. Cox

The lecture is on domestic violence. The voice drones on: "And the man who batters, blah, blah, blah . . .

and the woman who stays, blah, blah . . . and he . . . and she . . . and blah, blah, blah."

I have stopped listening; I can't relate. This isn't about me. And yet . . .

The voice, the room, students around me fade. Love, hate, and fear intermingle as memory comes flooding back. For a brief moment I am present in the past. Her voice echoes in my ear:

"God-damn you, Bitch. Someone should have killed you long ago. Someone should have beaten you raw, broken every bone in your body. God-damn you, Bitch!"

Even so, it is difficult to remember. Isolated incidents become fogged with time. What started it all? Whose fault was it? The signs were there from the beginning. But, breast-fed on guilt and denial, the stage was set long before she ever got there. Maybe it was inevitable. I don't know.

What started as a casual affair quickly developed into financial interdependency. When neither of us could afford rent on our own, we moved in together. Even then we were poor living together in one small room, doing what we could to make ends meet. It wasn't a living arrangement I would have chosen in more prosperous times. It was a time of desperation. Financially and emotionally, we needed each other.

She was an angry woman. We fought over money, sex, space. We made up. We made love. We ate, watched TV, slept. There were good times and bad times.

Often, she would tell me stories. Lying in bed, she would talk of her childhood, her past affairs, her drinking days. She told me of the fights she had growing up, of barroom brawls, losing and winning. I loved those times, the sound of her voice, the thrill of her adventures. The stories were almost always violent. Once she told me of giving an old lover a black eye.

"You won't ever do that to me?" I asked. " I mean, you wouldn't ever hit me like that?" She had cradled my head against her breast, stroked my hair.

"No, love. I won't ever do that to you. I'm here to take care of you. You don't ever have to be afraid of me." I drifted off to sleep, her voice comforting in the darkness.

This is what I loved most about her: she was stronger, more willing to fight than I. Her brutality would be my protection. Sometimes, she would ask me to marry her:

"You won't have to work. I'll get a better paying job. I'll be able to support us both. I don't want you to have to work."

This was her idea of a relationship. This was what she wanted: she would go off to work and I would take care of her needs at home.

This was not what I wanted: to be her housewife. No, I needed to work, to be out in the world, to make my own way. And yet, there was a sweetness, a seduction to her words. Her desire to take care of me touched some emotion deep inside. It held in it the promise of security or, perhaps, the illusion of comfort. Even though it wasn't what I wanted, it was what I too had always imagined a relationship to be.

But she was uneducated, with no real job skills. The reality was she would never be able to support me. Because this was the reality, she became increasingly angry. She accused me of spending money that never existed. When there was no money, which was often, she accused me of hiding it away somewhere and keeping it for myself. She would never admit that with me on unemployment and her working for minimum wage, there just wasn't much. She held on to the illusion that she could support us both. When the money wasn't there, she needed someone to blame. This was part of her anger. What started out as her wanting to keep me ended in frustration when she couldn't.

When we had been living together about a week, we got into an argument over the ironing. We had been fighting earlier that day. When she told me to iron her shirt, I blew up. "You're just as much a woman as I am. You can iron your own damn shirt."

"Sure, I'm a woman, but that's not my fault. You're supposed to obey me!" I laughed—I thought it was funny. Surely she couldn't be serious. After all, we were both women, weren't we? Before long, I came to realize just how serious she was.

She believed I was to obey her in all things, take care of her, satisfy her needs. If I didn't, she felt it was her right to punish me. She somehow thought that my being a woman was different from her being a woman. I was to be subordinate. The violence started. In retrospect, I knew it was coming. But, I just didn't trust that I knew. Denial mechanisms kicked in full force: Maybe I was wrong, maybe it was stress, maybe we all make mistakes. Maybe . . . this wasn't happening.

We were fighting—something petty. Later, I couldn't remember what it was about. Tempers flared, we exchanged harsh words. Before I knew what happened, I was pinned to the wall, my wrists crushed into plaster, her breath hot on my face. "I can hurt you little girl. Don't you ever forget that. 'Cause if you do, you're in trouble. I can do whatever I want to you, and there's nothing you can do to stop it!"

Later that night, she was sorry. She promised she would never act that way again. "But," she said, "*it is your fault.* You shouldn't make me mad like that. You should be more understanding. *I can't help it that I got angry.* You should just have given in to me." I would hear those words more than once. Was the violence my fault? I wanted to believe her.

When we had been living together for two months, she was injured at work. With her on Workman's Compensation, we were worse off financially than we had been before. With the injury began her problems with drugs. She had been addicted to drugs before, but had been clean for about a year when we met. But now, she lived for them—they became the one love in her life. I couldn't compete. She was totally absorbed. She chose and changed doctors by the drugs they provided, bought street drugs, traded drugs with the neighbors. Anything to stay high. Drugs became her main preoccupation, her one love. They took all her energy; I was merely an object, an appendage to take care of her other needs.

Did I say one love? Actually there were two: drugs and weapons. She loved them both dearly. One day in the park she found a club. A brutal weapon: a piece of wood wrapped in masking tape, with a leather handle attached to one end and twenty-six nails driven through the other to form a mass of spikes. Hand-made, with the sole intention of hurting. I felt it, felt the anger, the hatred, the fear in that weapon. She brought it home, cherished it, slept with it like a teddy bear.

There were times when, looking at her, I knew the woman I had loved was no longer there. She would become someone I didn't recognize. Her eyes would glaze, her mouth take on a sardonic twist. These times she was at her worst. Anger lay just below the surface, waiting to erupt.

As the drugs got worse, so did the violence. The question no longer was "would she hurt me?" The question became "will she kill me?" Money would disappear. There was no food in the house. Some days, she would threaten to beat me for imagined wrongs. If I was late coming home, she accused me of being with another woman. If there was no money, she accused me of hiding it. Still, I blamed myself.

And this was the hardest part—the night. Lying next to someone I loved, so afraid I couldn't trust enough to go to sleep. Listening to the lies until I truly believed I had caused it all, that I deserved the abuse. The hardest part of all, anger at myself for loving her, for being human enough to need love.

I fell away into a denial more frightening than reality itself. I watched her, knew her moods, when she was likely to threaten me, when the next incident was coming. Dazed, I walked around in the netherworld that lies between reality and pain. When it became too painful to think, I shut off. Anything to keep from listening to her threats which followed me throughout the days.

Our final fight came on one of those days when she was at her worst. We were fighting over whether to get a new TV. I could feel violence lying just below the surface, hear the hatred in her voice. I had long since learned to avoid her when she was like this—I got up and went for a walk. When I returned, she was still angry. I took a shower, went to the store—anything to avoid the confrontation. Hours passed.

When I returned, she started with how I was crazy, how I never wanted her to have anything. She claimed I was taking money and hiding it from her. Nothing I said or did could placate her. I was tired. Finally I had enough.

"You want to fight? O.K. I'll fight you. You think you're so much stronger than me?" I challenged. "Go ahead, prove it. I'll fight you."

We squared off. She came at me. "Hit me, why don't you? You think you're tough? Why the hell don't you prove it, little girl? I'll fuckin' take you apart. Don't try me!"

I didn't want to throw the first punch. I wanted to make her so mad she couldn't resist. Before, I always tried to calm her, to ignore her, to walk away. Now, I needed to prove something to myself—that I wasn't weak, that I didn't need to take this any more. "You want to hit me? Go ahead! Hit me!"

She came at me. But this time I knew it was coming. I was ready. We fought: kicked, punched, and bit. It was a fair fight, and neither of us was hurt beyond a few rug burns and bruises.

I don't remember what ended that fight, how it broke up. Just that, once again, I was the one to leave. Deeply shaken, I went to a neighbor's house, sat there drinking coffee and staring at the wall. My own violence scared me as much as hers; I had really wanted to hurt her. What had I become? This was the point at which I knew I had to get out.

After that, she still threatened to beat me, but now those threats rang hollow. We were evenly matched and for the first time we both knew it. Never again would she be stronger, more willing to fight than I. Her only comment about that fight was, "I see you got rug burns, too." She laughed. To her, the violence was nothing personal. She wasn't upset by it. Violence was just the way life was for her.

She never beat me again. But now, I was more afraid of her than ever. The threats changed: "You just remember from now on, you sleep with one eye open. 'Cause if you don't, one day you just aren't gonna wake up. I don't like you anymore and that's important. That's real important."

Finally I called a battered women's shelter. I didn't ask to be taken in. I believed that service was for straight women. As a lesbian, I didn't trust that they would see this as a domestic violence problem. I asked only for suggestions, any place I might go, any way out. To my surprise, they offered me shelter, which I gratefully accepted. I left her the very morning of my phone call, never looking back.

I had always defined domestic violence as a heterosexual problem. This is not the stuff lesbian fiction is made of. Never had I dreamed the possibility that one woman could so brutalize another woman. Nothing in my life had prepared me for this realization. In a world where man is foe and woman is friend, where separatism is the cure for all evils, something had gone awry.

Three years later, I am still afraid. No, not of her, not anymore. Rather,

I am afraid to sleep with another woman, afraid to let someone touch the innermost parts of me. Most of all, I fear needing somebody. Afraid that somehow, I really did deserve the abuse. The body heals quickly but the soul . . . that kind of healing takes more time.

The lecture is over. I pick up my books, close my notebook on an empty page. I should have taken notes, written down the "he's" and "she's" of domestic violence. This lecture is about heterosexuals. This isn't about me. ■

**Alive: A Diary**
Jane

*August 1984*

My husband Jim was leaving for the weekend with one of his girlfriends and when I tried to ask him something about the house, he punched me with his fist in the legs.

I went to the _______ Police. He does not know this. If he did, my life would be in great danger. This is the first time that I have been brave enough to go to the police but I should have done it years ago.

*Monday, Nov. 5, 1984*

Jim sat down on the couch beside me. He talked to me while poking his finger up beneath an afghan that he laid over his lap. He pretended that it was his penis and wiggled it around under the cover. Later he got a plastic glass and kept it over his penis so that I would not tempt him or hurt his privates.

Because he very seldom talks to me, I tried to initiate a normal conversation—to see what was happening in his life right now. I still get locked into "maybe I can make it all right." Some of his weird behavior has become so much a part of my daily living that I do not run away from it.

My husband began to question me as to my feelings about the physical abuse that has been a part of our marriage for about eight years. It first began on this very sun porch when he twisted my finger until I thought he had broken it. His reason (according to him) was that he did it for my own good because I was talking gibberish.

There have been many instances of physical abuse. I can't even recall all of them. There have been numerous death threats. The worse case was a beating that he gave me because, he says, I would not leave the bedroom. I wanted to talk to him and "he had no choice." On that occasion, he threw me to the floor in the hallway and proceeded to kick me in the back and sides with all his might. He was wearing shoes at the time. I went to the Women's Network and talked to the director, Janice. I showed her my bruises and injuries. She talked to me for a long while . . . helped me greatly.

Getting back to the night of November 5, 1984 . . . my husband began talking in a threatening manner, per usual. I told him that if he ever hurt me again I would not be alone . . . That my friends were with me. I was thinking, in particular, of Women's Network. He told me that he knew that my girlfriend Lois was screwing the entire Mafia and that I was going to get the Mafia after him. As incredible as this may sound, he truly believed it. He asked me—did I really claim to be a victim of physical abuse? He picked up a large glass and crashed it to the wall. He told me if the Mafia or anyone ever tried to hurt him, he would come get me and tear my daughter and me limb from limb.

This is the second time he has threatened my daughter Lisa in the last few weeks. The other time he said that he would bash her face in . . . His reasoning is that she did not appear to like him anymore. My daughter, however, does not know of the physical abuse towards me. If she did she would lose her temper and that would be extremely dangerous.

*December 18, 1984*

I returned home from work at about 10:00 P.M. Jim was returning from his women's exercise class, Jazzercise. He seemed agitated. I questioned him about it and [he said] he was upset about something a woman said to him.

I could tell he was also agitated about his girlfriend and about starting work on the night shift. The night shift always makes him nervous.

In the course of conversation he became threatening with no apparent motivation. Once again, he threatened the life of my daughter and myself: (I'll blow your head off and also Lisa's.) He removed his belt and began to wield it about. I tried to edge to a door but knew I was in a difficult spot to escape. I remained still as a mouse. He ranted and raved about everything, cutting me down once more.

By my remaining still, taking the verbal abuse without retorting—he gradually calmed down—he talked at me for an hour, pacing, a wild strange look in his eyes.

When he calmed down, I again suggested that he receive professional help. Again, he declined.

I am frightened about his continued threats toward not only me but, for the last few months, my daughter . . . He is extremely paranoid about the house and anything he owns. He has a great attachment to inanimate objects, really much more than to humans. It's strange because he is not materialistic.

I feel there is no protection for me. If he leaves, I must have someone live here with me. I don't know who. I don't think an order of protection would work. If his temper comes out, it would not stop him from breaking the door down. I don't think it would stop him if I change the locks.

I am becoming emotionally shut down. I can no longer cry. I am so used to having to become silent and take abuse.

*January 1985*

My husband has gone skiing with his present girlfriend for three weekends in January. He takes funds out of our joint checking account for his travel expenses. All of a sudden he has gotten on this insane jealousy kick. A man called about meeting time from the poetry center and he assumes I am having an affair with him.

He tells me that he would like me to get to the point where I commit suicide. He wants extra money now for additional household expenses. He has the money but will let the gas and electricity go off because he does not want to pay it any more. I believe he is taking additional deductions from his paycheck so that it looks like he is making less money.

When I ask him when he will leave, he says he is afraid of what he may do to me once he is gone. He is afraid of his loss of self-control. He is badgering me for money all week, harassing me, switching into frightening phases of near violence. I stay close to a door.

This has gone for the entire week and I am physically and emotionally at the point of total exhaustion.

*Feb. 8, 1985*

This has been a week of harassment by my husband.

On Tuesday night, the fifth of February, he began accusing me of having relations with men all over town. He called me a "fucking whore" and other terrible names.

This was a new turn of events because four years ago he came to my job and announced that he wanted to start dating openly, that he had been having sneaky affairs for years and no longer wanted to hide them.

I was shocked. I had no idea what had been going on but I guess I had secretly feared the reality of his comings and goings. He said he did not care what I did. He wanted his way and whether or not I liked it didn't matter.

Needless to say, his total disregard for my feelings fractured my very soul to the depth of my feelings. I had a horrible summer, watching him dandy up and go out with other women every weekend. He did it in front of me. He had no regard for my tears and pain. In fact, it was like he enjoyed it.

Now he is accusing a friend of mine, an older man also in my poetry group, of telling everyone in town that he has been "screwing" me for years. I asked the man about it and he was furious at this lie and damage to his reputation. My husband says he has talked to many men about their relations with me. I reply that he can bring them all into court, that I would love to know who they all are. He also told me that he has spies where I work . . . that someone calls him telling him about my meetings in the mall with different men . . . ridiculous! . . .

*Feb. 14, 1985*

Valentine Day. I went to the police this evening. I talked again with Lt. Brownell. I am afraid to have him [Jim] picked up, taken into custody or the state hospital because when he gets out he may kill me or badly injure my daughter or myself.

It has been another total week of harassment. He started on my daughter. He wanted to know where I was hiding money. He came for her and she covered her head with her hands. It shocked him and he stopped, thank God. She was terrified and left the house until 12:30 a.m. Usually, it has been only myself receiving his blows. My daughter said the look on his face was like a devil, not at all like his everyday look. It was horrifying and strange.

I live in terror but I am afraid that he will come for us if I make him leave. Jim tells me that over and over. I do not believe the Adult Abuse Act will have any effect on his behavior. It [his rage] is strictly impulse. I believe he is ill and can do great harm on anyone.

The police tell me that if he acts normal . . . the doctors at State would release him. I am stuck and frightened.

One morning I showed him detailed expenses of my bills, including tuition for my daughter's school. She is almost finished. I gave him another pamphlet from Men's Self-Help Center. This time he said he would read it. He knows at times that he is sick. Other times, most of the time, he denies it.

This has been the second week in a row of daily harassment without ceasing. Now his present girlfriend has come to town for the weekend so it will probably end for a few days. It is when he has days off that he is the worse.

On my days off I am seeing counselors, doctors, lawyers. I feel resentful. I did not cause this and now he is going to disrupt our lives. He wants our home sold. His crazy behavior is going to tear our lives apart. It is not fair. I feel anger, rage but most of all sadness—and fear.

When he came in the house the other night, I was sitting on the couch watching TV. The minute I heard him enter, my body uncontrollably began trembling. I could not control the shaking. If he had seen it, he would have been very pleased. When he talks to me, my hands become icy cold. I wonder how these years of stress are affecting my body, my physical health. I wonder if there will be people in the courts who will be compassionate. I must believe that there are . . . although sometimes I hear there are none. I must believe that it will work out all right. I must believe that.

*March 3*

My husband was home—the first weekend in a long while. Previously he had been writing checks out of our joint checking account to cover his traveling expenses, flying back and forth almost every weekend to visit his current girlfriend in __________.

I thought it a good opportunity to question him about leaving. He had been collecting boxes in the garage but always denied that he had definite plans. In the morning he was verbally abusive but did seem as if he would talk. Later in the afternoon, he seemed quite rational and in fact calm—could it be he was bordering on even being "nice"?

We sat on the sun porch and talked. He began talking about one particular time when we were out with another couple, my friends, since I have never known him to have a single friend, never a male friend—only secret affairs with women. He was telling me that while I was in the bathroom, my friends were laughing about something I had done—can't recall the occasion, very possible one of his delusions.

I "thought" he was talking quite nice. My daughter came home and was in her room for some time. She was very quiet so I got up and went into her room to find her very upset . . . . She said, "I can't stand this a minute longer. How can you let him talk down to you like *that*? I will lose respect if you put up with this for much longer."

That was the nudge I needed. I was ripe. I undertook the move that I had always been afraid of. I went back and began to question him again, only this time more fervently about when he planned to leave. He became agitated and jumped up to the calendar. "Tomorrow . . . . NO, Friday!" I believe he made this quick decision because he was not with his girlfriend on this first weekend and I felt he was being pressured by her to leave the house.

The rest of the week he proceeded to move his things out to the home of his ex-wife. She called me and said that he told her *he was moving in*. When she refused, he told her "I'm not asking your permission, woman, I'm *here*!"

For the better part of that week the pressure shifted towards her. He would come home calling her an Asshole, a sniveling Bitch, etc. His temper seemed momentarily directed towards her.

Friday arrived and I was home sick all week with bronchitis and laryngitis. However, as usual, he was totally unconcerned about my welfare. He continually tried to blame me for all his behavior. Luckily, I had learned in group that the abuser always tries to turn the blame 180° around so it did not bother me . . . .

I gave him a hug when he left and wished him luck. He snapped after twelve years—"Better luck next time! Good-bye!"

*Since my husband left the house on March 9, [1985]* he has harassed me with death threats.

In April—he went with me to the income tax office and created such an uproar that the woman we worked with told me that my husband needed counseling. I relented and let him have the tax refund just because he hassled me so much. He didn't deserve it.

In phone calls he has threatened me with the telephone wire. He has suggested suicide and murder repeatedly.

I now have a boarder, which makes me feel safer but probably means nothing.

*July 19,*

I met my husband, at his request, at Harry's Diner in ______ to discuss the house. . . .

He asked me if I did not have bad memories connected with our house. I said I was happy here with him gone and he replied that I would soon have bad memories. He keeps implying something about his airplane . . . perhaps he plans to crash it into the house. He speaks only of death.

I spent a lot of time trying to convince him to get help. He does not deny his mental illness. He does tell me that an order of protection, a police lockup, hospital lockup would only keep him away hours and then I would be in serious trouble. They would be meaningless

I wrote the police again tonight . . . called Women's Network, talked to Janice.

*After he left [in March]*, various relatives of his called me saying how they were sorry and didn't know what was wrong with him. His ex-wife complained of his temper and his "having some screws loose." His sister told me that years ago he had tried to [or had?] joined a woman's synchronized ballet swim team, that someone had seen him in a teenage bar a few years ago.

His family knew he was acting bad again. They were all very nice. I said nothing about the abuse, remained a listener . . . am very much afraid of him.

I feel relatively safe until legal action starts. He wants the house, apparently wants to rent it out to make money. His sister told me he wants to live in his other nicer home in the western suburbs with his girlfriend. He cares nothing about his former wife or my feelings. No matter that we own half of the houses.

It feels very good to relax in my home now. I would like to change the locks but he said that if he wants in, locks would not stop him.

I am very grateful for the help that I have received from Women's Network. Words cannot describe what that support has meant. I would like to go on with my life. I am not sure that I will ever again feel safe or trusting with a man. It will take a lot of counseling.

My daughter says she will never trust or feel safe with a man. She broke up with her boyfriend. I feel that Jim has left indelible scars here on these two women [self and daughter]. He doesn't care or accept any responsibility for what he has done.

We will need a lot of counseling. I know that we are still unsafe. I remember the look on his face when he made his last threats that he would blow off our heads. I'll never forget his face when he threatened that he would kill me if I went against him after he left.

I have tried to persuade him to go to Men's Self-Help Center, seek professional help but he scoffs at any kind of professional counseling. In fact, he has a very low opinion of government, law, any figures that are superior to him. He believes they, well, everyone really, is "crooked."

I don't know what lies ahead. I only know there is a little light in this house now . . . and that the spring flowers are starting to bloom. That must be a good sign, surely!

*Letter, received February 1990, attached to second installment of diary entries.*

Miriam,

I am very pleased that these journals will be perhaps helpful to someone else. I would like that. Thank you.

Getting my husband out of our house was a *major* accomplishment though he talked about leaving for three-four years. The day he finally packed up his car and left was a day I'll never forget. After he left, I raised all the blinds, raised my fist almost with Scarlett O'Hara determination and vowed: "I don't care if I end up a bag lady, I will *never* live this way again."

. . . . I was afraid I would not be able to survive financially—but my biggest fear turned out to be a blessing. I did better financially than when he was there. I made it by living extremely frugally. I have a job. I simplified my life and as a result have made it, not much money—but peace, no more trembling in my own home.

I owe a lot to Women's Network, the group of abused women in ________. If it hadn't been for that support I wouldn't have made it.

I have not had any significant relationships with men. It's been almost four years but I still do not feel as if I am interested. I have met some very nice men. I'm attracted to healthy men now! I have platonic male friends. I know I would still have difficulty being able to *trust* in a relationship. Time may or may not heal this. I've had counseling. (The day I was first able to cry again—at a movie—was a Big Step!) But I'm really happy living alone. I'm a poet and need that solitude. I have had quite a few of the poems [written during this period] published. I've been also published in literary journals, won and placed in national and local contests.

Since this time I have also converted to Catholicism. Deepening my spiritual life has been a great healing.

Sometimes I'm still afraid—like the other night when I had a call at 3:00 A.M. with no one there. Though he is living with a woman, I feel he checks on me. Women's Network told me he could appear one day—with who knows—a gun? He's a very sick man but as long as he has someone else to abuse, I'm probably not a target. It hasn't been easy but I take one day at a time and thank God for that one day. ■

**Crying Was My Middle Name**
Ellen Snow-Brown

When I was six years old my fourteen-year-old cousin raped me. I suppose that was my first terrifying experience with the opposite sex. I remember him as being very disturbed. He seemed to stay in some sort of trouble. When I told my mother what he had done, she was very angry and confronted his mother about his actions. His mother was protective and refused to believe that her son had done such a terrible thing. My mother decided to press charges since it was apparent that his mother had no intentions of doing anything about the situation. I don't remember exactly what happened to him except that he went to a boys' home. It was not a place unfamiliar to him. He has since been in and out of state prison for various offenses. For a long time I would have nightmares about the rape. How his eyes rolled around in his head, how he pulled my hair and hit me. I could never understand what I had done to make him do this awful thing to me. . . .

I have always felt like an ugly duck. I have always been very petite and quite dark complexioned. Growing up in the years before being Black was so "beautiful," being dark was a difficult thing. People felt being dark meant you were always up for ridicule, and ridicule they did. It certainly did not help matters that my last name was Snow. Kids would tease me saying, "How could someone so dark have a last name like Snow?" They made me feel as though all the odds were against me in the looks department. Once when I kissed a boy he told me it was nasty. He hurt my feelings so, I didn't try for a long time to form any type of relationship with the opposite sex. As a result of these things, I became quite shy and began to internalize the feelings of being ugly. Even today when I notice someone looking at me in an intensive manner, I begin to feel uneasy. I start to wonder what they are thinking about me. If they think I am too dark, too thin, or just plain ugly. If a man tells me I am attractive, my first reaction is not to believe or trust what he is saying. I feel as though he is merely making fun of me. . . .

James was the first boyfriend I had ever had. We began having sex when I was fourteen and he was sixteen. At the time James was still living with his parents. They had a garage at the back of their home. James and his twin brother had made a room out of the garage. It was very nice. That's where most of our sexual activity took place. Once we did it in a car but we didn't like it so we never did it again. I was glad about that.

When we started going together on a regular basis, I felt as though someone finally wanted me no matter what or who I was. I was to find out later that wasn't true. His feelings for me proved to be almost like feelings of hatred. . . .

At the age of fourteen-and-a-half I became pregnant. It was at this point in my life that my first experiences with physical and emotional abuse began. When James found out that I was pregnant by him, he started treating me like dirt. He would call me names such as bitch and whore. He would say that the baby wasn't his and then beat me up. I had little knowledge of what to expect from a relationship with a man, so I put up with his abuse because it was his child and I didn't want us to split up. I just wanted to be able to work things out.

But James wasn't satisfied with just mistreating me. He threatened to hurt anyone he felt I cared about. The threat that he held against me during these early years was to turn my mother in to the Welfare Department for receiving public assistance while working to make ends meet. He said if I told about the abuse, or tried to leave him, he would turn her in. I stayed. I didn't want my family hurt because of the choices I made regarding my relationship with James.

The day I went into labor, James was nowhere to be found. My stepfather had to take me to the hospital. James did come by later and the first thing he said was why was our baby so black. That hurt me badly. I suppose he needed to find some reason to ridicule me. But even in spite of this bad situation, we managed to work things out and ten months later we got married. My mother didn't want me to get married but I told her if she didn't sign the papers I would run away from home. I thought that I was in love and no one could tell me anything. I simply refused to listen. Finally my mother gave in and signed the papers.

The night of the wedding I was so scared and nervous. Walking down the aisle, my shoe came off. I stopped and put it back on. When I made it to the altar I was still nervous and frightened. The minister who married us was a former schoolteacher of mine. He explained the marriage vows to us step by step. I was so tired of standing, I was glad when it was over.

The first year of our marriage we lived with my mother. James started beating me up whenever my mother left the apartment. He never would give a black eye or harm me in any way that would be noticeable. He started cheating on me with other girls too. He eventually gave me the claps. He told me that he had caught it from sitting on a toilet seat. I believed him until I asked the doctor and he told me the only way to get it was by having sex. I told James what the doctor had said but he still denied it. He would lie and say that he wasn't messing around. But I never trusted him again. He had lied and once again he had hurt me badly. I felt dirty and I had thoughts of killing him for giving me the claps.

I eventually forgave him but I never could put the incident out of my mind completely. It was becoming, this forgiving, a way of existence for me, a prerequisite to maintaining our already destructive relationship. Two years later I had a baby girl. She weighed four pounds, eleven ounces. She was so pretty. At the same time I had our daughter, I found out that my husband had made his girlfriend pregnant. I was so hurt. They didn't have any respect for me. They would walk down the street in front of me. That is what really hurt me. He told me no one else wanted me and I believed him. His girlfriend named her baby after James. My baby was one month older than hers. I remember when she went into labor. James came running home and told me. He was so happy. Then he started to get dressed so he could go to the hospital to see her. I was so hurt that I started to cry after he left. I was never the same person after that.

I began once again to feel self-conscious about my looks and became quite paranoid about what other people were thinking about me. Some were bold enough to tell me to my face that they thought I didn't have a backbone in my entire body. But they didn't know all of the circumstances. By this time James had been living with my family and me for about two years. My mother was still working and receiving public assistance. James's very presence in the home complicated the situation. He once again threatened to report my mother to the proper authorities. Not only for working but for allowing him to live in the home. I truly believe that he would have made good his promise. So I continued to take the beatings and the flaunting of his girlfriend. It took a great amount of time but I finally accepted his behavior toward me with his girlfriend but somehow I never could have any respect for him again.

I started taking birth control pills. James was still treating me like dirt, fighting all the time. I started pulling out my hair and biting my fingernails. I stayed depressed and irritable. I thank the Lord that I still have my sanity. I really believe that my husband was ashamed of me because I am black. I stayed on the pill for about five years. Then the doctor told me to get off of them for about six months. He seemed to feel that my body needed a rest. I stopped taking them. The only other birth control alternative that I was aware of was the condom. Naturally James refused to use them. Consequently the first month I was off the pill I got pregnant. This made my third child.

I wanted to kill myself. Not because of the baby itself but because of the baby's father and how he felt about me. I thought husbands were supposed to love and be proud of their wives. The idea of abortion was not a consideration. For me it is just not the right thing to do. I suppose somewhere in the back of my mind during this period was the thought that I would not get pregnant. Loving someone along with the sexual act was what produced babies. I thought I was safe because I had long ago stopped wanting to have sex with James. He realized this and made me have sex with him. The more he forced me, the more I was turned off. At this point I had become so unfeeling toward sex with him that I started having thoughts that perhaps I was becoming a lesbian. But I suppose I was just responding to his negative behavior, attempting to justify his actions toward me. I thought here he was wanting to have sex with me and I was completely turned off. Something, I thought, must be wrong with me.

The one thing that helped me retain my sanity was my job. Oddly enough, James didn't mind my working but he would accuse me of messing around with the men on my job. I didn't. I was too scared and shy. I was working at a nursing home. I went into labor on the job, my water broke when I was passing out lunch trays to the residents. My supervisor called my husband and he came and got me. He took me to the hospital but he didn't stay with me and that hurt. I had our son without any emotional support from him. Six weeks later I was back on the job. I put the children in a nursery.

I joined the baseball team on the job. James didn't like it but I played anyway. He would pretend to be jealous but I knew that he would use this to start a fight. Somehow I learned to cope. Our children would tell me that while I was playing ball, James would be talking on the telephone to his girlfriend. He had threatened to whip them if they told but they told me anyway. I never told him that I knew. I didn't want the children to get into trouble.

I remember one night going to my sister's house with the children for a visit. When it was time to go home the children wanted to spend the night so I let them. I went home alone. James was out as usual. I was in the living room combing my hair when someone knocked on the door. It was one of James' friends. I told him that James was out. Then he asked me if he could use the bathroom. I hesitated for a moment then I let him in. I hesitated because I wondered if James was up to his old tricks of sending men to our door to see if I would let them in.

But this man seemed in great distress so I allowed him to use the bathroom. I went back into the living room and he went upstairs. A few minutes later I heard him call my name and ask me if I would come upstairs. I couldn't imagine what he wanted. I thought that something had gone wrong with the plumbing. I didn't think he wanted to harm me. When I got upstairs he told me that if I didn't have sex with him he would tell James I was having an affair with him. I became so frightened. I knew that if he told James this terrible thing that James would have no mercy on me. I was so afraid. I did what he wanted me to do. I was crying and so scared, he pulled me into the children's room. He slapped me and pulled my hair, holding me down while he had sex with me. It was horrible.

Then we both heard someone banging on the screen door. It was James yelling to be let into the house. I had locked the screen door out of habit after I let the man in. My heart jumped into my mouth. His friend jumped up and ran into the bathroom. As I went to unlock the door, I was crying and holding my stomach. It was hurting so badly. James called and asked the man about what had happened. He answered that I had let him in so we could have sex. After hearing the man's version of the story, James told him that it was all right. That he, James, knew that a man could only go as far as a woman would let him. I couldn't believe my ears. I really became frightened. After the man left James almost beat me to death. He threw me down the stairs, breaking my tailbone. He accused me of planning the whole thing because I had left the children at my sister's house. He kept me up all night. To this day I really believe that James planned the entire thing just to have the opportunity to really hurt me bad.

When morning came James went to my sister's house and told them he had caught me in bed with his friend. My sister later told me she had been scared to come to my house. She didn't want to see how badly he had beat me. I was really hurt badly. My face and body were all swollen. I didn't know what to do. This happened on a Friday night. It was one of the longest nights of my life.

Then on Sunday, he made me go to church. I cried like a baby. I sat on the back row hoping no one would notice my injuries and start asking me what had happened. I should have never allowed the man [James's friend] to come in but I never thought in my wildest dreams that he had rape in mind. I started having nightmares. James began forcing himself on me more and more, insisting that I give a verbal comparison of his performance to that of his friend who attacked me. It was almost more than I could bear. James started waking me in the middle of the night by hitting me with his fist. I almost had a nervous breakdown. I started going to see a doctor. He gave me some sleeping pills but didn't refer me to an agency for counseling. James finally got bored with the situation and started going out more, staying later and later, sometimes not coming home at all.

During this period in my life I was without a job. I had gotten laid off from the nursing home before the rape. James refused to pay the bills or buy food for the house so I had to get on welfare. My caseworker got me enrolled in a training program for nurse's aides. Even though James was rarely at home any more, when he did come home he would accuse me of messing around with men who were attending training programs in the same building. I finally completed the course and got a job at _________ Hospital, where I still work. I enjoy my work because I like helping and caring for others.

It was about this period of my life that James Junior's eye was badly damaged. James hit him in the eye with a switch. James said it was an accident and I believed him. He would whip the children but it wasn't his style to abuse them physically. I doctored on his eye myself and sent him to school the next day. That evening my son gave me a note from the school nurse requesting that I take him to a doctor. I took him to [the county] hospital. It turned out that his eye had been badly damaged and he had to stay in the hospital for about two weeks. Both my son and I were very upset and frightened. I began to think that he was going to lose the sight of one eye. It turned out he did lose partial sight in that eye. The doctor told me that perhaps in time, James Jr. would outgrow this handicap.

Over the years his sight in that eye became a little better but it will never be like having full vision. I tried to comfort my son and help him to accept what had happened to him, especially during his stay in the hospital. I would spend long hours there with him, sometimes spending the night if he was very upset. At these times I would leave [his hospital room] and go straight to work; often I was late.

Then my supervisor [at work] fired me for being chronically late. All this happened during Christmas time. First my son's accident and now I was out of a job. I was so upset and depressed. When, on the actual day I was fired, after gathering my things together, I walked toward the elevator and the tears just started streaming down my face. I just couldn't hold them in. About midway there a lady stopped me and asked what was wrong. I suppose she saw the desperation on my face. I explained to her what had happened and this wonderful person offered me a job in the Dietary Department. I was so happy, I thanked the Lord. I worked there for about three years. I worked hard to make ends meet.

James hardly ever tried to help keep things together. As a result of his uncaring attitude we lost our apartment and had to move in with my sister and her husband and their five children. I hated to have to do this but I just didn't make enough money to pay the bills and the rent too, not to mention food. It was so crowded in that house we could hardly move around. We stayed for about three months. I did all I could to make the situation more tolerable for everyone. I did my share of the household chores and helped out with the grocery bills every time I got paid. Then my brother-in-law must have become quite dissatisfied with the situation because he started going behind our backs telling lies abut how we weren't doing our fair share.

One day while driving down the street I spotted an empty house. We weren't sure who owned it but I began to make inquiries and found out. We rented with an option to buy. The rent was due on the first of the month but James hardly ever paid it on time. I would get upset because the owners were very nice people and I wanted to pay them on time. I ended up paying the rent, paying the bills and buying the groceries. When I wanted or needed something, I would buy it myself. . . .

James had me to the point where I felt like I was in prison. He could do anything he wanted to do but I couldn't do anything or go anywhere unless he gave the O.K. Most of the time he didn't. He didn't even want me to talk on the telephone. If I got a call, he wanted to know who it was. I didn't have any privacy at all. He would have his friends who lived across the street watch to see if anyone came over while he was away. One day I was outside talking to the lady next door. We weren't talking about anything special. After we finished talking I went into the house to start dinner. The children were outside playing. When James came home he came into the kitchen to see if I was cooking. Then he went across the street to his friend's house. When he came back home he asked me what the lady next door had been talking about. That shocked the shit out of me for him to ask me that. That's how I found out he had his friend watching me. It was as if he was afraid I might find out something he didn't want me to know or that somehow they would convince me to leave him. . . .

One day James and I got into an argument. He was talking about me and then he spit in my face. I was stunned. I was aware of what he had done; I just could not comprehend the reason for his actions. I was so hurt, all I could do was cry. That was my middle name: crying. Crying all the time. Out of all the things James had done and said to me, this was the worst. With the realization of how utterly cruel and demeaning this action was, I began to cry. It was as if someone turned on a faucet. The tears poured from my eyes, rolling down my cheeks for hours. I wished that somehow they would cleanse away the filth of this act. I felt so dirty. I felt as though my existence as a human being was of no value at all to him. How could I continue to go on? But then there were the children to think of. Somehow, I thought, I must survive. I stayed with him.. . .

One Saturday night I was sitting home alone with our baby. James was gone. A friend of mine came by to tell me about a party on the next street. She asked me to go with her. I hesitated for a minute. I thought James would come home, but he didn't so I left with her. I went to the party and guess who I saw? James. Hugged up with his girlfriend and kissing her.

I felt so hurt I just went over to where they were. He pulled me outside and told me to go home. I was so hurt I didn't know what to do. I just stood there for a while but he didn't know I was there. They came outside kissing but they didn't see me. I just left and went home. About three hours later he came home and started fighting with me. I was crying and praying to God to help me. I just felt like committing suicide. The only reason I didn't was because of my children. Who would take care of them? I kept wondering why. Why didn't he just get out of my life? Why did he keep doing these terrible things to me? I wanted to somehow make it right. I wanted him to embrace me with the same warmth and intensity I had seen him display with his girlfriend. I wanted him to love me as I loved him. But in my heart I knew that he never would.

I tried to go to bed. Somehow I thought maybe I could go to sleep, wake up, and it would have all been a bad dream. But the sleep would not come. Then it was time for me to go to work. I could not concentrate on my work. My mind kept going back to James and his girlfriend. I felt like there had to be someway to ease the pain. I started thinking of all kinds of wild things. I even thought of jumping in front of a car or jumping out of a window. But somewhere deep inside me the need to survive outweighed my need for immediate release from this awful situation.

God knows how I put up with it but I did until one day my mother and I went over to my grandmother's house to visit. I started looking through the telephone book and saw the number for Battered Women. I didn't call right away, hoping that James would change and I would have no use for it.

It was during this time that he gave me syphilis. I didn't know that I had it until one day at work I was talking with a co-worker about the spots on my hands. She told me that she had a friend who had the same thing and she had syphilis. So I went downstairs to the clinic and had a blood test. The results were positive. I was hurt. But the hurt was not as intense as in the previous situation when he gave me the claps. I suppose I had become immune to the hurt. I was more disgusted with the relationship more than anything else. I just cried. I cried because it was the only release I had available to me. I called James at work and told him what the nurse had said. He denied it. He said that he wasn't messing with anyone but I knew better. After all, I had seen him with his girlfriend. I decided to go to a private doctor and get my shots. I just didn't want to go to the Public Health Department to get them. I would have been too embarrassed. I was also afraid that I would see someone I knew. Then James decided to go to the Health Department. I had to go to the Health Department anyway. I had paid forty dollars to the private doctor and another five for additional shots I needed at the Health Department. I couldn't go back to work until I had the shots. I wanted to kill myself. I didn't want to have sex with James. He began to say that I must be messing around with someone else. But I wasn't; I was too afraid. Every time I looked at my hands the shock was still there. But in the midst of the shock I thought: How much more could I take? How much more humiliation and pain? How many tears did I have left? I had to do something. I knew that if I didn't, I would lose my mind.

Six months later I began to call the number for Battered Women. I would call everyday to see if they had a place for us, but they didn't. In the mean time I just endured and waited for my chance to escape. My car had been down for about six months. I had just got it running again and I needed some brake shoes. I bought them and James put them on. One day I was coming home from work and the car started making funny noises; then the wheel came off. A man came by and helped me put the tire back on. He asked me who had worked on my car and I answered that my husband had. He said that the wheel lugs hadn't been tightened on the tire. When the tire came off it rolled about fifty feet down the road and the lugs were scattered in the street. We got them and put them back on the car. Then it wouldn't crank up. I was so scared. I knew James would be angry and accusing me of being with someone else if I was late getting home. I called home and told the children to tell their father what had happened. I really wanted to get home before James. I didn't want to have another argument, another fight.

It never entered my mind that perhaps he had done this on purpose.

After all he had changed hundreds of tires and knew better. I thought it was just a freak accident. But no matter what the reason at that time, the fear of his anger and the abuse that would surely follow blocked out thoughts of how serious my almost being killed really was. It seems that the fear of sudden death in an automobile was somehow less frightful for me than the thoughts of the physical and emotional pain I would suffer from him if I in some way triggered his anger.

I had to pay the man to pull the car home. When I got home, James was already there. He was in the bedroom ironing his pants. He asked who the man was and I told him that I didn't know him personally but that he had just stopped to help me with the car. James asked me if he was my boyfriend and I told him no. James acted like he didn't believe me. He was very angry with me. My stomach felt like it was in knots. O God, I was so scared. I started praying to the Lord for help. James didn't get physical and I was so surprised. I thought for sure that he was going to beat me up. He put on his clothes and left the house. He was gone for about four hours. When he returned, he started yelling and calling me names saying that the man was my boyfriend. He said all women were alike. Whores. I told him I wasn't like all the other women he had come in contact with but I couldn't reason with him. Again I thought he was going to get violent but he didn't.

The next morning James got up saying that he would not be coming home that evening. He was talking to our daughter. She really loves her father. He told her that he might not come home until after Christmas. She looked so sad. I didn't have any food in the house except for one package of ground meat and he was saying that he would not be coming home. I was so upset; I was crying. I tried to hold it in. I went on to work and I guess I wasn't my usual self because my supervisor asked me what was wrong and I started talking, telling her everything. I was so upset and confused.

Then I started calling the number for Battered Women. They told me they didn't have anything open yet but to keep calling them back and I did. Finally the lady told me that they were looking through some papers and that they may be calling me right back. I waited as long as I could; then about 7:30 I called them back. The lady told us to meet her at the hospital. The children and I were running around getting our clothes together. All the time I was praying that James wouldn't decide to come home before we could escape. But we got away.

I was so glad and happy and scared. The children seemed happy with the decision to leave. I was thanking the Lord because if the Family Place hadn't helped me I would have killed myself. The people at the Family Place made me feel so welcome but I was still scared. The children seemed to be happy; they were taking it very well, a lot better than I thought they would. But I guess in a lot of ways they were just as tired of the situation as I.

There had been times I sat at home thinking that I was the only woman going through abuse. I would forget things I was supposed to do. My mind was messed up. But I thank God that I still know how to treat people. While at the shelter, I listened to other women talking about what their husbands had done to them and I didn't feel alone but it still hurt. Everyone tells me that I have a nice personality. That's why I couldn't understand why my husband treated me like he did. Since I have been on my own, I have been very happy. I am never going back to him.

As time grew closer for the divorce, I began to get a little nervous. James and I went to court for a hearing. It was the first time I had seen him since we left. I was sitting on the bench outside the courtroom when he got off the elevator. I felt him before I saw him. My mother was there and so was a friend of mine. One of the counselors and my lawyer were also there. No one came with James. James came and sat down by my lawyer and me. So we started talking to each other. He said that he had changed and as if to prove it to the world and me he had a Bible with him. He told me that I could have my friends over if I wanted to. He asked about the children and said that he loved them. He showed me some wedding rings and asked me how I liked them. He said that they were for me and he had just gotten them out of the lay-a-way. I told him I didn't love him anymore. But he still wanted me to keep them. I just put them back into his pocket. I was still feeling empty inside and he was looking into my eyes and saying that he loved me but I didn't feel anything.

The day came for the final court hearing. I felt strange. But I was not having any second thoughts about the divorce. My mother and I caught the bus downtown to the courthouse. I began to feel more and more nervous as we neared our destination. The ride seemed to take longer than normal and when we finally got there, it seemed as though my lawyer wasn't ever going to make it. I started thinking that she might not show up for some reason. But she did. I relaxed a little but then every time the elevator doors opened, my heart would pound so hard I thought it would jump right out of my chest. Then I would look to see if it was James. I was afraid of the final confrontation. After our last meeting and the way he acted, I just didn't quite know what to expect. I really was hoping he wouldn't show up. I just wanted my divorce. I didn't want to see him; I didn't want to hear his version of what happened to our marriage. I just wanted out!

I had to stand up in front of the judge and swear in. I told the entire truth and when I finished, the judge granted me the divorce. I was so happy. I felt like a heavy burden had been lifted from my shoulders. I was finally free from all the hurt and humiliation, from all the betrayal. I was free from the fear and uncertainty of his next attack. I was free to be whomever and whatever I wanted to be. I was finally free to not merely exist in this life but to actually begin living it.

But even in the midst of my joy, there was sorrow. The day after the divorce, I became quite depressed. I suppose that's normal. It took me a little time but I was finally able to shake the feeling. Now I am very content. It is hard but I know that I can make it.

Since the children and I have been on our own, we have all been freer to express and show our love and support for one another. We no longer have to try and fight through that dark cloud that seemed to constantly hang over our heads when their father and I were together. Naturally the children do miss seeing their father and no matter how bad the relationship between James I has been, I would never try to prevent them from seeing him. I let them go and spend some weekends with him and they really seemed to enjoy themselves. I would sometimes feel jealous thinking that they might want to be with him instead of me but those were my own feelings of insecurity, feelings that I quickly dispelled.

Long after the divorce was final, I would lie awake at night trying to find a reason for the way James acted toward me. I never could come up with a legitimate one. My big mistake had been staying with him, even for the children's sake. They were just as unhappy as I. But I know now that it had been the wrong thing to do. As a result there will probably be some things they will never be able to deal with but I have faith that they will not let this experience destroy their lives. For sure it did affect them, that was evident. They did at first show signs of unacceptance. They became sullen and belligerent. But with love, patience and prayer, we were able to work things out.

My freedom has become very important to me. I enjoy meeting and seeing men but I am not sure if I ever want to commit myself to just one man again. Perhaps one day I will find that special someone who will love and respect me. But, until I do, I'll continue to live the single life.

I don't mean to imply that it has been an easy road, because it has not. But I firmly believe that one can make it if they try no matter what the odds are in this type of situation. Since divorcing James, I have done so much better in every way. I am still working hard but I am able to take care of my household without the help of anyone. We might not have all of the luxuries but we sure do have the necessities. During this period since the divorce, I have purchased a new car. For me this was a major accomplishment. We have also recently moved into a house. I am not buying it, just renting but it is a start. I did try to buy one through HUD but they declined my application. They said I didn't have enough money in my savings account. But I am not discouraged. I will try again. Right now, we are happy to be living in a house.

In conclusion, I would like to say to all of those who read this story, I know and understand what it means to be labeled "battered wife." I say to you who are going through this turmoil, or those who find themselves still surrounded by the web of hostility and destruction: no matter how powerless you may feel, no matter how hopeless the situation appears, there is a way out. The door to the release is there, and it is open. There are people who will care and support you and do everything in their power to help you get out. But first you must find that door. Walking, running, or crawling, it doesn't matter. The important thing is that you must—and you can—get there. Your very life depends on it. ■

## Excommunicated

Wilma Goolsby-Gibbs

As far back as I can remember, there was always a tugging at my heartstrings for something more than mere existence. I felt it when I was small, an inner struggle leading me toward something different, something special, a place of my own. After a lifetime of searching for that place in which I could find peace, I felt I had found it in a small brick church.

For ten years I attended services making acquaintances with the congregation, young and old. There was always something going on: fund raisers, pot-luck suppers, prayer meetings, Sunday school, and night and special services. All three of my children and I were Baptized there, my youngest child being three years old when we started and thirteen when we felt the need to leave. He is now almost seventeen so the painful past is four years behind us and time does heal, for which I am thankful.

I didn't realize it then but peace comes from God. When I am happy, it is only by his leading and my following. When I need a friend, he is always there. He has always been as close as I let him.

It was while we were attending that church that circumstances began that would change our lives forever. My daughter, then fifteen, was sexually abused. My oldest son and I were both physically and emotionally abused and my youngest son was emotionally abused as well. All this abuse was committed by the children's father, now my ex-husband Jack, who was a minister of the church.

The children and I went several times for counsel to the pastor and his wife, and another minister in the church. At first I didn't know that we were not believed. Finally, they told me point blank that they thought we were lying about a man of God. I was shocked, embarrassed, and angry. It was hard because we knew we were telling the truth. We had gone to this church for so long by now that we felt as though we belonged. Now all of a sudden we didn't even feel welcome. It was as if we were being rejected by our own mother. I hadn't realized I was using the church for props until suddenly they got knocked out from under me. I was scared. My kids must surely have felt the same even though they never mentioned it.

In the days to come there were many conflicting emotions which made coping with everyday living difficult. One day I wanted to run away; the next day I wouldn't think of it. Some days I would think of giving up on life; then the next thought that entered my mind was "never." I wrote a poem entitled "I'll Never Quit."

Writing has always been an escape for me from the wear and tear of the moment. Although I have never found a way out of the suffering that resulted from the past, I have found a way to endure. When I am happy, I write. When I am sad, I write. My pencil frees me from the bondage of thought by letting my feelings flow from my mind to the paper.

My decision to tell our story has not been an easy one. However, the public must become aware of what is happening in the world today. Not only out in the world but inside American homes where families are supposed to love and protect one another. Maybe these pages will encourage other victims to turn in the perpetrators of their abuse, expose them for what they are, and find peace for themselves free from shame. These criminals must stand accountable for their behavior. They must be punished.

Although I look as normal as anyone else, there are emotional scars that will never heal and spinal damage that can still lead to other physical problems. Jack caused my whiplash when he choked me. I can still feel his hands around my throat, hear him slobbering and yelling, "I'm going to shut you up," or "I wish God would close that mouth of yours permanently," or "I'm going to rip your mouth out." Sometimes I thought he would kill me. Then if I would cry or scream out in pain, he would hiss, "Quit puttin' on—you're not hurt."

Today I can say that I am happy and love life, but there was a time when I was so unhappy that I stayed at home and kept the shades pulled down all day, sometimes for weeks at a time. I was ashamed to be seen and ashamed to see anyone as a result of the time I spent with my children's father. The truth is, he did so many things to us that it is hard to remember them all. Then I was like so many other women I have heard say, "Oh, he just slapped me around a little."

Now I know that is excusing something major. Allowing someone to abuse or molest my body is as bad as the church thinks drunkards and smokers are. Alcohol and nicotine damage the body they say. I say abuse also damages the body—someone else's body!—and can result in death. Abuse is a killer.

If abuse could be measured to see who actually suffered more, I would have to guess that although I suffered the most physical abuse at my ex-spouse's hands, my daughter Alice's emotional and sexual abuse surely outweighs all the rest. She was young and innocent, an unsuspecting child who placed her faith and trust in the hands of a madman even if we didn't realize his madness at the time.

The "grooming" period through which she went was horrible. She was granted special privileges by her dad behind my back under the guise of "Christianity." He said he was the head of our house. Many times he would get up in our faces, his whole head almost as red as blood and yell, "I'm the head of this house and you will obey me!" He also encouraged our daughter to go for birth control pills, which I found hidden under her mattress. I threw them away. He let her drive the car before she had a license. He tried to get me out of the picture. One day he wanted me to visit my mother; the next day he wanted to know why I had to go to my mom's so much. He would give me money to go grocery shopping on Sunday after church and tell the boys to go with me. Then he would say Alice had to stay home and do the dishes so that she didn't get to go.

She threatened to tell me many times but he told her if she did it would kill me. He said I'd have a heart attack and die. She knew I was taking heart medication at the time and was convinced he was right. The stress he induced at our house was so great that besides the 80 mg. of heart medication I took daily, I also had to take thyroid, nerve and ulcer pills. At one time I took as many as thirteen pills daily for stress-related problems. When I started coming off the medication—I quit some cold turkey—I had to come down 5 mg. at a time. I went through withdrawal each time.

Alice also started having nervous problems. She had so much pain with her period that she would have to be taken to the emergency room for a shot. Sometimes she wound up being admitted to the hospital.

When we finally got up enough courage to tell on him, we were knocked back down by the elders in our church. Because of past teaching from the church we believed that if we had a problem we should take it to the elders. When we did they did not believe Jack had done the things we said. We confided in these people with the truth and they said our accusations were false. Maybe their disbelief caused us to fight back.

After we told on Jack, we were given dirty looks by people we had gone to church with for years. Some of the members wouldn't even speak to us. I don't know where they were leaving God or what scripture they were using, but they sure excommunicated the wrong party. As far as our perpetrator was concerned, he was given more sermons to preach, more pats on the back and a cooler full of meat when I obtained a protective order against him. Why they did not believe what we told them is still a mystery to me.

On different occasions I found pornographic material at our house. I always confronted him with the paraphernalia and insisted he get rid of it. He was always hiding books. Once I sacked up a whole grocery bag full and took it to the church. When I arrived at church Jack was there. I took the sack to the office and told the pastor it was a sack of dirty books and they were Jack's and I had told him I didn't want them around because I was afraid the children would get hold of them. Jack began saying they weren't his, that he had found them under a bush beside the house. He said "the kids'" and I told him they were not the kids' magazines.

The pastor was quick to say, "Now, Wilma, you say your kids would not do anything like that."

And I said, "I did not say they wouldn't. I said these books are not theirs." Every time I tried to get their help, they refused me. The pastor even told me to "lay the axe to the root of the tree and let the chips fall where they may." The axe had already been laid, by a master feller, and the chips were being stacked as a result of the first blow.

Once when the pastor and his wife were visiting our home, because of an off-color remark Jack made, the pastor's wife called him a dirty old man. She didn't know how right she was. I am still mystified as to how she came to the assumption that he was a dirty old man and not believe he was guilty of the "dirty" stuff we accused him of. It seemed as if she was saying she could make the decision but we couldn't.

As a result of Alice telling on her dad, she spent time in a foster home. It seemed as if she continued to suffer for something she had not been responsible for. I am glad she told the truth and exposed her daddy for his wrongdoing. For one thing I did not wish to be married to a man who would commit adultery much less incest. Also, I did not wish to attend a church where incest offenders were patted on the back. Although I know there are good people there and some whom I am still close to, I will never allow any man to make a decision for me again, from the pulpit or anywhere.

I believe that as a result of Alice telling on her dad, there may be other girls [members of that church] who are in the same predicament as Alice who are afraid to tell the truth, afraid they won't be believed either. On the other hand, perhaps there are some who have told who would never have if Alice hadn't found the courage to turn in her father.

Alice was so mixed up at times, she has told me many thoughts she had during the ordeal. I remember she said at one time she thought all dads did it to their daughters. It makes me mad to think I was not aware of her trauma in a way I could help her. However I am glad she realizes how confused she was and that it was not her fault. I cringe when an incident reminds me of the past. There are so many things I'd simply like to forget. I sometimes think I have forgotten then, wham, another little reminder straight to the present.

I have heard people say how sorry they feel for a man who has been called into the ministry and has no support at home. I want to tell them I wanted to stay married, I had no desire to be divorced, and I would have gone to the end of the world with my husband. After he began preaching, the abuse and ridicule he directed at his family became worse.

During this period I noticed other changes in his attitude. He became quieter, often deep in thought, then wilder at other times, causing more confusion. He decided he no longer wanted sex with me, that he had no desire for marital relations and was going to "just serve God." I knew the Bible well enough to know this was against the scriptures but there was nothing I could do about it. He also started wrestling with Alice, spending more time alone with her, giving her "fatherly" advice, and putting her between us when we went to church. All these things were building in my mind and I couldn't shake the evil feeling.

I went back to the church. Another minister said that if Jack was abusing Alice or committing incest, she was as much to blame as her dad. In other words, if he was going to believe it, which he wasn't, he was going to blame the child and not the responsible adult. All the years we went there to church we were taught to obey the elders. This particular elder repeatedly told my daughter face to face that she had to obey her father.

I asked, "Anything he wants, we have to do?" His reply was that we wouldn't be asked to do anything wrong.

Looking back, I can almost pinpoint the day Alice's dad forced her into their hellish relationship. It was summer of 1981. She was fifteen, nearing her sixteenth birthday. She had been to church camp in Oklahoma. We were getting ready to spend another week at Camp _____, a local church camp. The pressure was so great that the presence of evil could be felt. I don't remember where I had been that morning, but I remember Alice crying all day. I tried to talk to her but she wouldn't listen. She screamed at her brothers when they said anything to her and acted horrible. Her dad excused her saying it was the "wrong time of the month." Even the sound of his voice gave me chills, but I couldn't accuse him without evidence. I begged Alice to tell me what was going on. She said nothing. I didn't know she was afraid telling me would kill me.

He started giving her money for makeup, not allowing me to discipline her, and letting her go places she couldn't go before. Along with her special privileges came meaner treatment. One day he was her buddy, the next he called her names derogatory to females and kicked or punished her. Once he spit on her.

Again, I went to the church for help and also complained through three different states attorneys. The pastor told me I didn't have grounds for divorce because Jack had not admitted his offenses to me and that God would not be pleased. The response of the church made me feel the web was being woven and no one could see except us. It was as if we were being tried and convicted by people who claimed to know the truth. I don't know at what point I realized they were wrong. They were not going to help.

When Alice told me her father did these things to her, I moved out of our bedroom but I stayed in the marriage because of my commitment to the church at the time. Eventually my husband admitted the incest but said Alice "tempted" him and it was her fault—a lie from the pit of hell.

Once my mind almost snapped and I held a gun on Jack to try to persuade him to tell the truth about his conduct with Alice. My son Jack Jr. stood in the hall and cried and begged me to come out. My mind kept thinking: what would my mother think, how would the kids feel in school if their friends knew? They would be so ashamed, it would be in all the papers.

I talked to a woman who shot her abuser. She said she doesn't remember thinking at all. There must have been a breaking point which she crossed that I hadn't reached. I'm glad I never stopped thinking.

Both my sons say they will never marry. I am hoping in time they will change their minds and meet someone with whom they can share a lifetime of happiness. Perhaps they are afraid they won't make good husbands and fathers or are worried they will be abusers.

Alice lives in Georgia with her husband and son. She went through many sleepless nights and a miscarriage before getting pregnant and was afraid God was punishing her for what she had done. When she became pregnant with her second child, she called worrying that her dad might harm the baby. She said she doesn't want her children to know he is their grandfather. Whatever their problems and concerns, I tell my kids: Be all you can be, do all you can do, and have all you can have without harming anyone in the process.

I now live on a farm with my new husband who has also been a great friend. I never thought I would again trust a man enough to marry him. However, I love married life and enjoy being a wife. Doc is more gentle than I could even imagine a man could be. . . .

There have been a few times in my present marriage when the emotional scars show up. One night I dreamed my ex-husband was after me and I was running away from him. I was still trying to scream when I woke Doc up. It was the break of daylight and when my eyes opened and I saw his dark hair, my relief was great.

Another time when I was reminded of the past was on an afternoon when Doc and I were cleaning the yard. I had taken a load of tree limbs off and was coming back toward the house with the empty wheelbarrow. I was tired and sat down in it and leaned back to rest. Doc was on the riding mower coming up behind me and I began to panic. The closer he came, the louder the engine became and the more my heart raced. I wanted to jump up and turn around to find out what was going to happen. I had to force myself to lie there, knowing he would not harm me, living with the fear of the past. He stopped, leaned over and kissed me, then drove on, never knowing that day what I felt. I didn't know at the time, however when I was allowing myself to be abused, I was allowing myself to be conditioned. Sometimes the sound of my ex-husband's voice caused my nerves to flinch. I wonder if I will ever be free from the conditioning. ■

**Will You Please Just Take Ten Minutes To Talk To Me!**
Interview—12/13/89
Penny Freeman and Miriam Kalman Harris

*Editor's Note:*

Penny Freeman is the daughter of Elizabeth Wilson, a woman I met through the hospital program. One Sunday evening Elizabeth called me at home for information she hoped would help her daughter. Penny had just escaped from her husband Ken [not his real name] and sought refuge at her mother's home with her young son Jason. All of them were frightened and confused. What should they do next? We spoke at length, and I suggested that perhaps I could help Penny untangle the issues and choices she faced by speaking with her in person.

I went to Elizabeth's house. In order to avoid upsetting Jason any further, the three of us went outside to talk, leaving Jason with Penny's stepfather. We sat in the dark courtyard, and Penny told her story. With every rustle of leaves, every passing car, the three of us would jump. Had Ken noticed that Penny and Jason were missing? Had he figured out where they were hiding? Would he track them down? Were all of our lives in danger? Should we call the police?

After about an hour, Penny felt better about coming to her mother's [Ken would be less likely to show up here than at various friends' homes], and we agreed it was the best place for her, at least temporarily. A counseling center for abused women was just a few blocks away. Penny could go there in the morning and join a support group. Both she and Jason could receive counseling, and Penny could begin to make definite decisions concerning Jason's school and day care—should she move him so that Ken could not "kidnap" him?—and her job—was she safe entering and leaving a building where Ken could find her?

In the ensuing weeks, Penny called and kept me apprised of her progress in "separating" from Ken, discussing the ins and outs of some tedious and controversial problems as they arose. The process of her journey to independence, the ethical choices she faced in keeping her son safe without breaking the law, typify the stressful circumstances abused women must endure when they choose to leave. I asked her to set up a second appointment for an interview so that we could record her story while it was still unfolding.

A few weeks after she left him, Penny received a letter from Ken. Had she been less resolved, had she received less support from family and counselors, she might have been unable to withstand the harsh accusations of his words. That she held her ground and kept her self-perceptions and goals intact is a mark of the strength of character Penny achieved after leaving Ken. The title of Penny's story is taken from the opening words of the first letter, which is printed near the end of the interview.

The day of the interview she received a second letter.

■■■

**Miriam:** Do you remember the date of our first meeting?

**Penny:** October 29, our anniversary. We'd gone out that Friday, and everything was OK. He [Ken] started getting real funny about it, like I owed it to him 'cause we rarely went out. In fact the last time we'd gone out was our anniversary two years ago. So, we were going to go out and have a nice dinner. Jason was at his aunt's house that weekend, and we went out to TGI Friday's, and everything was okay. But before we left [for dinner] . . . I told him if I had to beg him to take me out, he could just forget it.

So that was okay. And then when we got back that night, we'd gone to a friend's house that he does drugs with and stayed there. I wanted to go home—I was kinda tired—but he acted funny about going home. He didn't want to leave, but we eventually did leave without an argument.

Saturday there was a Halloween party we were to go to at the same friend's house. We had gone over there earlier that day, and I wanted to get back home so I could get things together before the party and get my costumes ready and stuff. He got angry and didn't want to leave, so I asked a friend of mine who was there if she could take me home. It was no big deal. If he wanted to stay, it was fine. I wanted to go home, and he wouldn't take me. He got mad because I asked her to take me home, and he ended up taking me home. Then he left and came back later that evening, and he was OK, fine. I guess he'd been drinking or something and calmed down.

So we went to the party, and it was about 1:00 or 2:00 in the morning. I wanted to go home—I was tired, I drank enough, ya know it was time to go home. He didn't want to leave, and I didn't have my house key, so I asked him for the house key. I didn't mind if he stayed at the party, I just wanted to go home, and he didn't want to take me. I just wanted the house key, and a friend of mine, Terilee, was going to take me home. He still wouldn't give me the house key. So I went home with them and stayed at their house, and then about 3:30 he came over there and picked me up, and he was mad because I left, and [he kept asking] why didn't I want to stay and stuff.

We got home and went to bed, and the next morning he asked me to go fill up the truck with gas and go get some cigarettes, and what he wanted was the deal with three packs of Camels and you could get a free video tape with it. So, I was to go get that and the gas. I went to the store and got a pack of Marlboro 100s, which is what I normally smoke, and I was trying to cut down so I wasn't buying cigarettes. When I got home and he found out I'd bought the Marlboro 100s, he just really got upset.

M: Why?

P: Because he told me to buy the three packs of Camels. I bought those too, but I also bought mine, the Marlboro 100s.

M: Why would that upset him?

P: Because he told me not to do that. He told me to buy Camels and we were trying to save money, and I bought one pack of cigarettes that are what, a $1.50? So, I blew our budget right there. And he left in a huff, and Jason had been at his aunt's all weekend and her car had broken down at my house Friday. So I had told her to take my car and leave her car there and then when I go to get Jason, I'd have her car fixed and I still needed a jump.

I wanted to get Jason, and Ken didn't want to and he said, "Why do you have to do everything now?" I missed him [Jason], he'd been gone all weekend. So he [Ken] left and I stayed at the house until 2:30 or 3:00, and then walked over to a friend's house and asked for jumper cables. Well it so happens that Ken was there too [at the friend's house]—I guess that's where he had been all that time.

M: So, it's like as long as he says it, that's the way it's supposed to be done. You're not supposed to disagree.

P: Oh, no, he sets the rules, and we obey. Otherwise he'll go into a rage and if you don't want him to go into a rage, you do as he says.

M: And he didn't hurt you—when you got the Marlboros?

P: No, he just went out in a rage and was upset and didn't tell me where he was going—just left and slammed the door, and when I got over there, I asked Carl if he had some jumper cables and he said yes and they were sitting in the garage. Carl got up to get the jumper cables and Ken said something about the cigarettes and I said it was none of [his] goddamn business, etc. And he jumped up, grabbed me by the arm, and threw me into a chair, I guess it was three to five feet away from where I was standing, and then grabbed me by the neck and kicked the cigarettes out of my hands and my keys and then was hollering at me and stuff. Then Carl came up with the jumper cables and I said, "Thank you." Then I left to walk home.

And when I got across the street, he came tearing down the street and around the corner. He came driving up and hollered, "Bitch, get into the car," and "Get in the truck."

I kept walking and he drove the pickup in front of me like to cut me off, and I got into the truck and he just flew home which was right around the corner anyway. I got out of the truck, and he got into the van and got it started and then he told me to get in the van, and I said to him, "I'm not going anywhere with you right now." He took it around the corner to get the tire aired up and then pulled it back up to the house. Then got in his truck and sped down the street, and he was going so fast that he almost slid into oncoming traffic. So I got in the van and was in the process of driving to Red Oak to pick up Jason, and the van broke down in Oak Cliff and I'd been crying the whole way, praying actually to be made free of Ken.

M: What do you mean by that, to be made free?

P: Well, I always felt trapped, like I was never ever going to get away, like there was no escape ever. I didn't know what to do, so I called Mom and told her I needed to talk. And she came and got me, and we went and got Jason. We talked and then got home, and we didn't know what we were going to do. I wanted to leave, but I didn't know what I should do. By that time I had been thinking I had been blowing this all out of proportion.

**M:** You mean you thought maybe you shouldn't leave?

**P:** Yes. And that's when we got home, and Mom called you, and you came over and talked to me and told me about the cycle and that stuff.

**M:** And that helped to hear about the cycle?

**P:** Yes, because it applied. I never thought about it, but it applied to the way our life had gone. Each time, I pretty much thought: he never put me in the hospital, never gave me a black eye—well he did, but I had forgotten about those times—but never anything serious. I always thought a battered wife was someone beaten to a pulp, so I had never thought of myself that way. I knew I was in an abnormal situation, but I never thought of it as that severe. It helped me to realize that it was not normal, that it gets worse. You told me it gets worse as the years go on, and it has. I just decided then that I wasn't going to wait around until I was put into the hospital.

Mom and everybody have been so supportive. I'm staying with them now. Then I went to the Family Place, and they did that checklist and there are twenty or twenty-five items on that list. The counselors ask you questions when you go in, and they check off things that apply to you. All but two of them he has done to me, and that was shocking. I couldn't believe it. And the counselor said, "Well, you fit the bill."

**M:** And I think that kind of confirmation is what you need to be strong enough to accept a letter like this, because that letter would devastate you in the state where you were diminishing it [the abuse], saying, "Well, I'm blowing it out of proportion." In that state of mind you would have read this letter and said, "Oh I've done terrible things to this wonderful man who has pulled us out of all of these financial problems, which of course he hasn't done at all. But until you can hold onto your perceptions. . . . I think that is what you get going to a place like the Family Place and hearing from other women. Hearing their stories confirms your own story.

**P:** Yeah, I'm not crazy after all. I didn't imagine all this; this did go on. And going [to counseling] on a weekly basis, things have been coming back. I'm remembering things that had happened and that's hard—to think and push it back because you don't want to remember it. You don't want to think of this person doing this stuff to you, and it's hard. It comes back slow, and it's hard to accept at first.

**M:** It's hard to imagine . . .

**P:** Yeah, that you put up with it . . . .

**M:** and it's embarrassing, like, "How could I have let myself be treated that way?" I think we all do that, we do it with people, we do it with jobs, with friends and then after things come to a crisis, we wonder, "Why did I let them treat me that way, why didn't I speak up?" And of course anything with marriage is going to be even more intense.

**P:** Yeah. It's hard to believe that I let it go on for so long.

**M:** But you didn't really, compared to some women. How long were you married? How long did it go on?

**P:** Six years. It went on before we were married, for eight years. He was already acting domineering, and I had choke marks on my neck at that time too, before I married him.

**M:** What was going on? What was your mother saying [the first night I met P]?

**P:** She couldn't stand him, couldn't understand why I would marry him, but at that time there was nothing she could do or say because I knew it all. I was going to do what I wanted, and I was involved in drugs too and that had a lot to do with it I'm sure.

**M:** You mean you were doing drugs with him?

**P:** We were both taking drugs then. Before we got married is when I quit. I haven't taken drugs since. That definitely had something to do with it, because you know it affects your mind and the way you think.

**M:** Uh-huh. Do they talk about that [during counseling] at all? How drugs play into the relationship?

**P:** We haven't gotten that far yet, what happens before the marriages. [We talk about] what's going on now and what kind of changes I'm making [in my] behavior. I've never had any inclination or desire to go back to him right now, since I've left. Ya know it's like I'm out of there, I'm free! I am never going back.

**M:** I think as long as you keep that memory of driving down the highway, hoping to be saved by a catastrophe—I think often people think maybe something will happen, maybe he'll get killed, to take choice out of your . . .

**P:** Yeah, rather than make me make a step, make something else happen. Throughout our whole marriage I used to pray he would die, that something would happen to him, and then I'd feel guilty because I was thinking that way and he had done all these things for us and he was such a good man and all this other crap.

**M:** Well, and he's supposed to be a good man, he's supposed to take care, that doesn't give him the right to hurt you. I think we forget that too, we make excuses for the people in our lives, and we remember the good things. But that's what you're supposed to be. You don't get rewarded for it. You're supposed to behave yourself. The reward for good behavior is not getting to knock your wife around, and I think we've just bought into so much of that, "I do all this stuff for you"—and what does he do for you? He does it all for himself as well!

**P:** He would leave and be gone, and I would ask him, "Where are you going?" And he would say, "It's none of your business." Then he'd leave and come home at 1:00 or 2:00 in the morning, and I wouldn't know where he'd been or what he'd done or whatever. A couple of times, he'd take off for a couple of days—several times he did that—and Jason would be ready to go to bed and say, "Where is my daddy?" I'd say, "Well, he's got to work late," and Jason would wake up in the morning and his dad would be gone and I'd say he had to go to work early, lying to him so he wouldn't know.

Well, what he [Ken] wanted, was to run around and do whatever the hell he wanted to, then to come home to Jason and me and have us at his convenience. And I said, "No, I'm not going to have anything to do with that. If you leave, I'm considering this marriage over." I meant, essentially, "Yeah, leave, don't let me stop you."

Yes, I would have loved for him to have left. I would have been scared financially. I never knew how I was going to do it, but this last time it just got to the point where I realized this was serious stuff here and that if I don't do something about this now, I'm doomed to this forever. I think that is why it worked this time, 'cause last year I tried to leave and be fair and tell him about it and let him know what was going on and everything. He kept me up, and

I work a full-time job.

M: You mean he kept you up all night? That's pretty typical too—have you heard other stories?

P: Yeah, that's what they said [at counseling]. He kept me up, and I got maybe an hour or two of sleep for four days, and I decided, well, give him another chance. Then I'd go to work, and he'd come home and the same thing: fighting and carrying on and then him saying, "I'll change," and begging, pleading, constant, all night long, and I'd lay down in bed and say, "I'm not going to listen to this anymore." And he'd shake me and say, "I'm going to keep you up all night, and no you're not going to do this to me, you're not going to tear the family up."

Then he'd start acting crazy. He didn't hurt me those four days, but he scared the daylights out of me several times when I thought he was going to. He was out of control, he didn't have control of the situation anymore, and so I decided to stay. Then the very day I decided to stay, he went out with one of his buddies to the Hard Rock Cafe. I didn't know where he was or what he was doing, came home, and he had wrecked his truck, brand new '88 truck . . .

The next day I went ahead and put a deposit down on an apartment and let him talk me back into staying that night. He told me he just wanted to go out one more time, and I believed him. And things were OK for three or four months. We moved into a house, he always said we had to have a house, 'cause we lived in an apartment, yeah, always blaming it on something we had to do.

■■■

M: Why was he smashing in his car windows?

P: Because he couldn't get his car started, and that is how he took out his frustration by hitting or kicking something. So, he was kicking in his windows, with his foot, a car window. I was in bed upstairs, and I looked out and saw all this going on.

M: What happens to you when that happens?

P: I get real scared because I don't know what he's going to do, all the violence. Whether he is going to get angry with me and come and throw me around. I kind of walk on eggshells when that happens. It's real scary to see someone act like that, because they are totally out of control. They are in a complete rage. You don't know what they are going to do. They are not thinking. It's like someone else takes over when they are acting like that.

■■■

M: You probably can't depend much on child support. If it comes, fine, but . . .What about visitation rights and custody?

P: I'm fighting for supervised. I'm not signing anything. I'll stay married to the man forever unless he gets supervised visitation. I'll keep protective orders on him forever. He's not going to get any other visitation unless it's supervised . . .

M: Because of . . .

P: Because of his drug habits throughout the past few years, the violence towards me and the emotional abuse towards Jason. I've heard that . . . if the husband is beating the wife, then eighty percent of the time they are beating the kids too or they will, and I'm not going to take that chance, mainly because of the drugs, and he's used drugs ever since I've known him. He used to take Jason where he'd pick up, and when I found out about it, we stopped that. A lot of times he'd just take off with Jason, and I had no say-so, and Jason was being influenced by these people sitting around in these drug houses and stuff. And again with the schools and stuff, he would get angry with me the night before or that morning and then he'd decide he wasn't going to pick up Jason, not call anybody to go pick him up, so the school would call me fifteen to thirty minutes later saying Jason hasn't been picked up yet.

That happened twice. After the second time, I started picking Jason up. One time I was fixin' to leave town, to go to Grapevine for a couple of hours 'cause I was doing side work after I got home with my full-time job. I was cleaning houses to make extra money, and again he was the one who pulled us out of financial distress [sarcastic], and I would have been gone for several hours, they wouldn't have known where to reach me, 'cause I had assumed Ken had picked him up. They wouldn't have known where to reach Ken. Well, thank God I decided to go by the school, and it was about five minutes to close and Jason hadn't been picked up. Well, that night Ken got home about 10:30 or 11:00 drunk. He had never even gone by, and his excuse was [that] I should have known to pick Jason up, I should have known he wasn't going to pick him up. The other time it was 6:30 and they called to tell me Jason hadn't been picked up, so I went and got him then. He's never actually been left for several hours 'cause that one time I checked and the other time I was home and they called me to pick him up. He still even . . . here's a five-year-old being left at school, and Ken didn't think that was wrong. He thought no, I should have known that he wasn't going to pick Jason up, that I should have known to pick him up without him calling me or letting me know, never made any arrangements with anybody, didn't call the school, nothing, just didn't show up, then shows up later that night drunk. I cannot let a man who does that take Jason for the weekend. There's no telling where he'll wind up. So I'm not going to do that. I'm going to fight like hell for supervised visitation.

M: That means you supervising?

P: No, a representative, some kind of social worker or something stays with Jason. I believe it's like a monthly basis for a couple of hours and hopefully he'll [Ken] get tired of that.

M: Yeah, he's not going to do that for very long. There's no fun in that, no power, and he's definitely a power person. What are the chances that he would just leave town?

P: NONE! He won't leave, 'cause I scared him that time I called the police on him—he hasn't been by since. He hasn't been by the office [since the time he left the letter], except for the time I was told he was driving around the house, and I did call the police that night and they put extra patrol. But I think he knows I mean business, and if he doesn't, he's gonna find out, because I'm not giving in, because I'm not gonna sacrifice Jason for what he did. He deserves to see his son—well, he was gone for several days, or wouldn't come home until after Jason's bed[time]. Well, he didn't see him then, it didn't seem to bother him; he wants to see him at his convenience and it's not convenient for Jason right now to do that.

M: What does Jason say right now about his father? Is he relieved or . . .

P: At first he wanted to see him. They got along real well, but Ken never really had a lot of good to say about what Jason did, and Jason often used to come home crying from soccer practice that Daddy told him he was not a good player, and Jason was one of the star players, and I'm not saying that because I'm his mother—he is a darn good player, and if he'd mess up or something Ken would only talk about what he did wrong, not that he was good. Even now Jason is always looking for approval in men, strangers even, any man he wants approval from, and I feel like it's because he hasn't gotten it from his father.

At first he wanted to see him, and he used to say, "I'm gonna go live with Daddy," and I'd say, "No, you're gonna live with Mom," and he stopped that after a while, and he's scared for me. He's going to counseling, and the counselor said he's seen a lot, and I didn't realize he'd seen that much—I knew he'd seen some, but I didn't realize how much. He knows that Daddy, that Ken, can hurt me, and he's beginning to feel like he has to protect me, and I guess that's because every now and then I get nervous about Ken, and he senses that in me so I have to stop that before it gets out of hand—it's hard.

M: But how could you stop it? The reality of both of your lives is that Ken is someone to be afraid of.

P: Yeah, 'cause I am scared. He is capable of doing a lot more, and I've just got to try to make it [seem] less. It's so obvious to Jason, 'cause he feels like he has to protect me.

Well, like he went to counseling today and he drew a picture: there was a house, and me and Jason were outside, and there was bright green grass where me and Jason were standing. There was a tree, and on the other side of the tree there was dark yucky grass, and then his daddy was drawn in black, and before he drew the house the counselor said it was just me and Jason, and then he said, "Wait, I have to draw a house," and she said, "Why?" And he said, "That way when Daddy comes, Mommy will have somewhere to go." And he drew the house and put me in the house and then where his daddy was he drew himself going over there and kicking him, like he was protecting Mom and that's not real good for him to be doing that. Yeah, he's working it out and that's good.

M: Are you sure he never hurt him physically?

P: Not that I know of. He's been rough with him, but not . . .

M: Tell me what you mean by rough.

P: Well, like Jason would be taking a bath, and he'd go in and holler and scream and Jason would be just tense. And things he would say, just rough, things you just don't normally say to a kid. You know, just let him be five. He doesn't know everything he's supposed to do. Of course he is going to misbehave, and it just bothered Ken. He had to constantly behave—that's why I'm sure it [the abuse] would have come to Jason, eventually.

M: What about spankings and things?

P: He, well, yeah, he spanked him, but it wasn't very often towards the end. I truly don't think he abused Jason. I think he was capable of it, but at this point I don't think he did. I know he'd be capable, and I know eventually it would have come into play, but I don't think he has to this point [except] because of the way he would talk to Jason, he's yanked him and stuff like that. . . .Shoot, I didn't know what battered women were. How am I supposed to know what child abuse is?

M: I just thought your mother said something about Ken using the belt on him to an extreme.

P: When he was younger, he used to spank him a lot, when he was little. Yeah, he quit doing that, and we got to where it was with the hand, and I had started to put Jason in a chair for punishment anytime I would try to do something to help as far as discipline and stuff like that because I don't like spankings myself, and he would always sabotage anything I did. He'd holler at me, "You need to spank him!" and if I was disciplining him it was, No, I was wrong. So therefore Jason had no respect for me because Mom is stupid, she doesn't know, 'cause the way Ken would talk to me while I was trying to discipline Jason, counteracting anything I ever did. I would get him okay for a week or so, and he would never set Jason in a chair. He would discipline him with a spanking or a shout—there were no other options.*

■■■

P: I had a hell of a time finding a lawyer, I called legal services and never got through with them, and until you put me in touch with that one lady—I can't remember her name—and she tried real hard to get me in touch with somebody, and I ended up going with my stepdad's lawyer, the attorney that did [his divorce], but nobody put me through to any kind of lawyer and this was weeks I had no legal help or anything.

I called [one of the volunteer lawyer services] to ask . . . some questions and stuff, and Ken had called me one day at work and said that I could not keep him from Jason, that legally I was wrong about that. Well, I called this

**Editor's Note: This kind of discipline is commonly recognized as child abuse .*

one lawyer, and she said, well, essentially you're afraid that he's gonna do just what you're doing, get him and keep him from me.

**M:** She was afraid you'd be charged with kidnapping?

**P:** Yeah, that's why I wouldn't let him [Ken] see him [Jason] 'cause of what he was doing—the drugs and stuff. He had no reason to have a kid, and that lawyer told me essentially I was afraid that Ken was going to do the exact same thing I was doing, keeping me from seeing Jason . . .

**M:** *[To the volunteers at the hospital, to fill them in on the issues]*: So the problem is that what the lawyer told Penny is the truth, that she had essentially kidnapped [Jason] from his father . . . but if she had let him see the little boy then Ken would run off with Jason and she would have been the one worried about it. She was afraid of the tables turning, so she just went into hiding. So the lawyer [working with a volunteer group set up to advise battered women] who is supposed to be in a position to advocate for . . .

**P:** Yeah. She didn't refer me to anything . . .

**M:** But what that does to a woman who's escaping a violent man and trying to protect her son is break down her self-esteem. It breaks down her perceptions and all of these doubts start to surface . . .

**P:** Then I called another one . . . but essentially after I talked to her I was like, God! Am I ready for a lawsuit here? And I was thinking maybe I am wrong about not letting him see his daddy 'cause it had been a week. . . .

**M:** Actually what their [the volunteer lawyers'] role is supposed to be is that they answer immediate questions and tell you what your rights are, and she [the lawyer] is obligated to tell you that you are essentially doing what he [Ken] would do, but in such a way that shows a sensitivity to your situation and an understanding of this mind set.

**Volunteer:** So do you think he [Ken] will come looking for you eventually?

**P:** I don't know. I don't think he will now. Now when he finds out about the supervised visitation, and I get that, that's gonna piss him off, and I think he'll come after me then, but I won't hesitate to call the police. That will make my day actually, because you [M] told me that they would make him go to mandatory counseling. I think I would do that.

■■■

P: A lot of people say, well, why did you stay? What caused you to stay this long? And there's other women that know what you're going through, and you can talk and then counselors are great, so had I not been going there I would not be doing this good, as good as I've been because. . . .

M: Well, you feel centered. . . .

P: Yeah, I feel confident. It's like I'm not beaten by every wind or whatever happens to me.

M: *[To volunteers]*: Oh, and she got a letter today that would blow anybody away who was not feeling affirmed, because according to the letter, everything was her fault. [This letter, dated December 11, 1989, would be the second letter she received from Ken. The first is included below, near the end of the interview.] When you're not emotionally strong it's easy for people to blame you and you buy it, we all buy it, we just do.

And I am amazed at the kind of strength she has shown—that she can just look at this letter and say, "He still doesn't understand the issues," whereas I doubt without your family's support and the counseling you would have been able to see it as *him* not understanding the issues. There would have been this confusion—who's right, who's wrong, what am I gonna do?

P: 'Cause I used to walk around, and my head was just going in circles. I had no strength you know and now, the Family Place, I just love that place.

M: That's good, it's a real resource.

P: Yeah, I go there. I just live for Tuesday nights. In fact today I had counseling because I had to work late last night. But I really do like the group, and then they have that twelve-week group and from what they told me it's ninety-five percent of the time the women who attend that don't go back into an abusive relationship. Because so many times the women leave they find another one, and I know I would 'cause I always have.

I've always been attracted to the jerks, no matter what they do they beat us somehow. So I want to go to that, where you commit yourself for twelve weeks, and it's real structured—they have something they work on each week. See, at open group anybody can come and go. You can talk about anything you want, but I do want to get into the structured one.

M: Are they having you keep journals?

P: No, but I have been. Anytime I have any contact from Ken, I write it down in my datebook. That way I've got the date and time, I just write it down.

**M:** That will be good for evidence in case there is harassment, of which there has been some. But, I think, so far, considering what could happen, he's come to her work and driven by the house, but all things considered, I think he's pretty scared of what could happen.

**P:** Yeah, cause I've never done anything this drastic before this time and that scared him, and a friend of mine, whose husband is friends with Ken, told me that it scared him, and I thought it would. I hoped it would, because I knew if I didn't do it the first time that he'd just . . . I'd never get away. He came into the office, he called me that day and wanted to see Jason, and that was the day I talked to that attorney, and she told me that [taking Jason was illegal] so I was a basket case already. And he walked in the office, and I had been fine. I turned around, and there he was, and I said, "What are you doing here?"

**M:** Were you scared?

**P:** Oh God! One of our patients—cause I had forgotten what I said or anything, all I remember is walking back and calling the police—and one of our patients who knew what was going on, she said my eyes got just this big. I asked him what he was doing there and then didn't even give him a chance to respond. I immediately walked into my boss' office and called the police, and they were there in five minutes.

**M:** And that was Dallas police?

**P:** No, that was Irving.

**M:** Was he still there when they got there?

**P:** Yeah, he was out in the truck writing the letter, and the one officer went out and talked to him. The other came in and talked to me, and the officer who was outside went over the letter to make sure there were no threats.

*Following is the letter Ken gave the police officer when he came to Penny's office.*

5:00 P.M. Thursday, November 2, 1989

Penny,

Will you please just take 10 minutes to talk to me! I have been patient and haven't tore anything up. I had allready [sic] packed my clothes Sunday, and was waiting for you and Jason to return so we could talk this out like adults. I don't understand why you won't talk to me, or even let your son see his father. It will go [us] in any direction you want it to, but you must do it in an adult manner. You also must take the responsibility as an adult and a mother. Just running off and hiding from the facts is not the right answer. [Heard that before?] I'm not going to bother you, but can you understand how hurt I am by not being able to see Jason. Jason and you are the main thoughts and people in my life and now youre [sic] both gone! The reason I got mad Sunday is that you broke the rules of low spending to have your own kind of cigs, as well as lying to me in the first place. Penny I will allways [sic] love you and Jason. Please, Please talk to me and let me just tell Jason I love him.

Ken

P: He "didn't tear anything up" [at their home] so that's supposed to be good. So I was supposed to be real proud of that. But he hasn't been back since, hasn't called—or he did call that one day he wanted to see Jason—and he hasn't called since then, and then he sent me the bill from the landlord.

M: So he's not living there?

P: No, he left and moved all his stuff out. I don't know where the rest of his things are. . . . Ken sent me his bill [the landlord had sent Penny half] with a note at the bottom of it, saying since I left . . . and since I didn't help him move anything out or clean it up that I needed to pay this . . . . He still didn't understand that I didn't want to be near him for fear of what he's gonna do, and I can't get over it after the protective order, you know, what else are you supposed to do? He thinks he has every right to do to me whatever he wants 'cause in the past I essentially [by her actions] said [he] could. He truly believes he can do whatever he wants. ■

*Tapes transcribed by Pepi Eileen Harris.*

## Section Two
# *Thoughts after a Rape*

Strange to think I have been raped
only once;
it felt so familiar,
so similar to things I had hoped were unimportant,
things we do not call rape.

The rape that we call rape
is only one rape,
a rape with perhaps more articulate rage
but still akin to all those vague rapes
that we do not call rape.

The rape that we call rape
has shown me those other rapes
I had thought were nothing.
I have named them now.
I know now that rape is nothing more
than ignorance of the sacred.

There are more rapes than we might suppose.

Chris Mandell

"My husband used me as a toilet," she says. "For fifteen years, I was his toilet." Suddenly, for the first time since the interview began, she smiles. "Like a place to pee," she continues. "He didn't beat me, but he'd throw me around a lot, call me names, then make love. *Make love.* He don't know the first thing. . . . Just a toilet that's all I am. Every night! Do you think that's normal? I think he's a sex maniac. But I've never told him that. I've never told anyone. I wish I had tonight, before I left."

For the first time, she details those fifteen years of daily rapes. But she doesn't use the word "rape."

Marital rape, also called spousal or wife rape, until recently has not been called rape. Traditional attitudes that view females as sexual property provide the key to understanding both wife rape and extramarital rape. Under such concepts, it is "unthinkable" that a husband could be prosecuted for raping his wife, "for the law was conceived to protect *his* interests, not those of his wife" (Russell 1982, 3). Feminist lawyer Catherine MacKinnon explains that traditionally the law had "nothing whatever to do with the problem of sexual inequality as it's experienced by women. . . . The law sees and treats women the way men see and treat women." Thus, rape laws were formulated as "male-seeing" and "male-serving," identifying female victims through the eyes of the rapist (Streibeigh 1999, 29ff).

Since the 1975 publication of Susan Brownmiller's landmark history, *Against Our Wills*, rape has been redefined and categorized:

- Real rape: stranger, traditional, or "popular" rape
- Date or acquaintance rape
- Incest or rape by a parent, usually a father but often a brother, mother, grandparent, or other close relative

Revised rape laws promoted primarily by feminist scholars and lawyers followed in the wake of these definitions. Historically, the protection of husbands from the crime of wife rape also allowed for the rape of lovers and daughters (Russell 1982, 257–269). Marital rape, defined as any "unwanted intercourse or penetration obtained by force, threat of force, or the wife's inability to consent," according to Violence Against Women Online Resources, "falls into three categories: force only, battering rape, and obsessive rape" (Teitelbaum 2000, 1). Motivated by power, "force only" rape uses as much force as necessary, like holding the wife down. Most victims of this form don't identify themselves as victims and therefore do not seek help, according to Annette Burrhus, lay training specialist for the Texas Association Against Sexual Assault (Teitelbaum, 1). "Battering rape," motivated by anger, combines sex as part of the beating. Victims who seek help or treatment for their injuries may describe both activities and thus can receive counseling. "Obsessive rape" involves torture and/or harmful sexual violence. Ashley Teitelbaum, communications specialist for the Texas Council on Family Violence, points out that women may "experience more than one type of marital rape throughout the marriage." Long-term effects, both psychological and physical, may be devastating and include anxiety, fear, depression, eating and sleep disorders, fatigue, vomiting, torn muscles, chronic negativity, and lack of trust. All too often, however, marital rape is viewed as less serious than stranger or date rape and considered a marital problem rather than a criminal offense (Teitelbaum, 6).

Whereas wife rape became a crime in California in June 1979, by the early nineties, thirty states still allowed husbands legally to rape their wives. In 1993, according to the National Clearinghouse for Marital and Date Rape, all fifty states agreed "to make marital/cohabitant/date rape a crime." And in 1995, "all the governments in the U. N. voted in Beijing . . . to abolish the marital privilege to sex on demand from wives."[1] Naturally each state and nation enforces these regulations according to their individual commitment and training programs. Nevertheless, even today exemptions from rape prosecution still exist for husbands in thirty-three states (Teitelbaum, 6).

Diana Scully's study of convicted rapists was predicated on her concern that rape studies "focusing on women can lead to blaming the victim and to perceiving rape as women's, rather than men's, problem" (Scully 1990, 4). "Rapist" traditionally signified "psychotic" and "sick," which tended to obscure the social conditions that foster rapes of all kinds. By rejecting the "disease" model of sexual violence, Scully rejects the idea "that rape is the result of a mental illness. . . ." (Scully 1990, 37). Amazingly, claims made by the disease model are not supported by empirical studies that indicate that "as few as five percent of men are psychotic at the time of their crimes" (Scully, 41).

While Scully points out that "sexual violence is complex and cannot be reduced to a single simplistic cause," her study indicates that rapists and other felons "believed strongly in the double-standard pedestal values," and held a "rigid, moralistic perspective on appropriate female behavior . . . consistent with very hostile attitudes toward women [which] related to belief in rape stereotypes" such as she asked for, caused, liked, or deserved it. These values "find general support in our culture" (Scully 1990, 89, 91).

Men who fit this profile are likely to commit sexual violence toward their significant others, such as wives, friends, lovers, dates, or acquaintances, as well as strangers, the latter of whom comprise those victims of "real" or "popular" rape.

Rather than assuming that rape is "dysfunctional behavior," we propose here that it is a "normal" outgrowth of a society that makes sexual violence possible. These writings reveal violence as a part of everyday life across age, race, economic, and social circumstances among people living otherwise ordinary lives. Sexual violence, including rape, coercion, threat of/or implied violence, and "pressurized sex," (Kelly 1988) accompany most forms of battering. The infliction of sexual humiliation is a form of power and control. Many men top off a violent incident with rape with the same casual attitude as they top off sex with a cigarette. In the previous section, we observed Yolanda Molina's experience of wife rape. Molina was exceptional in that even as it was happening (in the late sixties and early seventies) she was able to define sexual violence as rape.

In her poem, which names this section, Chris Mandell discovers that her encounter with "real" rape taught her to view those unlabelled experiences that left her feeling violated as rape in disguise.

Myrna Sharp's "Halloween Flashback" reverberates as a classic "acquaintance rape" scenario that forever haunts one woman's memories. The circumstances of this story demonstrate that rape is not limited to sexual assault. "Pressurized sex," with an implied threat of violence, is rape in the context of the range of women's experiences (Kelly 1988). Yet few legal precedents recognize such a range; few police departments would have taken a complaint from Myrna Sharpe seriously. Indeed, a hierarchy of credibility often becomes part of police policy: "Rapes by strangers that took place in automobiles were considered more dubious than rapes by strangers that took place in the home or on the street. All dating rapes that occurred in automobiles were held unfounded by the police . . ." (Brownmiller 1975, 366). And yet, even in 1997, with public awareness and high visibility of rape case statistics from the U. S. Department of Justice and the Bureau of Justice Statistics reveal that somewhere in America, a woman is sexually assaulted every two minutes.

In 1966, 307,000 women were the victims of rape, attempted rape, or sexual assault. Furthermore,

- Most rapes happen at home, and/or in a car
- Only about ten percent of rapes are reported
- Most rapes involve alcohol or drugs
- In eighty percent of cases, people are raped by someone they know
- Approximately twenty-eight percent of victims are raped by husbands or boyfriends, thirty-five percent by acquaintances, and five percent by other relatives
- Ninety percent of all women in the U. S. will at some time experience rape, sex-related assault, attempted rape, or sexual harassment.[1]

Credibility is central to the protagonist's experience in Anne R. E. Baehr's, "The School Is Gone." Typically, when a child reports rape, she faces either disbelief or blame for causing it. In this poem, as in Sara O.'s memoir "Baths," (Section Three), the teacher dismisses a young girl's claims. In "Violation," Barbara Rosenthal traces the multiple rapes that comprise her sexual history. How do mothers teach their daughters to conceal the violence they experience, to protect their abusers? What role does adult complicity play in teaching young girls they are vulnerable?

Patti Tana's essay gives rape "A Name and A Face," creating a language and response for acquaintance rape. Tana explores the subtle cruelty and manipulative behavior inflicted by a former lover who demands "love" at the point of knife, behavior that sets up an ambiguous response in most women. As Tana observes, "the legal system reflects society's attitude that a woman loses her right to say no to a man after she once has said yes."

J. Whitebird's "Daddy's Angels or Sodomy, To Begin With" resonates with painful realizations that incest is one of "those vague rapes" that make "real rape" all too familiar. How do women with a memory of childhood rape, whether by grandfather, father, or other family members, articulate their rage as adults? How do they reach resolution? "Apologies" confronts the theme of a mother's complicity concerning the abuse of her child. If rape is "ignorance of the sacred," then J. Whitebird's two stories confirm, "There are more rapes than we might suppose." ■

## Halloween Flashback

Myrna Sharp

I told you, at first, that it happened five years ago. But then I said, "It was ten, really. It's just that ten seems too long not to have recovered. Actually, it's been thirteen. I was thirty at the time.

I have a picture, Scotch-taped alone on its own page in my album, captioned in a blue ballpoint scrawl: "Halloween, 1978. To Live in Infamy." Huddled together are Pat, dressed in her black tutu, fishnet stockings and spike heels; Trish and Tommy, wearing identical Robin Hood costumes; and me, draped in my gold living room curtain and a paper Flying Nun's hat—jerry-rigged, tacky, horrible. Before we left for the party, Tommy took the timed exposure. The three of them are smiling. I look frightened.

Tommy drove. None of us knew whose party it was. A woman who worked downstairs from Pat was acquainted with some other people, house-sitting a large Colonial in the affluent suburb of Newton.

The four of us had sailed together on the Charles River all that summer and fall. Pat was my good friend, a ballsy broad whose aggressiveness I envied. Her long, shiny, black mane framed her horse-face, and she was built like a beer keg on stilts. Trish and Tommy were just plain cute: short, sunburned, newly engaged and happy.

That night we were looking for fun.

As we walked up the path approaching the huge, beautiful house, Tommy handed me his keys.

"You're the only one with pockets, Myrna," he said. "Do you mind?"

I jangled his metal key ring, heavy with what looked like thirty keys. "You must be the janitor!" I laughed, and we entered the party in good spirits.

Once inside the vestibule, though, I found myself suddenly alone, surrounded by strangers. Pat, Trish, and Tommy disappeared instantly, which made me nervous. I went into the kitchen but they weren't there. I grabbed a beer, then looked in the dining and living rooms. I couldn't find them. I peeked up the winding stairway, yet recognized no one. So I found a spot in the living room and leaned uncomfortably against a wall.

Where are the furniture and rugs? I wondered. All accoutrements of living were eerily absent. There was nothing but bare, gray walls and filthy floorboards, darkened with age and dirt, gravely in need of refinishing.

As Meat Loaf sang "Bat Out of Hell," I sipped beer and watched weird monsters. Vampires flashed fangs and dripped nail-polish blood, while Frankensteins fingered rusty neck bolts and eyebrow-pencil suture scars. Hideously grotesque, whole-head rubber masks obscured all recognizable traces of underlying humanity. Everywhere, ghosts and devils drifted and Kung Fu danced with Killer Bees. Secret selves and dark, subconscious wishes surface on Halloween, exposed once a year to the outside world—men were dressed as women, women as men. I took off my hat and curtain and threw them in a corner, feeling better in just my jeans and sweater.

Where the hell are Pat and the Robin Hoods? I wondered, hating to be alone in a crowd. Panicking slightly, I asked myself what Pat would do in this situation, knowing that she'd dance in place smiling until she caught someone's eye and then, if he didn't ask her first, ask him to dance.

A relatively normal-looking guy was standing next to me. Dressed in green camouflage fatigues, he was about 6'2" and very thin, with close-cropped, dark brown hair. He wore no mask, had no blood on his hands. Beside him stood a friend. Trying to be Pat, I smiled at them.

"My name's Joe," the G.I. smiled back. "How do you know Deb?"

Deb must be one of the housesitters, I thought and said, "I don't. I came with friends who have disappeared."

"I work with Deb," the soldier told me. "At the Flower Factory."

"That's near where I work, at City Hospital. I do biomedical research."

He smiled and lit a cigarette, then stood there stiffly. I knew I wasn't going to get to dance with this guy. We chatted idly, grinning self-consciously into our beers, until he asked, "Wanna smoke some dope?"

"Sure," I shrugged, Pat-like.

"Let's go outside."

I followed him into the frigid moonlight. Denuded trees loomed like gnarled skeletons, and our breaths frosted. I wished I had a coat, or at least my curtain.

I thought Joe would light up right outside the door, but instead he walked down the path, turned right at the sidewalk and headed toward the corner. His friend wasn't with us.

"Where are we going?" I asked.

"To my truck," he explained. "For privacy."

At the next street, he opened the passenger door of a red-and-black Ford Bronco. I hesitated, afraid to get in. But then I remembered the day Pat and I had met two guys at the Cape. We drove around with them and swam and drank, and afterwards Pat dated one for two months. I was overdue for a boyfriend.

"Mountain climbing," I joked to Joe as I lumbered up the steep step and got into the cab.

He sat behind the steering wheel and lit a joint, and we passed it back and forth.

"Is this your truck?" I asked, sucking the smoke deep into my lungs.

"It's from work."

Such vehicular access made me think he was a manager. I started to ask what work he did but was distracted by inch-wide, black leather bands circling both his wrists.

"What are your bracelets?" I asked instead.

"Weights. I started wearing them in 'Nam. I never take them off."

My stomach tensed as I recalled scary stories of flashbacks to terror and death. I had always wondered what it was like over there in that awful war, in any war, yet never knew anyone well enough to ask. I realized it took its toll on everyone, and I pitied Joe in a generic way.

We sat in silence for a moment, and then he leaned over and kissed me. It felt good. It had been a long time since I'd been with a man. He unbuttoned my blouse and caressed my breasts, but when he started to undo my bra, I stopped him.

"Let's go for a ride," he said, starting the engine.

I stiffened, but immediately thought of Pat, barreling bravely through life, always open to adventure. "Okay," I said and silently reprimanded myself for being so suspicious, so easily frightened.

Joe drove around, and I tried to make conversation. Pat was much better at it. I gave up and merely watched the moonlit scenery go by. Stately houses on dead-leaf-strewn streets were dark and deserted. There were no other cars on the road. I wondered where everyone was. After a while, I became vaguely aware that we were riding in increasingly larger circles. I looked at Joe. He was hunched over, clutching the steering wheel, jaw clenched, dark eyes glaring intently ahead. My throat constricted.

"Let's go back," I whispered. But he seemed deaf and kept mutely driving and driving. He wasn't speeding, and he stopped at every red light, but before long I didn't know where we were. We rode around for an hour or three hours, I couldn't tell. Finally, I recognized our location: we were on Soldiers Field Road, heading toward downtown Boston, not too far from a Massachusetts Turnpike "On" ramp. We could end up anywhere, I realized, and my bowels contracted. I forgot about Pat.

"I need to go to the bathroom," I told Joe, hoping that would convince him to turn around.

"Just a little longer," he said in a monotone, his eyes focused on some distant scene I didn't see. This was no manager at the Flower Factory; this was a disturbed delivery boy, a Viet vet able to hold only menial jobs.

"Please," I said gently, not wanting to antagonize him. "I really have to go."

Still, he didn't turn the truck around.

"My friends will be looking for me. I have their keys." I held up

Tommy's keys and jangled them.

Joe glanced over. "Okay," he mumbled, and, to my relief, turned around and retraced our route. However, once in Newton, he deviated. "I'm looking for a place," he muttered. I wasn't sure what he meant.

He pulled into a small gravel driveway behind a little brick building on a tiny patch of grass beside a chain-link fence. I had no idea where we were. It must have been a power station by a park or something. I don't know. I've never been able to find that spot, although on occasion I've looked, drawn over the years by some perverse curiosity to see the scene again and in daylight. Perhaps as proof that it actually happened. Concrete evidence. And even now, thirteen years later, when I pass the house where the party took place, my eyes lock onto that monument to externalize my pain.

Joe stopped the truck and got out and peed. I had no choice but to do the same. All that beer. Afterwards, he was waiting for me in the truck. He kissed me roughly.

"Let's go back," I said, now insistent. "Tommy will want his keys. What time is it anyway?"

He looked at his watch. "One," he said and grabbed me and bit my breasts with a terrifying single-mindedness.

Fear surged through me. I pushed him away, but he grabbed my wrists with such strength that I pictured them black and blue the next day. He put my hand between his legs and shoved his under my waistband. I pushed him away again, and he pushed my head down to his lap.

"No!" I said, freeing my head. Then, in one deft motion, he began to remove my jeans. Moonlight crashed through the windshield and turned his face cadaver white. From deep within two hollow black sockets, his eyes flashed ferocity.

It must have been then that I left my body. I'm not sure. I only know that at some point I performed a cold calculation: he could kill me if he wanted; blowing him wouldn't be as awful as screwing; and I might as well get this over with as soon as possible, with minimal damage. After all, I told myself, it's nothing I haven't done before. I lowered my head.

While it was happening, I worried about Pat and Trish and

Tommy. Would they have a spare key and take their car and go home without me? Then how would I get home? I prayed they would be there when I got back, that they wouldn't leave me, and that he would hurry up and finish fast.

Afterwards, as he zipped his pants, he asked me in an abruptly cheerful, conversational voice, "Have you ever been in porn films?"

"What?" I said in dazed confusion, trying not to vomit.

He tucked in his shirt happily. "You'd be good," he said, as if I should be flattered.

"Do you do that?" My voice seemed to come from elsewhere.

"Yeh!" he bragged. "It's a lotta fun, and it pays really well."

"Tommy will want his keys." I heard myself say. "Let's go back."

"Okay," he said and drove straight to the party house. As he pulled up to the curb, I saw Pat and Trish and Tommy on the sidewalk. Joe's friend was waiting for him, too. It was almost over—I was almost safe.

Joe killed the engine and, in a flash, suddenly turned morose. He collapsed around the steering wheel, cradling it in his arms, and peeked sheepishly up at me. "Did I do something wrong?" he asked apologetically in a little boy's voice. It was Looney Tunes time.

"No, uh-uh, nice meeting you, thanks for the ride," I said frantically, concentrating only on getting safely out the door. I'd seen all I wanted of the Vietnam experience.

"I *did* do something wrong, didn't I?" His face twisted with grief as he spoke from another world, continents away. He started to cry.

I opened the door. "Bye, now," I said and got out, as Tommy ran furiously up to me.

"Gimme my goddamned keys!" he yelled, grabbing them out of my hand. "It's two A.M! Where the hell have you been?" He looked like he was going to hit me. I wanted to kiss him.

Trish calmed him as Pat put an arm around me and bent down close to look deep into my eyes.

"Are you all right?" Pat asked.

"Let's go home," I said.

Walking to Tommy's car, we passed Joe talking to his friend, who looked concerned. They watched us pass, and I stared down at the sidewalk but, out of the corner of my eye, glimpsed the agony and grief on Joe's contorted face. I felt sorry for him.

We got into Tommy's car. I sat in the back with Pat. She was still trying to read my eyes.

"Do you want to go to the hospital?" she asked, and I thought that was the goddamned stupidest mother-fucking question I'd ever heard.

"Let's go home." I said, suppressing my displaced revulsion and rage. "Let's just get out of here!"

The next day, Pat explained that she had suspected I'd been raped and that hospitals provide partial proof. I told her it wasn't really a rape, it could have been worse, it was my own fault for voluntarily going with him. However, because of his porn movie comment, I did see my gynecologist.

I went about my business in shock. I think I stopped eating.

Two days later, walking down the hall at work, I must have re-entered my body, because it started shaking so uncontrollably that I had to hold onto the wall to get to my desk and sit down. I kept on shaking, even at night, when I'd jerk awake soaking wet from brief, fitful sleeps, jaws sore from grinding my teeth.

The following week, I sat—still shaking—in the middle of my office. When I was informed over the phone that I had tested positive for gonorrhea of the mouth, I collapsed and had to be driven home. That second assault, so soon after the first, seemed somehow worse. He had stolen my body and left it diseased. It could only weep.

Anyhow, like I told you, all that happened a long time ago. Nevertheless now, every Halloween, I stay inside and lock my doors. I shut off my lights, too, and sit waiting in the dark until the insistent knocks and evil laughs cease. I hold my breath until the demons depart for another year and go back underground, safely sealed inside the earth where they belong. ■

**The School Yard**

Anne Ruth Ediger Baehr

The school is gone,
but the space is here,
bounded by the same walk
that leads me now to the corner
where I lingered alone
to pick up autumn leaves
after the bell had rung.
I did not see the boy until
he stood before me. Something
in his face surprised: a shining in
the eyes, as if my being there
had been at his request.

We're both tardy, I said
as I drew back from his touch
and tried to run. His hands
pushing me down and closing
around my neck felt hot
until my breath was gone
and street sounds faded
into a throb I clung to in the dark.
Then light again, the sun
too bright, too close.

Glad to see a face, to know
I could breathe again, I stood
and ran, but he was faster,
blocked my path, and held me back.
Don't tell, he pleaded,
as if we had shared adventure
that would lose its magic

if someone knew. He put something
into my hand. My new aggie, he said.
Don't ever tell!

*I will heed the bell,*
I wrote a hundred times,
my left hand on my tender neck.
I told.
But the teacher did not believe
a boy had stopped my breath,
had turned my autumn leaves
into the shining marble in my hand. ■

**Violation**

Barbara Rosenthal

The first time she was violated, little boys from the neighborhood lined the crack of her ass with twigs. Her mother cleaned her out but didn't get angry. Not being punished made her very uneasy.

The second time she was violated her mother was at work and she could run home to an empty house from the man who locked her inside the front seat and lay on top of her and pretended to need her help fixing some hard-to-reach place under the dashboard but really was rubbing himself against her. From underneath him she saw Retarded Joanie ride by on training wheels and she thought of Joanie's peanut butter mouth and knew it wouldn't help to call for help.

The third time she was already fifteen and doing a little too much flirting. She liked the balding young man who played tennis and they took a drive in the country. She liked it when he kissed her. She pretended she'd go further but she never pretended she'd go all the way, and refused. He put a rubber on, awkwardly. His car had itchy gray upholstery and still she refused. "Turn over," he said. (She didn't understand.) "Let's have your ass," he said. (She'd never heard of such a thing.) He began to roll down the window and roll off the rubber. "Oh no, don't," she said. "You can't get pregnant this way, little fool!" They looked at each other and realized their bargain. The rubber stayed on as he entered her high gasping pain.

The fourth time was on a rainy night in Rome. The pensioner collected both their passports and made Enrico take two rooms. She and Enrico were drunk and she was only too glad to get laid. But Enrico began to get pushy. Enrico wanted everything too fast. Enrico tore her dress and tore her stockings. He pushed her down. He bruised her elbow. It was very damp and cold. Enrico bit at her. There was no pleasure, only clamminess. She pushed him away, and he threw himself down on her and shoved himself inside her faster faster faster, pulling on her shoulders for leverage, pulling on her hips. "Have you had it yet, baby? Have you had it?" She faked an orgasm but stayed until morning. ■

**A Name and a Face**

Patti Tana

I wanted hardness when I met him.
To be taken on the hard wood floor.
To see his hard mask soften.
To soften my hard longing.

But nothing in me wanted the hardness of the knife.

The lover I was seeking
became the stranger creeping to my bed.

Now I am humbled. I am just like anyone
who swims beyond the force of arms
swept by strong currents.

Now I am never more than a knife edge
from fear.

A new character stalks my dreams.
Rape has a name and a face: Fear
sits at the bottom of my bed chanting

Beware of lovers.
Beware of lovers who are strangers in your bed.

"Beware of Lovers" in Patti Tana's poetry collection
*Ask the Dreamer Where Night Begins*

In the summer of 1982, a man I was dating raped me. Two months before the rape my husband had divorced me and I was unmarried for the first time in my adult life. Many people warned me that I would be vulnerable, but I never imagined I'd find myself with the sort of man I had run away from my whole life—a violent man like my father.

I had met the man three years before at a course in the local library. After that we'd wave to each other on the rare occasions we happened to meet in town. When we met in a gift shop that summer we were both feeling lonely and rejected from the recent breakup of our marriages. He lived next door to a friend of mine and invited both of us to a July Fourth barbecue with our children. It seemed safe.

For the next few weeks we rode our bicycles together, worked in our gardens, had more cookouts. When I worried about walking in our neighborhood at night, he showed me the large knife he kept strapped to his ankle. Just before our divorce my husband had been attacked by muggers, so I was conscious of the danger in the streets. The knife seemed a practical response to a menacing reality and made me view him as a protector. Fearful of sleeping in the house alone with my six-year-old son, I welcomed his staying late. After the second week we started having sex. I was delighted to feel the flush of excitement again; I was delighted to *feel* again.

He was a machinist, used to making the world fit his needs. He fixed the doorbell so it rang every time. He tightened my bicycle brakes and adjusted the back door so it would lock. When he brought over a few tools to keep in the kitchen drawer, I thought of a friend's warning about not letting a man put his shoes under my bed or he'd think he owned the whole house. But I was so glad to have help with repairing the inevitable mechanical breakdowns that I didn't want to think about how expensive his help might prove to be.

One night he brought my little boy a quarter he'd made with heads on both sides. His children were visiting him, so we made popcorn and took the TV out on the upstairs porch for our kids to watch. Having him there restored my sense of family life.

Looking back I see there were signs of his potential violence, and I also see that I did not interpret this information correctly because my needs obscured my judgment. He claimed he'd had some bad breaks, and his scars elicited my sympathy rather than my wariness. I realized he drank too much; sometimes he drank himself to sleep.

Though he kept himself tightly in check, I sensed anger beneath the surface. He became jealous and made insulting remarks when I warmly greeted an old friend. One evening about a week before the rape, he snapped his belt off in anger at my son's childishness—a shocking replay of my own childhood beatings. Quickly, before he could hit him, I swept the boy out of the room and made the man leave my house. But after his own teenagers assured me he had never struck them, I gave him another chance. He swore that he had no intention of hitting my son, only scaring him, and that it would not happen again. I wanted to believe him

Although I have blamed myself for not reacting decisively to these warnings, now I am trying to understand how it happened. And I am sharing this story to alert other women: if you sense *any* danger, be careful about giving second chances.

■ ■ ■

One day, when I dropped my son off at his father's apartment for a visit, he said he wanted to discuss moving back home. I had never wanted him to leave. The man I was dating knew it, so when I saw him again I told him I did not want to go out with him any more because I hoped to have a reconciliation. I had gathered the things he had left around the house (records, tools, an extra shirt), but he became angry when I tried to make him take them.

He said he wanted to sit on the porch for a few minutes. Although I desperately wanted him to leave before my son and former husband arrived, I tried to placate him. I poured some juice and went upstairs to join him on the second-floor porch.

He had turned over a small redwood table and was carving letters into the underside with his knife. As he talked he alternated between pointing the knife at me to punctuate his words and jabbing it into the wood with hard stabbing motions: "I want to fuck you one more time. . . . You owe it to me."

At first I tried to reason with him. I explained that my mind and body were now oriented toward my former husband—surely he would not want to have sex with me when I did not want it. But the more I reasoned, the angrier he became.

Now he was shaking the knife in my face as he repeated his demand. Glancing down I saw he had carved "I LOVE" into the wood. I feared that if I named what was happening—rape—he might drop the pretense that the knife in his hand was for stabbing the table and stab me.

I felt I had only as much time to think as it would take him to finish carving the phrase. Should I jump off the high second-floor porch and maybe break a leg or try to trick him and run outside to a neighbor? I could have screamed and perhaps attracted someone's attention before he stopped me, but I was petrified of provoking him.

I was also afraid he would come back if he did not get what he wanted. Even if the police intervened in this instance because of the knife, I knew they could not keep him away from me in the future. I had to make him leave before my husband arrived to avoid a confrontation. There were no good alternatives. I decided to comply with his demand, hoping it would really be a "last time."

I felt my defenses were meager, but I tried to protect myself as much as I could. I needed a time limit so I lied and said my mother was due to arrive in a few minutes and I would have to call her to delay her visit. I reached through the open window for the phone in my bedroom, telling him he could listen to my conversation. When I called she understood the lie and asked if I was alone. "No," I told her, "______ is here now, but he will be gone by seven. You should be here by seven." Now at least someone would know he was with me in case he injured me and I could not call for help—and he knew it too.

He stood outside the bathroom while I put in my diaphragm. Through the window I could hear neighborhood sounds—surely he would not kill me with so many people nearby.

It was just after six when we went into the bedroom. As he undressed I secretly turned the clock ahead a few minutes, but the hands still moved with excruciating slowness. When I saw his knife by his pants on the floor, I kicked it under the bed so he could not get it easily.

Though we'd been having sex for two weeks, now his body failed to respond to his will; he could not reach an erection. That increased his anger. When I tried to help him so we could get it over with, he ordered me to lie on my back and not touch him. The more frustrated he became, the more frightened I felt.

Finally he tensed his body enough to enter me, but it was grueling for both of us. At one point a girl in the street gave a loud laugh, breaking his concentration long enough for him to curse her. I was most terrified when he opened his tightly closed eyes and stared as if he didn't know who he was looking at. I thought he might blindly strangle me or smash my face. His stare was so distant and fierce that I said his name a few times and told him who I was. Again he told me to shut up and kept on pumping to ejaculation.

When he went to the bathroom I grabbed the knife from under the bed, dressed quickly, and ran downstairs. I waited by the door. When he came down, he grumbled that the clock in the kitchen was ten minutes slower than the one by the bed. I shrugged. Then I handed him the knife as he left—I didn't want him coming back for it.

My mother arrived a few minutes later. Even then I could not bring myself to say that I had been raped. Instead I told her "that was as close to rape as I ever want to come." She held my shaking body as I spoke.

I was relieved to be alive and grateful that I could walk and talk and breathe but very afraid that he would return. I also felt my own limitations in a sickening way. Like so many other women who have been overpowered, I felt that a truck had run over me. Now I understood the desperate compromises people have to make. I was trying not to feel humiliated, to see that the shame was his and there was no excusing his actions. I did not blame myself for being raped, but I did feel fragile and foolish, broken and enraged.

Many other women's stories had taught me that the legal system reflects society's attitude that a woman loses her right to say no to a man after she once has said yes. In fact much of my rage came from feeling trapped not only by the knife but by this lack of protection. Even if I had managed to escape from that particular situation, I was certain that my family and I would live in fear of future attacks because the police would not protect us.

I was so convinced that the police would just dismiss me and so fearful that the rapist would take revenge on me for reporting him that it took my friends nine days to convince me to report to the police. I decided to file the complaint to establish grounds for an order of protection in case he returned. I also realized that I owed it to other women.

Two male officers listened to what I had to say, made notes, and ran a computer check to see if he had a criminal record. They said that the district attorney would probably not pursue the case, but that they could go to the rapist's house and "scare" him. I told them not to. They assured me that if he were to appear at my home again I should call them and they would respond.

Four months after the rape, my friend who was his neighbor informed me that the man had moved. But for years he stayed in my nightmares. Now I am less trusting of men—and of my own judgment. I no longer list the phone in my name. I no longer open my door to strangers. And my memories of that summer are slashed by the image of the knife.

For years I kept the table with "I LOVE" carved underneath to remind me of how people confuse love and possession, love and domination, love and rape. While I was being raped I did not dare name what was happening to me. Afterward, a friend who was helping me sort out my feelings said, "Now rape has a name and a face." Though I am still sometimes afraid, by writing about this rape I am naming what he did to me. ■

## Daddy's Angels or Sodomy, To Begin With

J. Whitebird

My father was an astrologer, among other things. He also studied the tarot cards and had a crystal ball. One of my clearest memories is of him at night, late, as he took the black velvet cover off the crystal ball sitting on the table in front of him. I wanted so intently to know what it was he saw. I moved closer to the table, peering into the huge clear marble balanced on the small wooden stand.

"What do you see?" I was three and I wanted to be let in on the secret. I knew something so mysterious had to be grand and powerful. He passed his hand over the ball, looked up from under his eyebrows the way I had seen him do when he played fortune-teller at the charity fairs for the school.

"I see a sleepy little girl going to bed."

Sighing, I knew I had been conned. But he was right. I was sleepy and, apparently, I was going to bed.

Where my brothers were then, or my mother, I don't know. I don't remember much of them at all before my father died. But I climbed into my little twin bed that was shoved hard against the wall in the one room that opened onto the kitchen/living room. The next thing is a little more vague, because it happened so often that I didn't think much of it.

Whether or not it was an actual sound, I don't know. It usually started after I went to bed, just after he sat down at the table with his cards and his crystal. A low chant, or perhaps just a vibration, I couldn't tell the difference then and I can't now. A hum, like the buzz of a microwave or sonar that assaults the ears, would float through the room. Then it would materialize.

First it was just a gray area, like a wall of fog, not quite transparent, not quite visible. Then it became a door that opened into the middle of the air in my room and the creatures began to come through. They were not exactly animals, but they certainly were not people, though their faces showed an intense, sometimes ancient, awareness. They walked on all fours or crawled. Sometimes they did something akin to flying. They came through in a parade stepping carefully onto the wood planked floor and then trailed into the living room. The first was usually a sort of crocodile, except for its face and hands, or feet, which were mostly human. There was a kind of bent-over bird that might have been a flamingo except it was green and wore a hat over its toothsome grin.

In the beginning they would linger a moment to stare at me curiously, as if wanting to know what possible reason I might have for calling them. Then, heeding that low hum, they would traipse into the other room. Later they did not concern themselves with me except to acknowledge my awareness of them. But, as often as I saw it, I was still frightened. Were it to happen to me today I would undoubtedly faint, but then I only turned my face to the wall, away from the fuzzy gray light, when they began to arrive.

I never went past the recognition: Daddy's beasts are here and on time as usual. But I do remember thinking he didn't tell them to go to sleep. I felt left out, till the angels came. I didn't think it was particularly remarkable, though they were very nice angels and weren't like the funny-looking beasts at all. They came to see me when I was sleeping. The next morning over breakfast, I was proud of having had my own guests for a change.

"Two angels came to see me last night," I told Mama. She was hurrying around the kitchen and paused only slightly.

"What color were they?" She wanted to know if I had seen some prowlers. I thought it an odd question until I remembered that most of my daddy's friends were some pretty odd colors too.

"Colored like us. One had brown hair and blue eyes and one had red hair and brown eyes."

My mother poured coffee, dashed eggs onto my plate. My father paused, looked sideways around the table as if searching for something he didn't want to find.

"Did the angels have wings?" Mama pulled the oven-browned toast out with a bunched-up rag.

"No," I thought back, "they just stood like feathers."

"And what did the angels say?" Mama sat down to concentrate on her own plate.

"They came to see me, then they went to see Daddy, then they came back to see me and said, "Daddy dies the twenty-first of May."

Daddy jumped so hard he spilled his coffee. Mama's fork hand slowed and she looked up at me with a puzzled expression. She turned to look at Daddy, but he had already left the table.

I didn't know what a month was and if pressed, I could count as high as I was old, three. I had no idea it was already the eighteenth of May.

Daddy wasn't sick then. In fact, the way I understand it, he never really did get sick. On the twenty-first he wasn't feeling well. Mama took him to the county hospital, Jeff Davis, the only one for poor people in the city.

The doctor checked him out, took Mama out in the hall and said, "Mrs. Green, there's nothing wrong with your husband." When they walked back in to give Daddy the good news, he was dead. Mama told me later Daddy had two dead sisters, one with brown hair and blue eyes and one with red hair and brown eyes. Both had died years before I was born. But it wasn't until she had the film developed from that old Brownie box camera that she found the picture of the death card he had taken or the death chart he had set up for himself that was marked May twenty-first.

It would be fair to say I was somewhat traumatized by being taken to his funeral, wondering what he was doing all by himself in that big shiny white bowl they called a coffin.

A lot of things changed after my father died. A lot of people came and went quickly, and I suddenly began to see a lot more of my mother, a not altogether pleasant experience. Still, it was better than going to the farm.

North always to Arkansas, then twenty minutes east from Little Rock was a forty-acre farm my grandmother and grandfather lived on. They had a fifteen-year-old Tennessee walking horse called Nelda, and my brothers kept a roan calf there named Valentine. The one time they let me ride Nelda she pitched me face first into the dirt. I couldn't run fast enough to catch Valentine. Grandpa's blue tick hunting hounds were never to be touched and, by that time, he had been forced to give up raising fighting cocks. So, there wasn't a lot to do on the farm for a kid my age.

Grandma usually had too much to do to entertain me and, having birthed fourteen kids and raised the eleven who lived, she wasn't much interested in starting over with me. Mainly I tried to stay out of her way, not an easy job for an inquisitive four-year-old. Had I been able to find my way down to the creek to hunt for arrowheads like Eric did, things might have been different. On the other hand, they might not have either.

My Aunt Phyllis says Grandma was a wonderful mother but that's not the way I remember it. It was possible, of course, that she just didn't like me. It was possible that by that time she was as crazy as Grandpa. It is more probable that she had just given up and didn't give a damn.

I had gotten up one morning, convinced my mother was coming f or me and told Grandma so. She harrumphed loudly that she hadn't heard from Mama, and I was a stupid little girl for making up stories. Nevertheless, I put on my one new dress, the red one my Uncle Walt had bought me for Dad's funeral (he refused to buy a black one, knowing I needed clothes). I sat waiting in the front room most of the day. Grandma kept telling me to take off my new dress and stop messing around in the house but I wouldn't. I knew my mama was coming.

It wasn't 'till late in the afternoon that one of the neighbors came running up to the house yelling that there had been a wreck down at the old bridge across the creek bed. Grandpa went down to investigate.

Mama had run off the bridge and rolled the car four times in the creek. She wasn't badly hurt, mostly scratched and shook up, but the old car was totaled. I didn't get to see my mama that day, they took her to the hospital, but Grandma didn't tell me I was stupid again.

So I didn't get picked up that day or the next. Mama had to go back home and I had to stay on the farm. Nobody, it was clear, liked that.

Perhaps it was raining; perhaps Grandma didn't want me to get into anything outside. I don't remember why I was stuck in the house after that. It was a small, comfortable farmhouse, the kind they now call quaint. The three rooms were small: a living room and a kitchen, and a bedroom with two doors opening on to both of the other rooms. I remember I was always envious of the quilt on the bed. It was pretty and soft, not like the scratchy Sears-made blankets we had at home. Grandma had let me lie on it and cry myself to sleep after Grandpa had broken his leather belt on me for not saying "sir" to him.

I've always loved cobalt glass. The blue seems restful to me or at least far removed from this world. Grandma had a highboy in the bedroom with a lot of little bottles on the top, one in particular was cobalt. I just wanted to look at it really, to hold it, to let my eyes sink into it the way my father's would melt into his crystal ball. I stood on the bed, on top of the beautiful quilt, to reach it, being as quiet as I could. I knew I wasn't supposed to be up there. I had to lean far off the bed to reach the highboy and my small weight tipped it just enough to make all the bottles on top of it wobble. I held my breath, unable to reach any of them. The coveted blue bottle was the only one to fall.

By the time it shattered on the bare wood floor I was off the bed and halfway to the living room. Grandma was raging, she screamed and stomped the floor. She swept up the pieces and called me names; then she told me she would tell Grandpa. It was the worst punishment I could imagine. I knew he would have another belt, and he probably wouldn't care if he broke it, too.

He must have heard her screaming because he came in almost immediately. I don't remember the words but I remember the huge sounds that came out of her mouth as she pointed to me. Grandpa grabbed my upper arm hard and spun me around so I was facing away from him. I was face first in the quilt at the foot of the bed and I waited for the belt.

He pushed me forward 'till I was leaning over the bed, raised my skirt and yanked off my panties. But I didn't hear the clank of the belt buckle and I looked back to try to prepare myself for whatever it was that was coming. He was still pushing me down with one hand while the other unzipped his pants and pulled a wrinkled piece of skin from inside them. I didn't understand the punishment and looked to Grandma for a clue. She was standing in the door to the kitchen with her hands on her hips. She made something like a growling sound at Grandpa, but only shook her head disgustedly and turned away.

The pain of that hard knob pushing up my behind was more painful than any belt had ever been. It was like a broomstick ramming and tearing at me again and again. It was the first time I'd ever been punished like that. I wasn't going to let them know how much it hurt. I bit into that beautiful handmade quilt to stifle my screams. Even if I had been bad, I wasn't going to give them the satisfaction of knowing they had that kind of power over me.

I realized cobalt glass was the most precious thing in the world and I knew the angels would never visit me again. ■

## Apologies

J. Whitebird

I remember. I was twelve. They called and said my grandfather was finally dying. He had been lying in a nursing home in Beaumont for two years. He'd had a stroke and tried to drive to town, to Little Rock, from the old forty-acre farm. On the way he'd lost control of the car and run through a hurricane fence. The car threw him like a cantankerous horse and dragged him 120 feet before it stopped in a ditch.

This was before living wills, before people even considered such things. He was hooked up to machines. The few times he came to enough to realize where he was, he would pull the tubes out of his nose; his arms would strike out weakly at the nurses who quickly sedated him. My Uncle Bobby insisted we "do everything we can." The fact that Grandpa didn't want to lie there full of tubes and Thorazine didn't seem to filter through to Bobby. But, as I was to find out later, Bobby had enough guilt of his own to handle, much less to worry about Grandpa's.

I'd always known there was something about my mama's life that had gone wrong. I remember overhearing a telephone conversation late one night—my mama's lowered voice saying, "What happened to me was a terrible, terrible thing . . ." My young imagination, at that point in my life, was a pretty terrible thing, too. I could invent all sorts of tragedies, from clandestine secrets to murder. That she had suffered incest did not occur to me. Twelve-year-old minds do not usually go that far. Since incest was a "normal" part of my life it didn't occur to me it might be considered terrible.

I also knew about the abuse, from several sides. I mean, I remember defending my mother to Uncle Bobby when I had been sent there for a year at the age of six.

"I know what they did to Mama," I said stoutly at the kitchen table one morning. Uncle Bobby had just come into the room. Aunt Alice had been comforting me. She knew too, things I never should have become aware of. I had been told stories very early about my mother's harsh treatment at the hands of her family, how they had beaten and abused her, made her do all the housework. How much of this is actually true would be hard to say. At that point it hardly mattered; I was six and I believed my mama.

Uncle Bobby stared at me, hard and unyielding.

"They made her do all the work and then beat her all the time, too."

In a move as smooth as Burt Reynolds in the detective shows, Uncle Bobby leaned across the table and slapped me out of my chair. Aunt Alice screamed. I didn't. I just picked myself up. What else, after all, could I have expected from him? Even at six I knew that much.

I think it was the first time I ever heard an adult use the word fuck. Aunt Alice told Bobby to get the fuck out of the house.

"I haven't even had my coffee, and this is my goddamn house," he said.

Aunt Alice stood up, held one hand to my head, smoothed my short hair back into place.

"Get the fuck out of this house . . . now." She didn't scream this time; she was real quiet. Uncle Bobby left right then.

Aunt Alice died a few years after that—cirrhosis of the liver, I think it was. She was an alcoholic; she had more reason to be than most.

Six years later, Grandpa lay dying in Beaumont. It was a Catholic hospital, though no one in the family was Catholic. A nun called, a Mother Superior, I think: Mr. Bledsoe was dying. Could we come?

We went into the room, all quiet and fearful. I had seen death; my father, cold and shoeless in his satin coffin. Grandpa was gurgling when we tiptoed in. None of the other children were there yet. They had farther to drive or were with less reckless drivers.

The tubes and machines in his room seemed to have increased, but I couldn't be sure. He didn't look any different to me. He was in that semicoma state I had watched for the last two years. Still, I believed the doctors knew what they were talking about. If they said he was dying, it must be so. At twelve I still believed a lot of things people told me.

I remember we stood around the bed: Mama, my brother Bill and me. Eric had been gone for two years by then. Bill cried and talked about a B-B gun Grandpa had given him as a young child. Then he went down the hall for a coke.

Mama went up and put a hand on Grandpa's shoulder. She kept it there while she said, "Papa. It's Betty, Papa."

I stood at the foot of the bed absolutely transfixed by this withered piece of flesh stretched out in starched sheets, plugged into machines that beeped and flashed. Through the haze I saw him emerge, saw the face take on the features of a human again. I saw him look up at my mother, saw recognition in those old blue eyes. He began to cry, pitifully. To this day it is one of the saddest things I've ever witnessed.

"I'm sorry," he whispered, cracked words out of the cracked mouth. "I'm so sorry." That small, dry hand came up to the paper face, tears spilling over the thin brown sticks of fingers.

"I'm sorry," he said it over and over again. It wasn't an apology so much as it was a confession. Mama looked surprised. She didn't look at me at all. She seemed embarrassed to have me there, at the same time assuming I wouldn't notice, wouldn't understand.

She was right. I didn't understand then. I didn't understand until twenty-five years later. Oh, I knew about how he had raped her when she was eleven—thrown her down, beaten her and broken her arm. I was old enough to tell her that Bill had tried to do the same with me. By the time I was twenty-three I had been in therapy long enough to understand about "dysfunctional" families: how the abuse is carried from generation to generation; how insanity is visited upon the sons and daughters of sons and daughters.

When my mother lay dying, I was thirty-six, a mother myself. Long since I had broken the chain, cut what strings I could, taken my losses and traveled as far away as fate would allow. My brother Bill called; Mama was dying. I should go see her in the hospital. I had steadfastly refused for the five months since she'd had her stroke. Did I have an agenda for this crazy old woman? Did I really have anything to say to the person who had neglected me, beaten me physically, and tried to crush me psychologically? Yes, I did. I wanted the war to be over, whatever it took.

My therapist, Dr. Sharon, would not let me go alone. She took me up to St. Joseph's in her little white Volkswagen. She wore her white lab coat and they let us in the Intensive Care Unit, though it wasn't visiting hours. The scene was much the same as the one I remembered when I was twelve. This time my mother lay still on the bleach-white sheets, machines that beeped and flashed attached to her arms and nose, a half-filled urine bag hanging from a catheter tube at the edge of the bed.

Sharon stood at the end of the bed, a few feet away, talking with a Sister who sat monitoring the machines. My mother had a stroke just like Grandpa. Watched over now by Catholic Sisters, she was lost in that semi-dream state of the near dead.

"Mama," I said. "I love you, Mama." Whatever pain was left between us, I wanted her to leave in peace. I wanted that worse than I wanted that peace myself. If she were at peace, then maybe I could convince myself that she had really loved me, that she had not meant to do those things to me. Most of all, I wanted to believe what she had always told me—it had been my imagination, she had never hit me, never slammed me into walls, never chased me screaming with the big rusty kitchen bread knife, never ripped my legs up with a willow switch I had to cut myself from the tree in the back yard. I wanted very much to believe she had not begun to call me a whore when I was twelve, had not blamed me for Bill's sexual attacks on me. This one last battle between us was one I desperately wanted her to win: to convince me, once and for all, I had been wrong, crazy, psychotic, to remember those things about my own mother. To this day I feel an urge to protest. My mother loved me, didn't she? She wouldn't do those things to her only daughter whom she loved . . .

Mama came up from the depths. She looked about her oddly, at the machines, at the bed, at the Sister on the stiff-backed chair. And then as if remembering something trivial, I could see recognition in her eyes. She knew where she was, knew she was dying. She had a small bit of business to wrap up. She coughed, tried to clear her throat, whispered in a deep gravel, "I'm sorry."

She drifted away as I stood open-mouthed at her side. She did not say she loved me. To this day I do not know if I would have rather she lied.

I backed away from the bed, trying hard to find space in my lungs for air. Sharon touched me, I think, led me down the hall. I found a bathroom and dived into it. I thought I would throw up my insides they were screaming so hard. I stood retching dry heaves at the sink. I stared into the mirror, I could make out my reflection, I could see my ash-white face. But I could not focus, could not breathe. In the mirror I could see Sharon behind me. I sensed rather than felt her hand patting my back.

"Is that really what happened?" I said to Sharon and the mirror. "She said she was sorry, didn't she? She said she was sorry just like Grandpa said he was sorry when he died."

"Yes, that's what she said. I heard her."

My worst nightmare had been confirmed: I was not crazy, I had not imagined the horror of my youth. Worse yet, neither was my mother crazy. She had always known. ■

# Section Three
## *Dark Pages*

Curse you father
for making me hear doors closing
in the breath of the men who sleep
beside me, dark pages turning
the noise of my son twisting in bed.
You lurk everywhere.
Dogs cannot bark you away,
the dawn brings only light relief.
You are inside me always.
I brace the gate
but still your footsteps creak
on every stair,
your eyes at my windows peer,
your car comes closer
closer down an endless street.

Patti Tana

Sara O.'s memoir, "Baths," which opens this section, recalls the violence and pain of her childhood, adolescence, and adulthood up to the time of her divorce. Subsequent diary entries not included here trace her progress as an adult, learning to be autonomous and to survive as a single parent. Sara presents herself as daughter, adolescent, wife, lover, mother, divorcée, sex addict, and finally, single parent and would-be supermom. The plot of Sara's journey moves as a circle, a cycle of victory and defeat that seems never ending. These cycles, which appear to her as entrapments, form a spiral wherein even as the pain in her life repeats itself, she grows more capable of dealing with that pain. Sara's struggle to write her way into a resolution becomes a model for understanding the way the writing/talking cure functions and its relationship to the concept of transcendence as we are using it in this anthology.

"Baths" opens with the flashback triggered by Sara's daughter's behavior. In this memory we find the beginning of Sara's assumptions about the world she inhabits, assumptions confirmed as other events resurface. When Sara complains about her father's sexual advances, her mother mistakes the concern in her daughter's voice as concern for the father, rather than for her own safety. "Don't worry about him," she says, meaning, "He'll be okay." Traditions the mother passes on to her daughter deny the value of Sara's personal experience. Sara's teacher, and later her aunt, confirm those beliefs, setting up a pattern that silences her in adulthood to the abuse she suffers at the hands of her boyfriend/husband. Sara's life typifies the lessons girls learn as they turn to women for guidance:

- Women do not believe what you say
- Women do not have the power to protect their daughters
- Women do not think sexual violation is worth "worrying about"
- A woman's job is to clean up (take a bath) the mess men make of our lives.

However, even as women are supposed to clean up men's messes, they are not expected to consider them serious messes.

Missing from the memoir is the information relevant to Sara's divorce trial: that Sara worked and had children while Juan went to college. Now Juan, employed as a professional with a large firm, pays minimum child support, while Sara works for minimum wages and runs her life around treatment programs that define her as sick and in recovery. And, worse, Juan maintains visitation rights in spite of his suspected sexual abuse of the children.

The labels of the treatment programs Sara joins help her articulate her past and thus give her power over it. Ironically, however, she sees herself as "sick," as needing a "cure." Thus, we meet Sara at a critical time in her "recovery" from both child and spousal abuse. She is learning to write and talk about her life, exemplifying the way the writing/talking cure works in the context of transcending violence.

In a private interview, when Sara handed me a typed version of her latest diary entries, she remarked: "Typing this up, I felt like I was watching myself through a window." As narrator, Sara achieves distance from her own pain and can reject her position of helplessness and assume the position of healer. With the power to tell her life from her own perspective, she is free to create a story that casts her as heroine and paves the path to transcendence.

Progress toward transcendence begins with the achievement through writing of distance from the old self. Remembering validates her sense of victimization and the source of her power to survive. She can, thus, celebrate herself as a survivor and heal herself as a victim. But is that enough? How many stories can she bear to survive?

To break free of the victim/survivor loop, one must reach for transcendence. To live in search of transcendence is to live in the grips of a paradox: as Sara writes and speaks her pain, she is doomed to relive it. But as she relives it, she learns to separate from it. She becomes, at the same time, closer to her past and more distanced from it.

The lessons of the past are beneficial only when we claim them, own them, by refusing to allow the past to own us. To let go of the past—to free ourselves from its hold—fosters a quality of strength through which we can embrace the many selves we have become during our lives. The liberating effect of writing our way out of the pain is part of rebirthing ourselves. The release we feel has to do with separation: giving our pain "a name and a face," an identity separate from our former selves.

Sara O's case is one of many; indeed some estimates indicate there are 25 million women survivors of incest in the U. S.[1] Statistics are frightening: [2]

- One out of four women in the U. S. have a history of incest, one out of eight men
- Ninety percent of women surveyed knew their sexual abuser
- Sixty percent of abusers were blood relatives
- Sixty percent of all incest survivors never told anyone prior to age eighteen
- Sixty percent are also children of alcoholics

- Seventy-five percent of incest survivors experience severe mood swings
- Forty percent suffer eating disorders
- Twenty-eight percent were raped as adults
- Thirty percent have been battered as adults.

In 1993, over 2.8 million children were abused by their parents, caregiver, or a person that they knew. In 1995, local child protective service agencies identified 126,000 children who were victims of substantiated sexual abuse; of these, seventy-five percent were girls. Nearly thirty percent of child victims were between the ages of four and seven.[3]

Most perplexing is the tendency for researchers to blame "children for the behavior of their adult molesters . . . . Girls have been alleged to have . . . an underlying unconscious wish (to experience) sexual trauma in childhood . . . a masochistic expression of the sexual impulse . . . ." (Scully 1990, 44).

■■■

Incest is but one of many forms of abuse children endure, violations that darken their psyches for the remaining years of their lives. "adam," Susan Harned Roth's cathartic poem, condenses language into a stream of pejoratives and recalls the Adam of Genesis who named the world and its creatures. So are we formed by the names our parents call us. Roth's "adam," Patricia Monaghan's "Home Movies," Marie Cartier's "My Father," and Ava Leavell Haymon's "In Which, On the Fourth Anniversary of His Death I Accuse My Father of Incest" allow us to explore the way language and experience shape our images of self and the way the past infuses the present with pain. Thus we discover the reasons patterns must be broken and new ways of living invented. All too often survivors must reinvent their lives without benefit of role models and without support of trusted friends or sympathetic parents.

"Breakfast with Father" shifts us back into J. Whitebird's distant past. Whitebird knew at age two exactly what she knows now, only she could not have put that knowledge into words or into the context of a larger experience. The journey of her life has been to articulate and thus transcend the experiences of her childhood. But the voice of the child/adult stands outside time and place.

"Gifts" offers a deep exploration of the way events in Patti Tana's childhood, especially her father's abuse of her mother, inform her adult life. Exemplary of Hillman's concept that case history "moves us from the fiction of reality to the reality of fiction," Tana's short story presents a reality as fiction in a gift that illuminates the dark pages of her past. ■

**Baths**

Sara O.

What I remember from my dad was he used to put me on his knee and would make me feel good. So he was horse ride on his knee, which make me feel good also. Then what I remember is taking a shower with my parents. I was able to see my dad and mom naked. What I do remember is she showing me what to do with towel put in shower. To tie it up and the water flowing down to hit my vagina. It will make me feel good. She used to do it to herself. Or to use the water bag tube that goes in your vagina. Another incident that I remember was I found my dad kissing me one night. He had beer in his mouth. He just keep kissing me. I wanted for him to stop but he wouldn't. Then what I remember from that, that it was morning and he stink like when a man comes. I got up and told my moma.

And she said: "Oh, he only pee on himself. Just go and take a bath. Don't worry about him—everything is okay!!"

Then from that day on I remember him always trying to be with me alone. When he did he would get behind me touch my breast and he would move in my back. And pound me again and again, kiss my neck. I would try to get loose but he was stronger than me. He didn't care even when I got married he tried to do it too. I remember one incident I was going to check the freezer so I could fill it up. And he came behind me and grap me and went for my breast. Oh I hated that so much I wish I could kill him then. So I just fought until I could get away from there.

And I tried to hide everything from everybody because they wouldn't believe me anyway. I tried one time and it didn't work so why try. I just want to be loved. All I wanted is to be believe in what was happening to me. Why can't they believe what was going on with my dad. His kisses were always so wet and I hate it.

The other man that molest me was when I was nine years old. The way it happen: my aunt had a man to clean the garden yard. I was visiting my grandparents. I notice the man was looking at me every chance he had. So what I did I tried to avoid him and be far away from him. After awhile I decide to go home because I was getting afraid of him. So I told my aunt if she could walk me home and she said she was busy. Then Jose was going to walk me home, and I quick said please not him. I don't like him the way he look at me. Oh it all right it be okay. So then he walk me home. He said that I was a very pretty little girl. I kept on walking pretending I didn't heard him. So by time we reach corner he ask me for a kiss and a hug. And I said, "No."

Then—next day he put his arms around and kiss me touch my top and down. I was too scared to scream. When I did get away I ran all the way home. My dad was already there and he saw how scared I was and he asked me what's wrong and I told him what happen. And took me back and put me in the car. What I could hear was dad telling my aunt not to ever let that man near me again. But they did not report it to the police. The man did stop going there. Then months after that he appear again by then I took more precaution. He never did attempt to do anything any more. I guess he was afraid of my dad.

I was thirteen years old when this boy and boys in class also tried to touch my breast. Some did accomplish and that made me very mad. I told the teacher and she said maybe it's your fault. So please go and sit down and laugh with them. So I sure didn't like to go to school any more. I was in the sixth grade.

This is about Leonardo C. in the year of 1968. I fell in love with him. Every time he wanted a kiss he would give me a Tootsie Roll. One day he invited me to his house and his sisters left me alone. He asked me if he could touch my breast and vagina. And I said No. Then he said I sing you a song then. Then he got the guitar and started playing it. Then he gave me the guitar as he was showing me he started moving his hand to my hips going down every chance he could. Then I got up and said No. Please take me home. When I got home, he later call me. And he said he was sorry and we couldn't be friend anymore because I didn't give in. And he need somebody to be with. I said I sorry but I cannot do it.

Then I decided again to go out again. I was very excited. I was about sixteen years old. I told my mom if I could go out. And she said okay. But be very careful and I said Okay. That I was going to meet him at school. Well I got dress and went. His name was Julio. He was a cousin of Alex whom I liked but he was dating somebody else. So I said, well, at least I can date his cousin. Well we started talking and walking around the school grounds. We went to the vocational building. I didn't think I was putting myself in a bad position. Well I trust him, I shouldn't but I did.

We were laughing and talking. Then he put me in the corner. He started kissing me and I said No. But he just kept on and on and on. Then he would say Boy you look so good. What a [illegible] Breast. Then he move [my] hands to try to touch him and I stop him and he force himself and touch me. He was acting very crazy. He just would [not] stop. And kept on stopping him from touching me. But he was stronger. Then he went for my dress and touch my vagina. Boy I hate that. Why do they always do sex? Why can't they be nice?

He finally stop. Then he step away and give me the peace sign and good-bye. Boy I wanted to kill him. Why are they all alike? When I got back I told my mom and she just said, "Oh don't worry about it. Just go take a bath and you feel okay." Well even when I finished taking a bath I still feel bad.

Then I met Juan, my X-husband. I met him on May 2, 1970. I must a been seventeen. What I do remember is I was finishing my ninth grade. Nobody knew nothing about him except that he was known for art and good grades. I remember he gave me a jewel box with some angel holding the box. I lost it at home. I never saw it again.

Then we stopped seeing each other. We started again in the tenth grade. Well I thought he was the perfect man. Boy now I know it was mine worst one. The first thing I told him was he was not to kiss me or hold my hand until I wanted to. Well it did okay for one year. Then I let him kiss me and hold hands. Then he wanted me to prove my love for him. I started to tell my mom but I was scare. So I remember that day. But my mother was too busy to talk to me. I then grab her with my two hands and said please I need to talk to you. No I, don't have the time.

Well I went on the date. Yes diary he did asked me to prove it. Well this is the way it happen. It was a Sunday afternoon. We went to eat cone ice cream. We went across the street to the high school grounds and sat down for a while. Then he got up and started looking around. I didn't know what he was doing. I followed him cause he was holding my hands. He knew what he was looking for and what he had in his mind. SEX. Then put me in the corner and started to kiss each other. I didn't fight. Then he ask me if I could suck his dick. I said, no.

Come on. I won't hurt you.

I told him I never seen a man before. To please don't ask me to do it. Well he put his hands on my shoulders and push me down. He had his pants down now. I had my eyes close I was scare. He said Sara open your eyes. It okay. I'm not going to hurt just open your mouth. No please I don't want to. Come on Sara it will be okay. So I just open my mouth and let him do it to me on my mouth. Then he realize I had my eyes close and he said look at it. Once you see it you will love it. It's my part and you love me please if you love me you will please me. So I open my eyes. When I saw it I'm sorry but I fainted. I was so shock I fainted. Boy then he didn't know what to do. He finally brought me to.

We went to get a coke. And he said he was sorry for forcing himself on me, that he wouldn't do it again. I couldn't said anything. Well I got time to go home. On the way home he didn't keep his promise he wanted to touch me and he wanted for me to do it again, sucking his dick. I hate him at that point and I said No. But he force me again and put it in my mouth again we were in the Civic Center Building. Everything happened so fast. He finally fuck me in the mouth and yes he did come diary. Boy I hated myself so much that day. I want for him not to do that.

Well we did get home. But this time I was so scare of what had happen I couldn't tell my mom. I couldn't hurt her. Then from there on he always wanted me to suck it. Boy, I always tried not to. He had that look in his eyes that made me do it. Anyway he always force me with his hands pushing me to do it. Yes I did break with him four times and end up with him again.

Boy when he want to finally fuck me it was even worse. He started asking to please prove my love for him. He want us to [be] one just like married couple. That we would be like them. I said NO. Well he finally got his chance. We went driving home. He took a different road which was kind of deserted. As soon as I saw what he was heading for I started to move close to the door. But he saw me and he push me close to him. Don't worry Sara. I won't hurt you. Trust me. I won't hurt you. I love you very much. Please I want for you to be mine. Only mine.

Juan it's not right we should wait. Then he park the station wagon. Then I tried to unlock the door. He lock it again. He started to kiss me and kiss me then he would start for my breast then between my legs. No Juan please STOP.

But he was out to get what he want. My virgin spot. He then got me so hot I just didn't stop him. When he was starting for me I keep on moving and moving to stop him. He finally lock me with his body. I could fight him no more. I hurt so much but he wouldn't stop. I keep on and on and he keep on and on and on. He finally finish and I was so scare of what had happen. My mom will kill me now. Now I have to marry him because no body will want me. Who wants a girl who has nothing to give? I had lost it to this man. Well he would get into argument about sick and he would slap me so hard I just did it just to stop him from slapping me around. He would used force every time he wanted sex or sucking his dick. Well that went on for five years.

We finally got married 8-16-75. In our honeymoon he want anal sex. Which he had force me before. I hated anal sex cause it hurt. I stayed in the bathroom. I thought he was asleep so I went to bed and he was asleep. Boy I was in for it. Then he said you are my wife and you have to satisfy me all the time. Yes, he force anal sex on me. What a honeymoon. Hooray, hooray! Bullshit I would said. Well sex was to be perform three or four times a day whether you or him in the mood, which most of the time he was. So I just did it to please him.

Then he had one friend which I knew. He asked me if I could call him for lunch. I was supposed to get him drunk and then make sex to him. Well I did as he told me. But I couldn't get him drunk. I didn't have the courage. Well that night we got into an argument and did sex to please him. Then he started taking me to the rated XXX movies. Then when we got home I was supposed to do as they did in the movie. Yes I did diary, just to please him.

Oh! Diary I remember one thing before. We were dating at that time I had gotten shopping with my Mom. And saw an old friend who invited me for coke. I asked my mom and she said okay. So I went. Well I took longer than I thought. I missed the bus home. And I thought there was another one. Well this guy wanted for me to run away with him. Well I was scare and said NO. Well who did I call but Juan to the rescue. Well what rescue he got me to tell him why I had miss the bus. He slaps me on both cheeks. He did take me home but I got put down all the way. And he said never to do him like that again. I belong to him because nobody will marry me 'cause I was his.

Well things didn't get that bad until I got pregnant. He was always mad. He wanted more attention and I couldn't give it to him. I was pregnant and was going through a lot of changes. Then he found out that I had to get an operation to have the baby. Boy we fought half way home. I tried to jump from the truck but he stop me. He said he might as well as a HOR [woman of the street] to have his baby because she could have a normal delivery. And I couldn't. I had to deal with him and also knowing that maybe my son would be born deform, dead or mental retarded. All he was concerned that I couldn't have a normal delivery. At least he was going to have a child. It didn't matter which way. The argument keep on. I finally said well tomorrow Sunday I will get dress and go to the movies and put myself in the hospital. Then when the baby be born we would get a divorce. Well then Sunday came and when I started for the door. He stop me and apologize. Well I fell for it again. Yes I care for him. We both went to the movies and he left me in the hospital. The baby boy who is now eleven years old, Luis Jose which I wanted to name him Jr. and he said NO and again he won again.

The worst argument was this one. Well it started like this. My sister came to visit. She had come to visit my home and my baby. The baby being three or four months I don't remember what. I do remember it was when Iran had those hostages in the airplane. It lasted months and months. Well I was a hostage in my home then. Here's the way it started. He came in from talking with my sister. Remember she came to visit me and the baby. He started asking me is there anything you need to tell me. No I don't have nothing to tell you. Why? Well you sister said you do. No I don't.

**Juan:** Well I think you do.

**Me:** What do you mean?

**Juan:** Well it's time you know about it.

**Me:** What do I need to know? I was so scare of the way he was acting. I have never seen him like that before.

**Juan:** Okay. I tell you. Well I have been having an affair with your sister.

**Me:** No I don't believe you. I started to cry. How could you do this to me? Don't you love me?

**Juan:** Yes. I do. But she love me too.

**Me:** But I'm your wife and I have done everything for you.

**Juan:** Well things happen. I did enjoy it. But she said you have something to tell me.

**Me.** Well at that point I didn't care my feelings were so destroy I could not think. So I told on myself. Yes. There's something you don't know about me. I did sex with another guy.

**Juan:** What did you say? Say it again.

**Me:** I haved sex with somebody else. He was so mad. He slap and close his fist and punch me on both sides. I was bleeding from the mouth.

**Me:** Don't you want me to say the truth? You said to trust you. You would not hurt me. Why are you hitting me?

**Juan:** I'm hitting you because you desire to be punish. I'm your husband and you desire to be punish. Now tell me when did it happen?

**Me:** Well it happen when you were in college. We weren't married then. It doesn't make any difference. I wasn't your wife.

**Juan:** But you were my fiancée.

**Me:** That doesn't mean I was your wife.

**Juan:** Yes because you were suppose to be only mine. Nobody else. You could of waited for me.

**Me:** NO. I mean yes. Well you told me if I need someone that you would understand. So I guess that why I did. I thought you wouldn't get mad. Why did you tell me it was okay? Now you tell me it's not.

**Juan:** Now I want for you to tell me everything that happen that day.

**Me:** Why it's happen and that's the past.

Then he got his belt and said: Take your clothes off.

**Me:** Why. What are you going to do?

**Juan:** Just take your clothes off. Now.

**Me:** Okay. But don't get mad. I only love you. Why are you mad? Please forgive me, Juan. Please forgive me.

Well diary. He did not forgive me. He hit me with his belt all over my body. He didn't miss a piece of my body.

**Juan:** Open your legs, and lay still.

**Me:** I lay still and open my legs. He then ran the belt between my legs and I was so scare and crying not knowing what he was doing.

**Juan:** Now put your "butt" up so I can see your pussy. Your ugly pussy which you gave to another man. You should be very proud of your self for giving it to somebody else. Well this is what you get.

**Me:** He then got the belt and hit me and my pussy and butt again and again and again and then he turn me again and hit my back until he finally got tired. I was bleeding from my mouth which he had hit me with the belt and fist. Yes. He got tired. Now he was resting. I was laying still. I didn't want to make him upset. Then he jump out of the bed. Now he pull my hair. Do sex to me.

**Juan:** Pretend you're doing it to the other guy come on show me how you did it to him. You love sex, you couldn't wait for me. Come on show me you bitch. Fuck me you Bitch.

**Me:** Juan please stop. I love you. Why are you asking me to do this? Can't you understand I love you? I married you, didn't I?

**Juan:** (Pounce on the mouth) No. Now I'm asking you to make love to me as if I was him.

Well, diary, I did. I make love to him even though all my body was hurting. Well the night finally end. He got what he want. Suck his dick and made him come. Then he kiss me and put his arms around me.

Well, the next day he went to work. I stay and took care of the house and son. When he return the stage was on again. Get undress and be hit. When one night he had me make love to him and all the sudden he hit with his fist and then I lay and he got up and started smoking. He then order me to open my legs and lay still. Oh God please help me. He then got his cigarettes and burn my breast very slowly and laughing everything he did it. He also burn my vagina. After that say again what happen with the guy. When finish he would hit me with his fist and then perform sex again. Then after many nights being put through hit or belt.

One night he was a little more dangerous. He said I think I want a divorce. Well, I said Okay. We will get one tomorrow morning. He jump up his bed and hit me with his fist on my mouth. I thought he wasn't going to stop this time. Well he did and went to the closet and got the rifle out. Boy. God I up quick, but not quick enough for him. He said, stay there and he hit me and I was laying on the bed naked.

**Juan:** Open your mouth.

**Me:** No

**Juan:** (Pounce on the mouth with fist) Open your mouth.

**Me:** I think he hit with his fist so much I finally open my mouth.

**Juan:** (Rifle on his hand and straight to my mouth.) Now do you want a divorce?

**Me:** What choice do I have but to say NO.

**Juan:** Okay you will never divorce me. I will kill you first before you ever intend to leave me. Do you hear me Sara? I'll kill you.

Well, diary, there wasn't a night I rested. He was either hit or doing something. One night he ask me to lay still on the floor, of course naked.

**Juan:** Now open your mouth.

**Me:** What are you going to do?

**Juan:** Just open your mouth.

**Me:** He then got his penis and started pee on my mouth.

**Juan:** Now drink it you Bitch.

**Me:** I started to get up and he put his feet on me, and I took his pee. There was also other night he made me get the next door neighbor's dog which he was like a Doberman. But it didn't work so he make me bring the English setter we had. Yes he put the dog so the dog's penis be in my vagina. Please Juan Stop It.

**Juan:** NO! I won't. You have to do what I tell you now. You do desire this. This is the way you are dirty and don't desire to be love by a man.

I was so tired of being beat on. I tried call some people. A family counselor. But they said they need his name to report him. But then I said please I can't don't do it. I'm afraid and I hung up the phone.

I never knew what kind of a mood he would be. But there were nights I pretended nothing was happen. By that time I was tired. I left the house and got my baby. I walk the wrong direction. I pass by his mom house. She stop me and I told them I was leave him. They convince me so I stay. His mom said you know how Juan is. You better keep your mouth shut. He doesn't like people to know his business. Well I stayed.

Then next time I tried to leave I told my brother-in-law. He didn't believe me. He came and tried to talk to Juan. Well Juan got upset that night and beat me up again. Well I'll never tell again. Sometimes he would hit me down on the bed and do sex to me and force me to suck his penis. He even make me eat my food from the floor. He said I didn't deserve to eat on the table. If I didn't do it he would beat me up. There was one occasion we were fixing the bed and we put a nail on the bed. But I put it wrong and he almost hit me with the hammer. I got up and run to the kitchen. He got me and slap my face and pull my hair. My son was next to him and he said "Yes, daddy hit her."

*[Note: handwriting changes here from straight and round to slant and smaller.]*

Sometimes he was in the mood of crazy sex. He would ask me to get different long and round things so he could see me fuck myself and sucking his penis. Then he would come and I was suppose to take his liquid. I hate it when I didn't do he would hit again and again until I did it. Boy if only I would have the courage to stop him.

You know, Tina, [her counselor at the Family Place] there were times I couldn't even go to sleep when I wanted. He had to approve it. Sometimes I was so tired I slept sitting down and pretending I was watching TV. He eventually realize it which made him mad.

Well, he put me through a lot of things. But the good thing is I'm alive.

I left February 28, 1987, and stayed with Dawn and Alfred and their two kids. They help us for ten days. Then I decided to go to the women's shelter. I was very scared that Juan would come and get me. I would sit in front and watch the door. I wouldn't let my kids to leave the shelter. The lady whom I owe is Sharon. She said, even if Juan try to open the door he really wouldn't have a chance. The police would be there before he broke the glass of the door. (Now the door is not of glass anymore.) From there on I started try to get a job. My first job was at the donut shop. Then Kelly Girl which was okay. But the hour were so hard. I tried working at Hyatt Hotel but I felt that I would be very easy to be a pick-up girl. So I tried something else. I finally tried clerk with the state. I have tried very hard to keep this job. I have been there two year. I only wish that I keep on growing and that I will never put myself in another position like this. I'm finally able to say NO to men and trying to learn to be alone and like myself. I have my counselors and friend Sylvia which I have also learn from her. So please if you ever in a position or situation like me. I got out you can too. It's hard but it's worthwhile.

Juan still give me a headache but I'm learning not to get upset.

Oh, Tina, I also remember he used to make me masturbate myself and he was filming it also. I hope those videotapes and pictures are destroyed. Well, I think this is it for now. I hope I can recover from this one. (writing it all up.) ■

**Mother**

Kathleen A. Sitarski

And with what
were you preoccupied
from the moment of my birth?

Instead of lullabies
you hummed death threats. ■

**adam**

Susan Harned Roth

she could not say what he called her
but wrote this list from memory:
stupid numbskull fatass asshole.
there was always a place in whatever life
she lived for these words which she carried
in an old suitcase that fell apart at the worst times:
jerk knownothing fatso horse's ass.
no matter how small the space she occupied
there was always one hanging in the closet:
horse's tail shit little shit big shit bitch.
sometimes she dressed in them and walked
like a naked fool through the streets:
creep clumsy dirty filthy ugly as sin.
sometimes she stuffed them in a drawer and locked it but they
always found their way out
through the window of a dream somewhere:
dummy spoiledbrat spoiledrotten bigmouth.
they especially liked to gather on the bed
when she and her husband made love
and slip down her throat to occupy her skin:
stinking smelly nokidofmine.
her mother always said oh don't pay any mind
he's just teasing and really she was very lucky
because even though he would rage and rage at her
his face a bag of red hot coals
he was a good father who never hit her:
all he did was name her. ■

**Home Movies**

Patricia Monaghan

A Japanese meal has been made,
and sake bought and warmed, and
the kids dressed up in kimonos.

The conversation is
instructive, for the children,
somewhat bawdy, for the rest.

At least one mention
of Panmunjong. Then
a bilingual song or two.

The daughters bring out
the wood dolls from Japan and show
how the elaborately dressed hair

can be removed, leaving the head
momentarily bald while another
wig is brought from the case.

As the children grow sleepy
a sheet is tacked against the wall
and the projector is brought out.

There is a little game to play
with the sake cups, so that
everyone is drunk by the time

the movies begin. Aerial views
of Korean fields, paddies, blue
distant hills. Smoke and flame,

real war movies. The men drink
and retell the squadron jokes
while the women clear and clean.

The children, holding their dolls,
watch the silent bombs land
on the bedsheet, over and over. ■

## My Father

Marie Cartier

My father sold me to a neighbor cop,
"A hundred bucks for good sex . . . 'till you drop
sex." On top of me, his breath and his weight
come back to me years years years too late.
I hate him. . . . Dad . . . gave me a lollipop.

My Dad. My Pimp. The cop customer. Top
of the line. A cop. My Dad did flip-flops
for guys like that. "Yeah, that cop's no lightweight."
    My father sold me.

To a cop. I told Mom, Why does he plop
me in his lap? Blue uniform eavesdrops
into me, his hand marks my cheek: dictate
shame. I am scared. I tell Mom. Ha! Checkmate.
"Don't cause a scene." I stop. I become his prop.
    My father sold me. ■

## In Which, On the Fourth Anniversary of His Death
## I Accuse My Father of Incest

Ava Leavell Haymon

It's just like you, you god-besotted woman hater. To die
today, dragging off after you half the mythology of middle winter.
Groundhog's day—when all that's left of the future's a shadow
of the lack of it. It's Candlemas. Celtic Imbolg. La Fheile Brid
in Ireland, St. Brigid's Day—according to *The Golden Bough* "a heathen
goddess of fertility, disguised in a threadbare Christian

cloak." It's also Feast of the Purification of Women, a Christian
holy day, handy annual reminder of who's dirty. Chances are, you died
to celebrate that, but maybe, deep down in your freckled genes, a heathen
grandmother stirred like a seed in mud, refused to spend one more winter
in Mississippi. Enough horses sweat/men perspire/women glow. Her breed
of women doesn't cotton to hold-your-knees-together and stay in the shadow

of your man. No mere man cast a shadow
big enough to knock the sun off her. And enough Southern-accent Christian
trinity "PraiseFathuhSuhnAn'Hoe-leeGhost, All-men"—grisly parody of Brid,
radiant Goddess of three faces. Blasphemy, she declared. No wonder you died!
But where do you leave me? four years later at the fulcrum of winter,
my own throat and red-haired ancestors crying out for heathen

vengeance. Creeping above ground, I cringe like the groundhog (heathenish
superstition anyway, you'd say), not so much afraid of her own shadow
as terrified she'll see the quickening winter
sun as I saw it once, my Christian
father's John-the-Baptist severed head, dying
scream a long no-o-o-o-o across the sky. I'm bride

to too many lovers. Bride
double-bound to father/husband, Beast and Prince alike. My heathen

scarlet heart's blood thumps toward rage, rage, to gush out, die
fighting, to drag these shape-shift shadow
trysts to light. All the while, my Christian
blood, blue blood of veins and martyrs, soughs wintry

toward a drowsy surrender, toward the ice-choke secrets of winter,
the blasted kernel, family shame veiled with the eldest bride.
In two sides of the same mouth, I chew Christian
bread and sacramental wine, and heathen
wedding feasts of meade, venison. I swallow hard. A shadow
falls across the table—my own, the outline curling in to die.

Hunched in the white glare, she risks a cautious breath. Dying winter
gathers its last storm. Is it her shadow summons the cold? or the bride
tearing away her veil? purple heathen lips, face pale and old as Christ. ■

**Breakfast with Father**

J. Whitebird

The child sat upright in the crib, balanced on her ample bottom, her legs splayed out in front of her. Toes had ceased to be of interest. However many there were, they fit nicely on the ends of her feet and functioned fairly well. They wiggled, spread apart, and stretched back and forth, did all that was required of them. She had explored them as fully as an inquisitive twenty-month-old child was capable of—quite extensively.

She was not hungry but did not remember eating. Time in her crib stretched endlessly across the days. She knew how patterns of light from the window in the wall beside her crib moved through the room. It was a universal repetition that she instinctively recognized. It was calming, reassuring, but impossibly long. She could barely remember from the beginning of the cycle to the end of it. It still seemed early, the paned light was only halfway across the floor, still elongated. Through the light that sailed in front of her she could see the tiny motes drift through the hazy, honey flavored air.

At first she did not pay any attention to the small sounds coming from the kitchen, one wall away. Mama and John were having their breakfast. At least, by the angle of the light, that was probably it. Mama had eggs and toast on a plate and coffee in a thick white mug beside it. John, on the other hand, still drank his breakfast, much like she would take her bottle to bed. She envied him his comfort. She called him John because that's what Mama called him. Her older brothers called him Dad, when they were around, which wasn't not very often. They always left when the light was still long and thin across the floor and returned when it faded to a dim glow on the far wall.

John, on the other hand, was always there. She liked to play with him; he was more fun than Mama or the boys. Once John put little tape shoes on the bottom of the cat's paws. My-Tease jumped about on her tiptoes, trying to remove them. The dainty-looking white cat pawed the air, shook her furry feet and meowed pitifully until John took the shoes off. She had worried for a moment, until, tape removed and My-Tease's ruffled fur smoothed down, the little cat curled up in her lap and purred for petting.

Mama was usually glum, sad about something she could never quite understand. Mama was a large woman, stocky and solid. She went to work in the morning looking angry; returned home at night tired and sad, often crying. This morning she waited for Mama to leave so John would come play with her. The routine was always the same. John would bring her coffee in a small white cup, not as big or bulky as the one her mother drank out of, more her size and easier to hold. It was not the same color liquid that filled her mother's cup either. Mama drank dark brown coffee, not a very appetizing color. But her own coffee was a warm buff color, sweet and thick. She and John would sit in the tiny front room and have their breakfast together. She with her coffee cup—she was terribly proud of that—and John with his huge silver tumbler.

First he would bring her coffee. Then he would bring in another bottle, clear, with a light, golden liquid and fill up his tumbler. Sure to let her watch, as he always did, he broke a fresh egg into the tumbler. She would laugh to see the heavy yolk plop into the scotch and sink slowly to the bottom.

It was all part of the game: John would turn up the tumbler and drink the liquid all at once, trying to see if he could finish it before the egg drifted to the bottom. She would lean out of her crib and watch. She could tell when he opened his jaws wide to take in the egg. Whether he won or not she could not be sure, but she always laughed anyway.

It seemed that coffee was late this morning. She was not aware of it but time divided itself differently for her than it did for Mama and John. It was a still, live, endless entity that sustained her in its wholeness. It was only when she felt the first gnawing of hunger that she turned her attention to the sounds coming from the kitchen. She noticed vaguely that they were different from the usual morning squeak of chairs, clinks of cup to saucer, scrapes of fork on plate. The voices were not muffled and low as they usually were. Mama's sounded shrill and angry, but she could not make out the words—they went too fast. There was a heavy scrape and a bang. Someone had knocked over John's big wooden chair. Curiously, she listened. She put out her hands as far as they would go to the crib bars, white and squarish in front of her. The painted wood felt cool and smooth. The shouting in the kitchen grew louder; her fists clinched around the bars. She felt her shoulders tense; a strange grating tingle ran up and down her back.

The room exploded in sound and energy. Mama came running from the kitchen, John behind her. Mama was screaming garbled, frightened sounds. Tension filled the room. Her nose picked up the scent of burned air, blue, charged and crackling.

What was happening? She pulled herself to a standing position holding onto the sides of the crib for support. She was unaware that she was holding her breath. Her hands seemed to become embedded in the bars of the crib. Mama turned to face John; she had nowhere else to run in the tiny house.

John caught up with her. His hands closed around her throat in a swift, almost imperceptible motion. From her crib she stood absolutely still, a repulsive curiosity building within her. She saw Mama's head lean back, away from the hands, heard a gurgle deep in her throat. John stood, feet solid, electric energy oozing from every inch of him. He seemed so much larger than Mama all of a sudden.

In that instant, time changed, slowed down, became a thing she could pick apart frame by frame. She was, at once, aware of every movement in the room: the light through the window, the swirling dots in the air moving faster; her father's hands, powerful, large and pale as they squeezed Mama's throat. Mama hanging limply, her face turning red, then bluish crimson. John's hands produced a slight shaking motion that rippled Mama down to the hem of her dress. Mama's back was bowed; just the tips of her black shoes scraped the floor. John kept shaking her and one of the high heels kicked off with a clatter.

John was hurting Mama. She understood that, knew it without having the words to know it. Mama's tongue extended from her mouth, purple and thick. John had not so much as changed his stance, his face rigid, feet planted slightly apart, his hands set like stone around Mama's soft neck.

"JOHN!" She heard a voice say. Her breath came back to her, entered into her as the sudden understanding of time and its physical limitations. As if from a distance, she watched her mouth open again, form the one word, over and over.

"JOHN! JOHN! JOHN! JOHN!" The room filled with its tremor. She could see the walls bouncing it back, could taste the whirlwinds of air, first expelled, then returning to her lips. The waves of sound rolled toward her father, toward the white, fixed hands. It did not occur to her that she could affect anything; she did not know that was her intent. She continued to hear the word push itself out of her mouth, surprised at the autonomy of her own voice, surprised at the repeating sounds that echoed in the room.

Time slowed to a drip; one second only slightly connected to the next. The jerky motions of John's hands, the fluttering of Mama's body, moved from one second to the next in stop motion, one complete motion, disconnected from any other, then another motion, another stop . . .

"JOHN! JOHN! JOHN!" The voice kept screaming. Wave upon wave of sound finally reached the shores of his consciousness. He turned his strange bone-colored face to her in the crib. She wondered where he had gotten that face; it was so different from the one she knew. His eyes swung around quickly, enraged at being interrupted. A shock pounded into her, a body blow that shook her to utter weakness. She had never seen eyes like that; she could not hide from them. She could only let them scorch through her. They were not his. They were of a different animal altogether, staring relentlessly at her, unaware of who she was, unresponsive to the repeated sound of his name.

She stared back at John, struck motionless by the maniacal eyes. Then the moment began to turn, began to drip into the next eternity, as she stood, hypnotized, at the side of her crib, blending with the molding and the thin white bars. Something was happening to John's face. It shifted. The eyes, the glaring hatred and animal fire, changed, melted, transformed, became human again as she watched. She saw the shade pass over them, a waterfall cascading across his brow. Swift and painful came the eyes, the change. Swift and excruciating came the understanding into her tiny body. This, too, then, was a part of who she was, was a part of the species she sprang from. She did not know the word insanity, but she understood implicitly the frightful reality of it.

John's face softened, color returned. He recognized her, heard his name being called. He looked at her curiously at first. When his humanity returned, he glanced down at his hands, at Mama dangling limply from them. A gasp came from his throat; his hands dropped to his sides. Mama grabbed a chair arm and slid down to the floor. She crawled away from John, toward the light of the window. Mama sat crumpled there, one hand holding the weight of her body, the other touching the reddened skin of her neck.

The room had stopped shouting. She still clung to the sides of her crib, waiting. Mama coughed and sputtered a little, a few drops of blood spilled out of her nose and fell in the path of the advancing light. John stood staring, his eyes dull.

Very slowly, he moved. He stepped carefully, as if over the bones of her innocence, over the stripped skin of time that had been her short childhood. He eased himself into the black wooden chair Mama had used a moment before. He did not look at her; he looked at Mama. She was covered in dust. It lay on her dark dress in uneven stripes. Mama looked at the floor, patting at her throat.

She relaxed as the charged air began to drain out of the room, replaced by a long slow breath, syrup heavy, that settled against her skin.

Her arms and legs ached; a sharp pain suffused her lungs. She watched Mama; Mama was okay. She turned to look at John.

He was staring at his hands, as if asking them an important but unanswerable question. They posed mute before his face, fingers open and extended. Slowly they came up to his face, took the burden of it off his shoulders. He fell forward into his hands; the sound of sobs began to permeate the dark air. His shoulders quivered.

She surveyed the room once more: Mama on the floor, now a normal color, breathing and looking about, cast a sad look at John in the chair. John, cried loudly, human again, the animal gone . . . at least for now. She leaned back; her own breathing slowed to a normal pace.

She was aware of herself for the first time, conscious of being a mixed species, part human, part her father, part whatever beast it was she saw in his eyes . . . *the power of that beast to transform, the rage of it to decimate.* The realization ingrained itself on her soul, a great power and a greater fear. The burden was much too heavy for her childish body and she sank down on the mattress of the crib, her hands slowly releasing the bars.

Her diaper was wet; she knew it would be a while before anyone changed it. ■

## Gifts

Patti Tana

The first Hanukkah after the divorce, Jack sent us gifts. It was strange and scary because he had never given anything when he lived with us as our father. Never took us on a picnic or to a drive-in movie, never played games or made things with us, or sang us a song. We weren't sure whether to accept the gifts, but we didn't know how to send them back.

I grew up with a brother three years older, Fred, and one four years younger, David. My oldest brother, Herbert, was the child of my mother's first marriage to a man named Sam, who had abandoned her. Herb went away to college when I was three so he was home only for school holidays or when he was on leave from the Navy.

Once when I went with Mom to visit Herb in college, I thought the streets in Albany looked like him—long and skinny. Later, while in the Navy, he wrote a book on weather that had pictures of clouds. Mother kept it on her bedstand and I'd often look at the pictures, feeling proud of him. Then he married a hometown girl, and they moved far away. After that he seldom kept contact with us. I had looked forward to his visits home from college or the Navy when he would dance with me, teasing me good-humoredly that I was his "Royal Highness," and I was disappointed when he distanced himself from the family. But I understood. Jack had become his stepfather when Herbie was ten and I can imagine what his teen years must have been like.

From my own experience living with Jack, I can remember only rare times when he came home in a good mood. Returning from his work painting houses, he would try to wash off the paint stains, but the smell of turpentine and dots of color remained on his skin. He'd sit on the cushioned armchair in the living room and I'd sit on his lap, my body turned sideways so I could scratch off the flecks from his face and hair with my fingernails. I loved leaning on his big belly, loved the roughness of his cheeks and the smoothness of the bald spot on top of his head.

But what I remember most about Jack is his anger—cursing, screaming, hands lashing out. We lived in a minefield. No matter how careful I was, he might explode. We all got smacked, but when he unstrapped his leather belt Freddie got most of the beatings. He stuttered, perhaps because of being hit on the head, we thought, and he had a perceptual difficulty that was finally diagnosed and corrected with glasses when he was an adult.

We'd make bets on whose turn it would be to cry at the dinner table. I can still picture Jack at the head of the table and Mother down at the other end banging her fist on her chest: "The food lays right here. The food turns to poison."

> David and I are laughing as we eat dinner. I start to choke and spit my soup in Jack's direction. He turns red, stands up—noodles and pieces of carrot clinging to his skin—and starts slapping me. David dives under the table shouting, "MAD DOG! MAD DOG ON

> THE LOOSE!" Flailing her arms to ward off the blows, Mom tries to step between Jack and me.

A big lace cloth on the dining room table draped down to the floor. The table legs had claw-shaped feet and above the claw was a fierce lion face with an open mouth and pointed teeth. For years little David would crawl into the lions' den around five o'clock and wait to see what sort of mood Jack was in when he came home from work, wait to see if it was safe to come out.

My most vivid memory of his coming home is the time he walked in the front door and fell flat on his face on the living room floor. Just keeled over. His breathing was hard and loud and I could see his tongue coated a pasty yellow in his open mouth. Mother came running from the kitchen and we dragged him over to the couch. When she went to call the doctor I untied his shoelaces and tried to take off his shoes. I was afraid he was dying. Then Mother came back in the room and told me, with a mixture of resignation and disgust, that he wasn't going to die—he was just dead drunk.

Though I often saw him drinking whiskey and beer, often smelled them on his breath, I didn't connect his drinking with his violence because he was always so volatile. Even in public there was the danger that he might pick a fight with a driver over the right of way or get into a brawl with some guy in a parking lot. If my mother talked to a man, a merchant in town or even the rabbi, Jack would become enraged.

> The congregation is honoring the choir with a dinner. Mom sings in the choir and she is excited about getting dressed up. I go with her to the five and dime to buy sequins for a plain black dress. When we get home I hand her the shiny sequins as she sews them in a pattern that radiates from the neckline. Since the sleeves are short, she also sews sequins up the length of her long black gloves in a pattern that looks like a climbing vine. Then she winds her salt and pepper hair into a French twist and I help her pin in a bright flower.

I wait in the foyer to watch Jack's face as he sees her walking down the stairs. As she begins her descent, I imagine hearing the music that plays for Loretta Young's grand entrance. Perhaps I am humming the tune.

Jack's lips start a smile, but freeze as Mom comes closer. "You look too beautiful," he snarls. "I don't want anyone seeing you look like that! Take it off—" As he grabs her dress and rips it, sequins fall to the floor.

I never understood why he was so possessive of her; I never saw her give him cause for jealousy. I do know that I was their "new start" instead of a divorce after my mother read a misdirected letter addressed to Jack from a pregnant woman begging him to marry her. Jack had been stationed at Fort Sheridan, Illinois, for a year during World War II, and when he was released from the service his mail arrived home before he did. She gave him a second chance. They packed up the two boys and moved west to Venice, California, but my mother hated the transitory feeling out there and the sand in the house, in the clothes, in the food. One year later, when I was three months old, the family moved back to New York State.

Mother liked to tell me how she put a wide-brimmed yellow bonnet on my head and carried me in a wicker laundry basket all the way across the country by bus: "I sewed lace around the basket and padded it inside, and everyone would look in and say how beautiful you were!" And then a shake of her head at the turn in the story: "It took three days to cross Texas. At one rest stop Jack re-boarded the bus and it pulled away without us while I was warming your bottle." She had to run after the bus carrying me in the basket. She'd end the story by telling me that even though she had felt her family was "complete" when she had a daughter, she was sad because she knew "how hard life is for women, how we have to pay for everything."

Mother never forgave herself for the passion that produced Fred. "What right did I have going out with anyone when I had a child at home?" Her parents were always feuding and they were divorced when she was a teenager, so she had married her first husband at seventeen, without finishing high school, to have a home. Then he deserted her when she was pregnant with Herbert at the age of twenty. My grandfather, her beloved Papa, took them in after she gave birth.

I think about how lonely she must have been, working to support her baby through the Depression, not having enough money to buy him a pair of shoes, at times not even a quart of milk or a carrot. When Jack's eye caught her on the subway, he followed her home to her father's small Bronx apartment. Fred, their "love child," was born at the beginning of the War. Some things my mother is ashamed of make me proud of her—her struggle and her passion. When I think about it, I'm sorry that the struggles were so long and the passions so brief.

For Jack was a liar. Was he two years older or twenty? Was his name Jack or John or Joseph? Van Glubt or just Glubt? Did he lose his pay or gamble it away? Where did he go for days on end and whose lipstick stains were on the cigarettes in the car ashtray? It wasn't until after she married him that she found out that he'd been married three times before and had served time for bigamy in Sing Sing.

When I was almost old enough to go to school my mother talked to Jack about a divorce, but he raped her and made her pregnant again. Abortion was illegal and she had no money. Though her rabbi and her doctor, a Catholic, agreed that Jack was pathological; they told her abortion was immoral when she sought their help. And so she had David. By such conspiracies are lives determined.

Even though Jack had a prison record, the State of New York issued him a gun for his weekend job as security officer at Bear Mountain State Park during the summer. So I grew up with a gun in my father's dresser when it wasn't strapped to his hip. Sometimes the whole family would go with him to the Park, which meant crossing over the Jan Peek Creek from our home in Peekskill, passing Camp Smith, then driving a winding mountain road to the Bear Mountain Bridge that spanned the Hudson River—at least a twenty-minute ride. Jack would race against his own time until he made it over in twelve minutes, a harrowing journey. As we careened around those cliffs, Mother begged in the front seat, "Slow down,

Jack! Please slow down!" while I huddled in the back seat with my brothers.

Living with Jack meant living with the threat of death not only on the highway.

Night. Voices from behind the closed door of the master bedroom at the end of the long hallway. When I sleep in the middle bedroom at the top of the stairs I sometimes hear the squeak of their bedsprings, then my mother crying. This night David and I are in the bedroom at the other end of the hallway, the one with walls of tin, and Fred is in the middle room. Herb is visiting home from college, sleeping on the sofa downstairs.

The voices get louder — his cursing, hers pleading.

Now Herb's footsteps climb the stairs. My brothers and I meet at the landing. The nightlight throws our dim shadows against the hallway walls. Herb is wearing dark pants and a white t-shirt. The rest of us are in pajamas. I hold on to my little brother and look up at the faces of my big brothers.

The shouting continues — what should we do?

Herb tells me to take David back into our room and close the door. David hides under the covers, but I watch from our doorway and Fred watches from his.

As Herb reaches to pull the chain for the hall light, something falls in their room and he calls out, "Stop! Stop that now or I'll call the police!"

Silence.

Suddenly their door bangs open and Jack bursts through the doorway

—a bull loosed from its pen—"You call the police and I'll kill you! You hear? You goddamned son-of-a-bitch—I'll kill you!"

Mother is behind him trying to hold him back as he bears down on Herbert. "Jack—no—please no!"

Everything is arms and shouting: my mother—unable to get beyond Jack in the narrow hallway, Jack trying to shake loose of her—I'll kill you too!"—pushing her back toward their bedroom with one arm and grabbing Herb with the other.

They wrestle together, elbows and shoulders knocking against the walls, until Herb stumbles down the first few steps and catches himself on the banister. "That's it," he says firmly, "I'm calling the police."

"You call the police and I'll kill you all—I swear I'll kill all of you!" Jack calls after him from the top of the stairs, shaking his fist, then turns to the rest of us and sweeps us into his threat. As he turns, Mother manages to slip past him and follow Herb down the stairs.

For many years I couldn't remember what happened next. In my desperation, had I imagined that the police came to our house that night? If they didn't, why didn't they? Had Herb called them?

In a recent quiet moment I asked Mother about that night, that darkest night. "I ran down after him and pleaded with him not to call the police," she responded.

"Why," I asked, knowing the answer.

"Because it would have made it worse. It would have made Jack more violent. "

Back then we used to say to her, "Answer him, Mommy! Why don't you answer him?" And she would tell us, "Because it will only make it worse."

"Try. Won't you *try*?"

"All right. I'll answer him back for one week and you'll see."

For a few days she did stand up to him and answer him back. And it was worse. The level of violence did increase. So she went back to swallowing his abuse and nursing an ulcer.

Around this time I began to feel sometimes that I was going to faint, that "the whole world was blacking out." The doctor put me in the hospital for four days and tested me, but he couldn't find a physical cause. I overheard him asking Mother if I was under any stress and advising her to get me counseling.

"My daughter's not crazy!"

Though she did not get me the help I needed then, it was not long afterward that she decided to file for divorce. Finally her youngest child would be in school all day. I was ten, Fred thirteen.

Jack laughed, predicting that she'd never last. "I give you three months and you'll come crawling back to me on your knees." He bragged that he'd never give her "one red cent" and warned the merchants in town not to help her by giving her credit.

And then while Mom was in Alabama overnight finalizing a quick divorce, Jack pointed his finger at me and said, "I'm going to work through you to get back to your mother." I was in their bedroom watching him pack his things, black and brown and blue socks in separate piles on the dresser near his gun, his shirts laid out on the bed. "You're my only daughter and I'm going to work through you."

I didn't know what that meant, but I was scared. I had seen his temper and it scared me. When she came home, Mother tried to assure me that I needn't fear Jack any more. She even laughed when she discovered that he had taken her diaphragm from the drawer of the nightstand.

But when I looked from my schoolroom window, he would be there in his car waiting for me. I couldn't tell the teacher why I was staying so late after school. Divorce was considered shameful. Being a child from a broken home, shameful. Mother had told us to say our father was "transferred." I would stay as late as I could, then sneak out a side door and race home.

Once Jack was sitting in the living room when I arrived. Trying not to show fear, I went directly upstairs, pretending to need the bathroom. Instead I tiptoed into my mother's room and dialed her number at work.

"He's here," I whispered. "What should I do? Hurry—please hurry home!" I was able to intercept David at the back door and send him across the street to Judge Peccarora's house for safety, yet somehow I felt I had to stay in my house and pretend not to be afraid while my mother sped home in a taxi.

In some ways, I was most afraid of Jack during the year after the divorce. We used to lock the front door, but like most of our neighbors we'd never felt the need for a back door lock. Now it was clear we needed one. I developed the habit of looking over my shoulder as I walked. He would drive along behind me and ask if I wanted to go for a ride with him. "No," I'd say, and keep walking, my heart thumping in my chest.

And then at night I'd have to be the brave one, watching over my younger brother. Since Jack never sent money for our support, Mother worked by day as a salesclerk and at night as a waitress. When she became a corrections officer, she had to take her turn working the night shift. Fred would be out on a date or working as a busboy on weekends. Mom would call to bless us at bedtime, but her blessing could not quiet my fears.

Looking back I see that one of the most hurtful aspects of my experience was that I learned not to talk about or show my fear to other people—not to the doctor, certainly not to Jack, not to my teachers or neighbors, not even to my brothers or friends. The one friend I did confide in, the son of my mother's best friend, abused my trust in him by taking advantage of me sexually when we became teenagers.

I felt some pride when recently I realized how brave I must have been at eleven to go with my mother to the lawyer and swear out a complaint against Jack. I told about how often Jack followed me and about his being in the house when I came home. I told that I was afraid he would hurt me. The lawyer typed what I said on a long sheet of paper and asked if I was willing to say what I'd told him in a courtroom so we could get an order of protection. I said yes and signed my name.

■■■

So it was with great apprehension that we opened the gifts Jack sent that first holiday: a toy drum set for David, an English racing bike for Freddie.

Mom said Jack sent the drums to taunt her because Herb's father had been a drummer. Maybe that was his reason, but for David it was the first of many drum sets and the start of his fondness for jazz. He spent hours tapping rhythms along with his records, sometimes with a savage insistence and sometimes keeping an even pulse. I grew up with his drumbeat as background music. Though there have been long silences and deep philosophical differences between us as adults, our friendship lasted through his Air Force time in Vietnam and beyond. Handling bombs in Da Nang understandably increased his sense of vulnerability and tension. After an early discharge from the service—he refused an appointment as an M. P.—he lived with me and my husband for six months. He met his wife in our home and we remained friends through his college years too, laughing together and having good times. We parted following a heated argument about his feeling toward our mother and his response to my bearing a child: "How can you bring a child into this world?" he demanded angrily. Since then he's become a successful chiropractor in a nearby city. After ten years of silence, we renewed our contact. David is the brother I was closest to, close enough to be playmates and a comfort to each other. He is part of the music of my childhood.

The English racer Jack sent Freddie didn't last long. He didn't know how to work the hand brakes so he crashed into a parked car on his first ride. The doctor had to wrap his rib cage with wide strips of tape. Growing up I had trouble with Fred's militaristic disposition and his bullying, though I realized even then that he was compensating for his own awkwardness. He'd tease me about how I looked, about getting my period, about learning to dance. He'd rub against me as we passed in the hallway or barge into the bathroom when I was taking a bath. As I was collecting his arrows at the target in the backyard, he impulsively shot me in the left knee. I still have the scar.

David and I used to say, "Fred's god is Money," because he wouldn't give a nickel to us little kids for ice cream or a quarter for the family's breakfast milk. Fred blew a harsh trumpet and listened at night to distant voices on his ham radio. Instead of public high school he attended the local military academy. When he was discharged from the army he said, with mixed implications, that they had trained him to be an assassin. After college he married his high school sweetheart, became a teacher, moved to the West Coast, and later became a chiropractor. He lived near Herb, who had become an optometrist, but they never got along. I visited Fred only three times, and each time he told me that he felt cursed, acting like his father in relation to his own daughters. At the same time, he needed to reinterpret the family history to find something good about Jack in an effort to respect himself. He even wanted me to chip in for a detective to locate Jack, but I refused. In order to identify with good qualities in Jack, Fred heaped blame on Mother. Nothing I said could free him from the need to be like the father and to denigrate the mother.

A few days before his forty-second birthday, Fred died of a heart attack; Herb died two years later at fifty-four. Fred drank to excess; Herb smoked three packs a day. Both died in their sleep without having made peace with some of the people they had lived with. Though my contact with Herb when we were adults was infrequent, he was a decent, intelligent man who used optometry to help people. He was the one who detected Fred's perceptual problem. I visited him the three times I was on the West Coast and he stopped by to see me during the two times he attended a conference in New York. His first marriage and his relationship with his children was stressful; however, before he died he found a few years of happiness with a woman who had been his dance partner. Perhaps we could have been friends if we lived closer, but perhaps not. He used a stinging wit to shield himself from genuine contact, and he could not open his arms to close embrace. Neither Fred nor Herb seemed to find much satisfaction in the money they made. Haunted, driven men, they resented their mother for the strength she exerted to raise all of us and support the family. They had a mocking attitude, making fun at other people's expense. And neither had the slightest idea who I was.

The gift Jack sent me that holiday is not only lost but forgotten.

About six months later, though, I did have a dream about a crate of oranges from Florida. Fat bright fruit that smelled like blossoms. Attached with a wire to the wood slats of the crate, a tag addressed to me from him. While getting ready for school the next morning, I told Mother about the dream. She said not to worry about it. The lawyer had told her Jack left town to avoid facing the courts. But when I returned from school that afternoon, Mom called me into the kitchen and asked Fred to repeat what he'd just told her. A man had stopped him on the street as he was leaving school and said that Jack was living in Florida and was sending us a crate of oranges. Then I told him my dream. Mom's eyes moved back and forth from Fred's to mine: "Are you making this up? Are you playing a trick on me?" We said we couldn't have because Fred left for school before I woke up that morning. None of us had any way of knowing Jack moved to Florida.

We never did receive oranges or anything else from him. Never saw or heard from him again—but I still have dreams.

Some dreams are the long shadow Jack casts down that narrow hallway and the car that follows me down an endless street. As a teenager I was afraid to be alone in a room with a boy. Sounds at night still set off alarms in my head and I reach for the phone to call the police quicker than would most people. I can see that my attempt to push back against my fear has sometimes caused me to take imprudent risks. I still have a hard time expressing anger and responding to other people when they express theirs. At times I placate rather than risk incurring their anger and then I rebuke myself for such compliance. Sometimes I distrust my judgment and this vulnerability has made it difficult for me to trust men.

At the same time, I can see that the need for a father to be proud of me has made me seek approval from men. Growing up, I would fantasize that other men were my father: teachers, fathers of friends, even the school janitor. I came to think my measure of a man was how good a father he would be. Not a bad measure, surely. But for a long time I was blinded by my own desperate longing. I had to learn there was little chance of my judging clearly. The reality was that all I saw was Man equals Father. Discrimination was often doomed by wishes.

I used to have dreams born of the terrible longing for a father's love. The night before I delivered the commencement speech at my high school graduation, I dreamed that Jack was standing in the back of the auditorium, radiant with pride. I awoke covered with hives and delivered my speech to a full auditorium, but he was not there. It was a long time before I found a mature friend who understood this need and made it a comfortable part of our friendship, thereby setting me free from the futile search for a father, or at least reducing some of the distraction in my contact with men. Even longer until I found pride in myself.

Now I am living with a man who is an excellent father for our child. Despite his example, I see that our good-natured teenage son is infected with the cultural message that he is privileged because he was born male. That he is entitled to opportunities and pleasures females cannot assume. That if women do share in the richness of life's offerings, it is at the expense of men. That brutality and crimes against women need not be taken seriously. Because I am a survivor of domestic terrorism, I am conscious of how the assumption of privilege can lead to tyranny and violence. I do not want to raise an enemy—I hate the thought of it. Against the unhealthy image of woman as slave, toy or bitch, I try to set the image of woman as friend, partner and companion. It's a hard job, and it goes on.

The night before my wedding I dream that Jack comes to see me alone in the temple. I stand at the altar and he stands at the doorway. He holds no gifts. We look at each other and say nothing. He does not ask forgiveness nor do I offer it. ■

# Section Four
## *On the Grinding of Axes*

Now this is the grinding
of teeth into pale dust
for bearing this man's
insult, his macho hubris,
white salt rubbed in the wound
and how rage can turn
into claws of retaliation
or wrap itself in
a winding sheet of grief.

Manya Bean
from "On the Grinding of Axes"

We women! We have axes to grind: with our husbands and lovers. With our fathers and brothers. With our mothers who betray us through complicity or through active abuse or by enduring abuse at the hands of the men in their lives. With teachers, clergy, lawyers, doctors—with a society that teaches us to accept images of ourselves without question.

Manya Bean's poem invites us to re-envision traditionally accepted images of women, especially the common literary and cultural metaphor of the Madonna/whore. The Madonna (or virgin) and the whore are traditionally the "pornographer's obsession" (Griffin 1988, 21, 43). Juxtaposing stories of the typical housewife/Madonna experience with stories depicting pornographic images demonstrates the ways our self-images imitate cultural values that divide soul from flesh. Since this dichotomy plagues women and not men, we see it as a value that gives men more privilege than women, thus promoting a double standard that requires women to be more virtuous than men.

To grind axes, we begin with our mothers, "For we think back through our mothers if we are women"(Woolf 1929, 79). Lynne Conroy's "Slings" and Jill Wasden's "Star Sapphire," like Patti Tana's "Gifts" in the previous section, present daughters who grind their mother's axes and, in so doing, call attention to the hypocrisy underlying traditional marriage and the "happy housewife" myth. The daughters characterize their respective mothers as "typical" housewives/Madonnas who pay an enormous price for the accoutrements of middle-class respectability.

In "The Dark Side of the Moon," Jan Barstow grinds her own ax with society. As a young housewife, she trades one pedestal for another, transforming herself from "Madonna" to "whore" by stepping off the housewife pedestal and onto the stage as a topless dancer. Bristol's story reverses social clichés and sets the abused woman free through what she defines as her control of male eroticism.[1]

Susan Radtke Tong's "Sisters" demonstrates that the key to our escape from oppression lies in our freedom to articulate positive metaphors of feminine strength. For Tong physical and emotional strength is a weapon of self-defense and a measure of self-esteem.

"Zone Documents," Lynne Conroy's collage, explores pornography as a medium that transforms women into lustful temptresses, desiring—and therefore deserving—violation, rape, and oppression. Again we discover the Madonna/whore split in Conroy's unfortunate circumstances: a single mother and sole support of her infant daughter, Conroy must earn her living as a projectionist at a pornographic movie house. Irony builds through the juxtaposition of images that connect rape, pornography, and "snuff."[2]

The diary entry, "Gun Control," is evidence of the games people play that normalize violence and make it seem commonplace to hurt women. Conroy's portrait in words of the violence of pornography is here transformed into the pornography of violence. These two unrelated pieces, written close to twenty years apart by two women who had never met or spoken, demonstrate the connection between degrading images of women and hostile action against them.

"A Drop of Scarlet" draws on Cynthia E. Matthews' experiences both as a battered woman and as a counselor and expert witness.

Announcing the themes that will be addressed in the next section, this short story grinds another ax, that of one woman for another in a movement where the plight of all women breaks down the walls that hold us imprisoned. Matthews transforms the image of "scarlet" from a symbol of shame to a badge of honor that celebrates self-defense. ■

**Slings**

Lynne Conroy

Mother had a cast again and I was betting I knew why.

We sat in a restaurant that had blue Margaritas and "Catch of the Day—Cajun Pompano—" written on a blackboard. It was the kind of yuppie cafe that she acted as if she liked. Mother waited for the Absolut martini she'd sent the waiter running for. The white plaster envelope on the lower part of her left arm was probably cutting into her skin because she rubbed it all the time she talked. Her friends would hear about this new restaurant. She was telling me what she said when this one said that and so on. "Could you believe . . . ? Have your heard . . . ? I don't want to seem . . ."

She thought I might be losing weight but that it was probably my new haircut with the height on top. It made me look younger. Were Indian print skirts like the one I wore coming back in style?

She mentioned nothing about the cast or how she got it.

"Your father was going to come with me today," she said.

"He's not my father. My father's dead," I told her, but she knew this. She also knew how I felt. I was glad that her husband didn't come. I've told her before that I don't understand how one woman can marry two such different men. When I was ten, a drunk driver killed my father during a sun shower on a slick interstate. Too soon Mother remarried—a man who manufactured leatherette billfolds, passport cases, and luggage that I wished he'd use to pack up and get out. A month after their wedding, he smashed her aquarium with his fist, spilling guppies and glass all over her Oriental rug. He didn't like the way she put the wastebasket outside the cabinet under the kitchen sink. He thought trash should stay hidden.

I had helped her put the wriggling guppies into a teacup. She cried.

I said, "It's never too late, Ma."

She answered, "I made my bed. I'll lie in it."

■■■

Fifteen years later, she was still with him. I think of myself as a patient woman. And forgiving. But I don't want to be as patient or forgiving as Mother.

She was saying, "Honey, don't be like that. He tries hard."

"Tries hard to do what? Throw you down the stairs?" I asked. I was at their cocktail party last year when he got drunk, threw all the guests' coats out, and Ma down the stairs after the coats.

She winced and said, "He hasn't done that sort of thing lately. He was just upset because his mother had to go into a nursing home the week before, and all I could think of to say was that everything works out for the best."

"I hate it when you make excuses for him. Did he hurt your arm?" I asked.

"No, I was walking Perky, and he yanked on the leash, and I fell on the ice." Perky was her twelve-pound beagle. He was fourteen years old.

We were quiet. The waiter brought the Absolut martini and picked up her empty glass. Mother told him that he might as well bring another.

"Are you sure you don't want something," he said to me.

"How about lunch?" I suggested, but Mother frowned.

"Don't be a party pooper. Have something," she said.

"Shirley Temple with a bonnet." I conceded.

The waiter put his pad away. "I'll remember that order," he said and left.

She finished her drink and looked out the window. Rain was beating down, overflowing the downspouts on the restaurant. "I hate it when they put onions in these, don't you? I didn't ask for onions." She placed the onion and its toothpick neatly into the empty glass.

"Have you gotten that arm x-rayed?" I asked.

"I had everything done when it was set," Mother stated, as if she were talking about a new hairdo. A blond woman with wrists as thin as saplings, Mother has had a grapefruit for breakfast for as long as I've known her. She's expert at counting calories in everything from Sara Lee cheesecake to tunafish sandwiches. I'm not sure when she started downing martinis, but I know she's never worried aloud about the number of calories in one.

"Did the doctor say your arm was broken?" I asked.

The waiter put down another martini and my Shirley Temple. Half the glass had whipped cream in it. I tasted it, then licked the smudge of froth that the spoon left on my lip. I ate the half-moon of orange and chewed the rind.

"Hairline fracture of the upper or lower 'tibet' or something. That looks like about four ounces of cream. Let's see. Half a cup. They wanted to know how I did it. It's none of their business," Mother said, flipping through her *Paige Craylock Calorie Guide* that she carried around in her Fendi bag. "That must be about 491 calories. Approximately. We don't know how much sugar they put in there. I told them I fell on those concrete stairs going down the back. You know the ones."

"They probably meant your tibia." I spooned more cream into my mouth. "Can you tell me about the x-rays, Ma?"

"There's really nothing else to tell," she said.

I got to the bottom of my drink and started to make slurping noises with the straw. I looked at Mother. When I was little she'd say those noises made her crazy.

She looked at me, one of her old looks. "Do you have to do that? Listen, let's go to the Jewelry Building on Roosevelt Avenue. I know what I want for my anniversary. Pear-shaped diamond earrings. I want stones at least a carat and a half each. I saw them on a countess in Europe. When I die, you'll have them."

"Ma, do you have to buy your own anniversary gifts, too?" I asked, licking the straw. I couldn't stop it; I went "m-m-m." I smacked too. She started to laugh. I made her start to laugh.

"You're awful. No! Your father has me on his payroll as a consultant. This year I decided to use the fee for earrings. Normally I spend it for help to run the house. You pick out some gold hoops or something, too. It will be our secret. Now, can you let sleeping dogs lie?"

Mother picked up the check and pulled out a MasterCard with her husband's name on it. She put the bill and the MasterCard on the edge of the table. A busboy came by and said that he'd take it to the register.

I decided that I wasn't hungry anyway. I put on my pea coat. I was cold. We watched the waiter erase the daily specials and wash the blackboard with a sponge.

A button hung from my coat by a few threads. I pulled it off and held it in my hand while I picked at the threads. My fingers felt numb. If my father were here, if my real father were here, I'd say to him, "Help her get through this. Help me get through to her." I'd say, "Help her." I'd say, "Help me."

I put the button in my pocket.

She signed the charge slip and put the MasterCard away. I thought of her two safe deposit boxes filled with jewelry. When Mother turned around to pick up her Harris tweed jacket, I touched her hand that was poking out of the cast. She looked up at me and held my hand with the tips of her fingers.

She said, "Cold hands; warm heart." ■

### Star Sapphire

Jill Wasden

Everybody else in the family had blue eyes so I faced the fact early that I was an outsider. Being a stepdaughter with green eyes, I learned to watch out for things.

I was looking under their bed when I saw the dishes—blue and white china—a whole box of it, new. I got a tingly fear that this might turn out to be another of Mom's secrets from my stepfather, the man I called Dad. Their own kids, Karen and Donny, were too young—six and three—so it was up to me to keep the family's secrets secret. 767 Elaine Street with its nice lawn in L.A. County was a hidden war zone, and we could get caught in the crossfire if my attention strayed.

In sixth grade science class I read about barometric pressure and recognized right away that we had it at our house. You could watch a storm coming in for a long time. The air moved in thicker and thicker until it bogged down in a deadly stillness, and then exploded.

Sundays were the worst. Mom taught Sunday school and Dad was a church deacon. All five of us went to church together every Sunday, though my little brother who was only three just sat on a chair in the nursery. The nursery teacher took a picture of him like that, with his white hair and sad blue eyes, waiting for us. As soon as we were in the car going home, Mom and Dad would start in arguing about the Reverend Fix's message.

Saturdays were okay. Mom was always good about taking me to the library. Every Saturday morning she drove me downtown for another six books. The huge rooms were cool and quiet, always the same, no barometric pressure there.

After the library, I helped her with the grocery shopping while Donny and Karen scattered all over the store. They whined and begged for candy until she'd yell, "You kids!" and, "Jan, take them out to the car." She was edgy anyway, thinking of Dad back home, chugging Jim Beam.

I knew how much she depended on me to help her with it all, even though she acted mean. But she wasn't mean. Her main problem was she couldn't shut up during the times she most needed to. There was nothing she could do to stop Dad's secret drinking, but she couldn't stop from trying. She stayed busy trying to work, cook, clean it away. I tried too, but nothing I did could fix it for her, not vacuuming or ironing, or even talking to her about it.

"It's not your fault, Mom," I told her, but she just looked at me as if she'd already lost.

Dad focused on keeping Mom's attention off his drinking. He had hundreds of empty pint bottles stashed in the garage in different cubbyholes and one thirty-gallon garbage can almost full. We kids were used to it. Karen brought home an empty whiskey bottle once in her doll carriage. "Here, Dad, for your collection," she said, proudly offering it up so it wouldn't be a secret from us. I don't know why he thought Mom didn't know what was under the lid of that garbage can.

One Saturday in June Mom and I went downtown alone and after the library instead of going to the Safeway we drove farther. Mom parked in front of a big store that had tall windows and jewelry on velvet display trays. Inside, the carpet was pale gray and thick. Everyone spoke in whispers, quiet as the library. We sat in straight-backed velvet chairs like queens. It was wonderful.

"Jan, I want your opinion," she said. I helped her choose a necklace with a blue star sapphire in the center. The salesman wore a gray suit and clear fingernail polish and smelled of English Leather cologne. Driving home Mom told me Dad didn't need to know about the necklace—it was just between us.

But I don't think she wore it even once. When I asked her about it she looked at me funny. I wasn't supposed to ask questions, especially about secrets. She said she still liked having it, just knowing it was hers, whether she ever wore it or not. I worried it was the same with the dishes—only they were going to be a lot easier to find.

Mom's secrets played a big part in my life, and I had my own secrets from Mom. She took long showers with Dove soap every day before starting dinner. She filled the bathroom with steam and delicious grown-up woman smells. Sometimes I just sat breathing in the thick mist of her shower and sometimes I prowled around her bedroom.

Most of the stuff I found in her drawers and closet was normal woman stuff I was curious about. It took more than feminine hygiene equipment to surprise me. But that box under the bed worried me. She was getting ready for her shower when I asked her about it.

"Dishes?" she asked looking in the mirror as she gathered her thick dark hair into a barrette without looking at me. "What dishes do you mean?" Her face was like the silhouette of the cameo women you see on pins.

"In the big box under your bed, Mom."

"I don't know what you mean, Janine."

"Those blue porcelain dishes, Mom. In a box like they just came from the store."

"Jan, I've asked you kids not to nose around in my things. Why don't you let me have my privacy?" she asked, still not looking at me. Her bare breasts swayed when she reached to slide open the mirrored medicine cabinet. The erect brown points of her nipples repelled and fascinated me. My chest was still flat, though I expected it to bloom any day.

I drifted to the doorway and leaned against the shiny gray tile counter Dad had built. I slouched on the counter with my chin on my knees and listened to her hum "Rock of Ages" in the shower while I tried to rub the dry bumps off my elbows. Sometimes it was hard to believe I was really her daughter.

The new shower got built because Mom's doctor said it was tub baths that were causing their marital problems, giving her infections. Dad was a building contractor so he started right away on the blueprints to add a new bedroom with its own bathroom, one with a shower.

Mom yelled above the spray while I sat there on the counter in the thick perfumed mist.

"Jan, bring me a new rayza, hon. This one's all dull!"

I crept off the counter and tiptoed into the bedroom. "Okay, Mom," I yelled, and walked back into the bathroom so she wouldn't know I'd been there all along. At least I could pretend to respect her privacy.

When she wasn't around, I loved to look through her drawers at her bras, which she called "bru-zeers." The points stuck up like twin tent sets in neat rows. Once I tried on the black strapless one using safety pins but it wasn't any good, an eleven-year-old draped in an empty holster. I scouted tampons and black silk stockings like an addict for forbidden adult stuff. I was driven to know her private business, dangerous as it was.

I also loved to look at her jewelry. Dad took eight liberty head dimes and made them into silver earrings and a bracelet for Mom. It amazed me that his huge hands could cut around a woman's face on a dime. He said it was easy, he just concentrated.

In his private time Dad invented things. He was always tinkering with stuff, mostly coins and electrical gadgets, turning them into something else. One of his masterpieces was a silver dollar wall clock, a circle of twelve silver dollars with delicate aluminum hands I watched him cut from the bottom of a pie tin. He mounted it on the master bedroom wall above their bed.

The only excuse I had to touch him was when I talked him into letting me put curlers in his hair while he read. The pink rubber cylinders dangling against the shadow of his beard made me want to laugh, but I acted professional until he closed the book and shook his head. He dabbed at the gadgets bobbling off his scalp with the hard palms of his hands and laughed as if he'd just noticed them.

"That's very nice, Miss Hairdresser. If you're about through with me, I think I'll go off to bed now until my next appointment," he said.

I pulled the rollers out. Our time was over.

They seemed happy. I thought of all those glass booze bottles building up a volcanic power out there in the garage hiding in the garbage can. Look out when Dad dropped that last Jim Beam bottle on the heap that set Mom off. It wouldn't matter then that Mom was five foot two and Dad was six foot three.

She told me how glad I should be that Dad was so good to me. "After all, you're not even his and that would make a difference to a lot of men." I knew it made some difference to him. When he looked at my little sister, his blue eyes lit up. Not when he looked at me. But still, the only person he ever yelled at was Mom. And Mom yelled at all of us.

She was always running around doing something, anything, distracted. You never knew when you'd find the mayonnaise jar down with the cleaning stuff and the Ajax in the refrigerator. But it was better not to mention it. Most of the time Mom was fun. I could tell she thought kids were funny. Like my lists. I liked order in my life so at night I wrote down all the things I needed to do the next day, what I would wear, things like that. When she saw "Get Up" at the top of one of my lists, she laughed and grabbed me up in a dazzle of her Shalimar perfume.

Mom, who was from Georgia, was always making jokes on herself about not getting onto California ways. Her saying "dollas" instead of dollars was a standard joke if I got into teasing her. She'd say, "One dolla, two dollas or how many dollas did you have in mind for me to mispronounce, little miss?"

One time I came home from school and she was out front pushing the lawnmower in white shorts and a black bra. I couldn't believe it. Thank God I'd come home just then.

"Mom, what are you doing?" I shouted above the noise of the motor.

"Mowin' of course, silly sally."

The Jewel Tea truck rumbled up the street. "But Mom, you're not dressed!" She stopped and looked up and took off running for the front door, her laugh flying behind her. But I couldn't laugh about it. What if someone had been with me? But I knew better than that—I never invited anyone home.

Dad was serious except when he was drinking. He read the dictionary and the Bible through as if they were novels. He didn't like to go out much, except for church and the Masonic Lodge. His fun was country/western records, sad songs about foggy rivers and cheating hearts. Mom, who was from Georgia, said her family thought the problem with Dad was that he had too much gray matter. But I liked him being so smart.

Still he wasn't one to show off. Say I'd come to him for help with an algebra problem, the first thing he'd say was, "Now Janine, if you can't figure it out, smart as you are, I don't know why you figure I could." I knew it was his way of building me up. Everybody knew how brilliant Dad was. I'd heard the Reverend Fix tell my mother about it.

"Your husband has a brilliant mind," he said. "Well as I know my Bible scripture, he's a hard person to win an argument with." Mom had to agree with that.

I thought their problem was each other, as if they were allergic to one another's ways. It seemed that Dad was against stuff and Mom was in favor of it. Restaurants, for instance—Dad didn't believe in them.

"What kind of fool would pay that kind of money for food that isn't as good as I get at home?" he liked to say. But Mom didn't take it as a compliment to her cooking. They couldn't go out alone together because another thing he didn't believe in was babysitters. So on weekends we were all stuck at home together, breathing pressurized air.

But that spring while Dad was adding on the master suite I was lulled into thinking that we were a "normal" family. Dad measured and hammered and took long pulls off his pint bottles to "keep his energy up." Mom left him alone. I guess she figured he deserved that much for his efforts. I started skating and taking Karen, who was seven, to matinees, leaving Donny at home with them. I was nervous about it, but when we stumbled out of the theater, dizzy and headachy from so much darkness and candy, there the three of them were to pick us up, just like a regular family. Donny stood in the back seat with his shiny white hair pressed flat against the back window, craning his neck, watching for us with clear blue eyes. He felt safer when I was around, and I shouldn't have left him with no one to watch out for him.

That same spring there was a sixth-grade Daughters and Fathers Dinner, an awards banquet. I was getting an art award. Mom said to ask Dad to take me. "Don't worry, he'll tell you no if he doesn't want to go," she reassured me while she smeared wax on the dresser top and bore down to rub it in with her silken arms.

I worried about it and waited for Mom to fix Swiss steak for dinner, Dad's favorite. When I mentioned the banquet, he looked at me as if he just landed on the planet and needed a minute to place me.

"I'm proud of you," he smiled after what seemed like a long pause. "It's a date." I wanted to jump up and do something I was so glad he said yes, but I knew how shy he was with me in the affection department so I just passed him more potatoes.

The banquet and getting ready for it was the best time. For two weeks Dad and I practiced dancing in the living room, he wearing his size 13 dress shoes with me resting my stocking feet on top. He swirled us around the carpet in huge waltz steps. "Just imagine the Vienna Woods, and it's easy," he said. For the banquet he wore his perfect black jacket and white tuxedo shirt. He was the tallest dad there.

I saw this as my chance to win the summer book reports contest for elementary school kids now that things were peaceful at home. I loved to read anyway, the way you could get into a book and pull a safe world up around you. *The Scarlet Letter* was my favorite. Hester Prynne's red "A" gave her away—for me it was my green eyes, but we were both outsiders. Fourteen book reports had won the year before, so I planned on doing at least fifteen. First Hester Prynne, then my other favorite *Kim*, the story of the scared child in India.

Trouble started again in August as soon as the remodeling was finished. The first weekend the tools and paint were put away we all went on a visit up north to see Dad's parents. Mom and Dad didn't talk. I was in the back seat with Donny's and Karen's sharp elbows and knees all over me while they slept. I couldn't close my eyes anyway with them so quiet up front—I had to stay alert. Then Karen and Donny woke up with pink hot faces, hungry. Restaurant after restaurant went by until Dad found Erma's Eats Diner and we straggled in. I watched our fingerprints form a film on the Formica as we ate friend chicken. Mom drank her coffee and looked away from the rest of us. She twirled a piece of hair around a finger and hummed "Old Rugged Cross" while Dad dropped quarters into the jukebox and ducked in and out of the men's room. Trouble brewed. The barometric pressure rose.

The next Sunday I went skating while Donny took his nap and Karen pushed her doll buggy around the neighborhood. As soon as I pulled open the back door I heard it, a neon silence crackling trouble. Time slowed, my ears developed radar. I heard a crash and their thunderous voices—Mom and Dad swearing at the top of their lungs. The dishes—he must have found the blue-and-white dishes. Or the necklace. The star sapphire. I made for the louvered closet in the living room and hid. I held my breath praying she wouldn't say the three words. Don't say it . . . don't say it . . . don't . . . Mom . . . Please . . . . But she did.

"You're a drunk!" she shouted.

The slow pounding of my heart beat against quick popping sounds, low grunts. They fought crazily for all they were worth, while I watched through the slats like a coward. I crept out when Mom landed on the floor in front of the closet.

"Come on, Mom!" I said, pulling on her arm. Her eyes were wild like a cornered cat. When she flew out the front door I was on her heels. We ran and ran and after a while I felt my book in my hand, *Kim*. I must have grabbed it on the way out. We didn't stop running until we got to Grandma's house, a long way. Mom had so many bruises it hurt to look at her. Her calves had purple spots, and all over her arms. For the first time I didn't want to see her naked.

We stayed eleven days with Grandma. My winning the book report contest was in danger, with me having just the one book, now overdue, and no car to go to the library. I thought about my sister and brother at home with Dad. Karen was probably glad the first morning no one was there to put a comb through her tangled hair before school, but I knew how she'd feel when she came home that first day and we still weren't back. Donny probably wore his red pajamas all day.

Mom told me not to worry, that Dad would have to sober up to take care of his kids. I was glad I was only his stepdaughter or I might have had to stay there too. I could picture him lying on the floor next to his forty-five record player with his eyes red and bleary, wailing drunk, singing along with Hank Williams. With us gone, he wouldn't know any better than to stay drunk, and the kids [would have] no one to take care of them.

But as soon as her bruises turned yellow we went home and school started. I checked to see if the necklace and the dishes were still hidden. They were. I got back into my books.

One Sunday in late September I went out skating after church. I knew it was risky, but I did it anyway. When I came in both kids were screaming and Mom was sprawled on the floor with a broken broom under her. When I saw she had blood coming out of her ear, I ran and called the police. She looked small, like a broken porcelain doll, when the ambulance men carried her out. The bruises were huge and purple on her white arms, her face was red and shiny and growing into a shape I didn't recognize. I thought of the peach I dropped once on the Safeway floor. I wanted to see if her eyes were still blue on the inside but her lids were puffed shut.

I ran behind the cart that they put her on, trying to see something "normal," something uninjured. Then I saw her red toenails, still pretty, still my mother. She said my name and something like "cloth" or "cover." I understood she wanted me to get something to put over her face so I ran back inside past where the police had Dad against the wall and into their bathroom where I grabbed a hand towel with crocheted edges—my grandmother made it. I put cold water on the towel and heard the ambulance screaming again. I ran back down the long hall out to where my mother was, but when I got there they had gone.

I told the police I would call a relative, but I didn't. I didn't feel like explaining things. I made Spaghettios for the kids, and we watched *The Wonderful World of Disney* on television under my Navajo blanket so we could stop shaking. Then Donny was crying and Karen started in with she wanted her mommy and where was her daddy. I said, "It's time to get our jammies on and I'll read you a story," in a strict voice to make them feel like someone was in charge.

I took them to the master bedroom to have the story on the king-size bed. There were blue and white china chips everywhere. I didn't look to see if the star sapphire necklace was still in its velvet box in the back of Mom's underwear drawer. I didn't have to. I could hear it beating like the telltale heart behind the wall in Edgar Allan Poe's story.

I went to get a comforter out of Mom and Dad's closet and saw Dad's black dress shoes, neat, with wooden stretchers on a shelf. It was awful, seeing those dance shoes. They were from a different life, when I was a different girl. Everything had changed. I remembered Dad in the hallway with his arms cuffed behind his back. He looked weak, his head tucked down, not even tall anymore.

I read them a chapter from *Kim*, telling about the boy in India on his own with no parents. After they fell asleep, I lay awake trying not to picture Mom lying in the hospital or Dad in jail. I got up and kneeled by Mom's bottom drawer and opened the star sapphire box. My heart beat loud looking at the stone on its bed of white satin. There it was, gray blue with black points in the center, like my mother's eyes. I knew I wasn't going to win the book report contest. ■

## Sisters: A Re/membering

Susan Radtke Tong

I remember once my cousin asked my uncle if she could learn gymnastics. He said no, because she would develop muscles. I remember this because when I began to study martial arts everyone I knew told me the same thing. Women I worked with, women I hung out with after work, my mother. Why, they would ask me, do you want to get those "muscles" in your legs? Everyone but my sister.

Everyone but my sister told me I'd never get a man if I was too tough. Men don't like tough women. My sister didn't talk about men, she just said, good, you're doing a good thing.

My daughter has my sister's laugh and her voice sometimes. When we're all together I often confuse their names and call my sister by my daughter's name or my daughter by my sister's name, and then they are confused and we all laugh.

My sister's been married a few times, that's a fact. I didn't know for a long time that her first husband beat her. I only knew she grew more silent, and in that silence something went out of her—and she possessed herself a little less. She became mute, but I got stronger, and maybe she made a connection between those things and hoped her lost self was going into me.

The first time I saw a mark on her face, the thought of anyone hitting my sister was so foreign to me that I believed her when she said she slipped on the stairs. But how many times can my sister slip on the stairs? How many times could I let her slip before I stopped believing her words and listened to her voice? When she told me the truth, I said—leave him. What could be more simple, I thought, leave him. He hurts you, so you cannot stay here because he will hurt you again. But she wouldn't go. I made her come away with me, to stay at my house, away from him. And she began to awaken at my house, with the locks on the doors, and she would say—you're strong—with no reproach in her voice.

She began to long for her things, her clothes and pictures and combs and brushes. You're strong, she said, help me. Of course, I thought, they're your things, you should have them. So we waited one night until her husband was away and we went back.

Why should we be afraid? This is my sister's house, we are not thieves. But we were, thieves prowling in the darkness, letting ourselves in the back door so the neighbors wouldn't see. We packed by moonlight, silently, quickly—don't let him find us here. She needed my strength, and I know why now. The air of this house was alien, it reeked of danger and violence. And then we heard his car. Trapped in the bedroom window, he caught us, like deer frozen in his headlights.

Time became our enemy, our limbs were rushing, reaching for the door, but his time had accelerated and ours slowed; we couldn't get away. This is the nightmare: you must run, but your legs won't move and the evil is bearing down. He caught her by the hair, pulling my sister away from me. I screamed, but silently. He was yelling at me, but I heard nothing. I only saw her eyes as he pulled her away, mute, endlessly receding. Then the noise came, the sound abrupt as the motion; he flung her body against the wall, his fist still twined in her hair. My body released, and time was mine again. I took him from behind, I had to leap to reach him, and take him by the throat. I will hold onto you until you never breathe again. Taken by surprise, he reached blindly, and tried to shake me off. And then the deluge came—like rocks the words fell from his mouth—whore, slut, bitch, cunt, dyke. I'll kill you—he said. But still I held on. He spun and tried to throw me off. Then he thought of the wall. Twice he slammed me against it, and the second time I felt the sharp twang of a breaking rib, but I did not let go. At last he fell, crumpling forward so that I did not trust him. He is cunning, he will try to trick me. I still held on. Not until my sister pulled me away, begging me to run with her, did I let go. We didn't look back, we got away.

You're strong, she said, and there was no reproach in her voice. ■

**Zone Documents**

Lynne Conroy

*11/15/76*

I have no time. No time for friends. My baby is my joy and my life. She eats because of my work projecting porno films in the Combat Zone.

I joined the Motion Picture Machine Operators Union and they assign me work shifts in the State, the Pussycat or the Pilgrim.

I can take their joke but it burns my guts.

I vomit this work every morning.

This work haunts my dreams.

I fear blinking these days because of the images burning between my eyes and my eyelids.

I make $75 a week take-home.

I get food stamps so there is milk on the table.

Most days it is worth it.

When it is not, I wish I had the money for us to live in the country.

Days, the baby is in a nursery.

She grows quickly.

Nights, I work in the Pussycat Cinema.

I miss her growing.

She said to me, "I wouldn't work porn. I'd be supported by my friends...."

Was she saying I am responsible for porn?

I do not have the option of supporting my family with a stipend from husband or family.

FRAME

Six traveling salesmen rape a woman whose arms and legs are amputated.

NOW PLAYING AT YOUR LOCAL THEATER

Lily

Is evil

Is possessed

Is mad with desire

To do what most women fear.

**Psychiatric Evaluation**

I. General Information

Lynne Conroy, a twenty-six-year-old divorced white female, is a film projectionist. . . . She is the primary source of this history which appears to be reliable. Anxiety is the precipitating factor which caused her to seek psychiatric help. . . . Ms. Conroy is a short young woman of medium build and average looks, wears her hair closely cropped, wears dangling earrings, and dresses in heavy pullover sweaters, loose fitting workpants and hiking boots, generally projecting the image of a no-nonsense feminist. Fairly anxious, she relates in an aggressive demanding style that with probing gives way to an extremely insecure, self-dramatizing though even engaging manner.

*12/13/76*

The vice squad busted "Spanish Fly" today. The sergeant and the boys were visibly taken aback when I opened the door to the projection booth to give them the print. When they started to laugh, I shook. There is an agreement between the union and the DA's office that projectionists will not be busted. But these cops threaten to take me to headquarters. Or to a party to which they are on their way with the film.

"We need a projectionist," they hoot.

"Y'eat hot dogs?" the sergeant guffaws in reference to the film which is about a case of hot dogs injected with Spanish fly. Shortly after the cops depart, the management brings up a second print of "Spanish Fly." On screen, the fucking resumes.

*12/15/76*

Too much rape. Too much death. I am numb. I even expect it.

Frame

The maniac pulls pantyhose from his face as he yanks the blood-tipped lance from the vagina of the woman he murdered.

Now Playing At Your Local Theater

Life is a ball if you're a lucky stiff.

*12/30/76*

As I pack up the print to ship it to the next theater, I run a razor blade down the center of the 35mm film. I am protected by the next union projectionist who will not report his "brother's" negligence because it would reflect on the union.

Frame

Gang rape of a pre-adolescent female.

Now Playing At Your Local Theater

Baby Maria. . . .There is nothing she wouldn't do to fulfill her secret fantasies.

*1/16/77*

My tool kit includes:

1. 16 Craftsmen open-ended box wrenches.
2. 8 Allen wrenches in various sizes.
3. 5 Craftsmen screwdrivers.
4. 4 boxes of fuses of different wattages.
5. Hemostats.
6. Razor blade.

I carry my tool kit to work on the subway. When I feel strong, like today, I consider it a political act. This morning, I grease the intermittent, clean the upper pad rollers, log the bulb hours used the previous day, clean the gate and use the razor to edit the film. I am, after all, mother to a very young woman.

*2/15/77*

Something in the way that National Labor Relations Board lawyer shut the door steeled me for his next statement. My upper teeth had already clamped against my lower teeth when he chuckled intimately, "Y'know, when we all saw your case, y'know, that you worked at the Pussycat, we fought over your case. We thought you would be a real hot tomato."

**Psychiatric Evaluation**

Recommended Treatment:

Ms. Conroy's demandingness and relative non-compliance are to be anticipated as initial obstacles to forming a working therapeutic relationship.

*2/28/77*

My head is a video deck. Rewinding. Replaying. Repeating images all night long. The way to end these is to make my own.

Frame

The butch artist seduces the blonde femme who was 'frigid' from the time she was raped by her father. Their 'lovemaking' is performed with an assortment of plastic items and the blonde reaches climax with a man who opportunely steps in.

Now Playing At Your Local Theater
Her name is Alice.
Her friend's name is Claudette.
Their world is cruel and beautiful.
And lonely.
Until they meet Frank.

*3/8/77*

Jane introduces me to women in the Prostitutes' Union of Massachusetts (PUMA). I am shy. Man-made fear keeps us from being at ease with each other. But, I want to know Rebecca, Lee and Arielle. And how we all survive the Zone. We talk about making a film about us women.

I study for a union admissions test. It is the first written exam given in the seventy-year history of the union. This exam will be administered to the first women trying to enter the union. They tell us they are upgrading the skills of the membership.

*Written Entrance Examination*

Each examiner will take into account how difficult the question is. You will receive two points when he judges you have answered a question correctly and completely.

Question #241

What is the most critical cleanliness problem area in a Western Electric 1B Soundhead?

Answer #241

The light gate and its slit.

March 21, 1977
Dear Ms. Conroy,

Your presence is requested at the next regular meeting of the Local on Sunday, April 10, 1977 at 9:30 A.M. in the Hotel Bradford, Tremont Street, Boston, for the purpose of obligating you into membership. Before the start of the meeting, would you contact Mr. Buckley, financial secretary, for the following:

| | |
|---|---|
| Initiation Fee | $500 |
| Quarterly Stamp | 23 |
| Initial S.R.D. | 15 |
| Total | $538 |

*4/10/77*

Before they initiate me into the union, they read my papers from the NLRB, ending with Fuch's letter withdrawing the charges. Even if they allowed me to respond, and I were not frightened of them, they would not fathom the harassment I have endured.

Amid hoots, they ask me to leave the room so they can vote on the admission. I leave; I raise my chin high, so high they can't see my tears of humiliation. I can raise my chin because I hear Marge Piercy's poem about the woman who was an "Immaculate Exception." And I know why I am so scared.

*4/11/77*

Mad hattered pimps party through my sleep.Burning hundred dollar bills in my face. Handing me razor sharp lilies that slash my hand when I reach out.

In the overexposed morning light, I call Lee.

"What's a pimp?" I ask.

"Any man to whom a woman gives a chance to take her money. Pimps usually don't stop a woman from leaving. They think, 'She could never find a man as good as me.' Some prostitutes allow themselves to be defined by the status of the pimp for whom they work. A pimp can be a business agent; he may take care of the kids."

"Why do they hate us?"

"I think it is because we do not want to take care of men any longer. We want, too. We want money, sex and pleasure."

"What is going to stop rape and battering?" I push on.

"A society that clearly indicates a woman's worth extends beyond her sexuality."

*4/15/77*

Arielle was busted today. Another woman using her apartment let in a second man to wait while a trick was in the bedroom. The second man was a cop. The woman was charged on three counts but her real name was not discovered.

Two counts were charged to Arielle. Running a house. Accepting money from a prostitute.

The other woman is scared. Two previous arrests. This time, do time. She doesn't show at her arraignment.

Cops return for Arielle. They arrest her on three counts. She has a baby due in November. A baby born in jail is taken by welfare.

Four counts of us go to the Tombs. We take bail money from rent money, diaper money, food money and pay checks. Landlords will have to do with less.

I collect this money but the officer has to ask me three times what my occupation is before I hear him, smile and lie. I am scared of jail. Scared of walls. Scared of being walled in .

*4/15/77*

On a scrap of harsh brown paper towel that is jail toilet paper, Arielle copied poetry from the walls of Cell B-3 Suffolk County House of Detention. Once out, she reads to us:

Fight for Revolution
And there won't be any jails.

Jails will be for pigs who made them.

Keep your mind strong and fight
Strong and Fight
For Freedom.
Women Unite. ■

**Gun Control**
Miriam Kalman Harris

As director of an emergency intervention project for battered women I often received calls at home from the volunteer counselors when they confronted cases so complex they needed consultation on how to handle them or so heartbreaking they could not bear to keep the stories inside. When my phone rang late one afternoon, I was sitting at my computer. As the counselor spoke, I began to type along to the tune of her voice, taking notes of what she was telling me. Later, I recorded this following account in my diary.

April 9, 1990
Carol's call

"Saturday we had a referral from the intensive care unit upstairs. One of the nurses had a patient she thought might need our help. Sarah and I took our assessment form and went up to see her. I had never been up in the rooms before—everyone I've seen has been in the ER and, although often they are seriously injured, I've never spoken directly with anyone who had to be admitted.

"Our patient was twenty-four years old. Her boyfriend shot her in the vagina—took a gun, stuck it up her vagina, and pulled the trigger. It was some kind of game they played [while] tripped out on crack cocaine. He says he didn't know the gun was loaded. Can't figure out how it got that way."

"He was there?" I asked.

"Yeah, he was there. Weird looking guy. But he left the room after the first few minutes. I was glad. But tell the truth, I could hardly bear to look at her. She seemed so small, so young and vulnerable. And I think she was still in a state of shock. Her first concern was that she'd never be able to have a baby. But it turns out her uterus and ovaries were unharmed. It turns out the bullet shattered her large and small intestine. I can't remember how many feet she said they'd removed. It turns out she had to have a colostomy—she'll have to wear a bag for the rest of her life. That is if she doesn't die from the peritonitis.

"When we walked out of that room, I thought I was going to vomit. I went into the bathroom and just stood there a while—sort of gagging. I kept seeing her face. For the rest of my life, I think I'll see that poor girl—woman?—lying there with that bag. For the rest of my life, I'll never forget her. I'll always remember. I'll always remember . . ."

We were silent a moment as the horror of such a scene began to form images in my brain and I am sure continued to whirl through Carol's. Yet immediately I felt a sense of rage. "Carol," I asked with what I could find of my voice, "did they take turns at this 'game'? Did he hand her the gun and have her aim it at his penis?"

"I didn't ask."

Nor would I have asked, I thought later. I was afraid I already knew the answer. ■

## The Dark Side of the Moon

Jan Barstow

I took off my shirt and studied my body in the mirror. The rhythm drifting in from the radio seemed to sweep over me, and I began moving with the music. Usually when I dance, I feel beautiful, powerful, in control. On this day I felt distanced from my body, plagued by so many questions:

> Why did I become a topless dancer?
> Why did I sign a contract to have someone else's baby?
> Why did I get an abortion?
> What happened to the money?

Why did I hide an ex-convict from the law?
Why didn't I get help after he raped me?
Why didn't I get away from the men who oppressed me?
And most importantly, why didn't I take the children with me when I finally left my husband?

In the beginning, I didn't know any of the answers. I couldn't even have asked the questions. I didn't know anything about family violence or battering; I didn't know I was abused. I had no black eyes or broken bones. But I knew a lot about a broken spirit.

I didn't know that I was a battered woman because my husband, Ray, controlled me more with fear than with beatings. Ray controlled me by threatening to leave me, threatening suicide, throwing chairs, and slamming doors. In the first years of our marriage, he smashed a red phone against the wall and kept it in our bedroom to remind me not to make him so mad again. I was afraid of his anger. When Ray shook with rage, I cowered. Ray was not violent to other people, but early in our relationship, he learned how to control me through my emotions. The more I tried to stand up to him, the more violent he became. And the more afraid I became of his anger.

In the summer of 1986, I ran away from my home and from the responsibilities that I could no longer carry. One year later, in desperation to put my life together, I went before the court to seek custody of my three children. I lost. The following year, I appealed to a jury in a last effort to determine the fate of my children and of my future as their mother. Ray's attorney, the psychiatrist, the court-appointed guardian, and the attorney who represented the children all were against me. Society does not forgive a mother who moves away from her children, no matter what the reason.

It's not easy to explain where the problems began.

My childhood seemed normal enough, though my father didn't live with us most of the years I was growing up. My mother raised five children alone, and I remember many happy years. It was important to my mother that my sister and I be "ladies"—that we learn proper etiquette, that we never smoke, drink, or curse, and that we keep a high moral profile so we wouldn't get a bad reputation. We were raised to be dependent and refined, even though my mother worked as a teacher in order to support us. My mother did everything involved with raising a family and keeping a home, and I wanted to be just like her.

On the few occasions when my father moved back into the house, life became more tense. My father was highly emotional, and he didn't like the demands that children made in his life. When he was home, my mother spent her time nursing him through his depressions and catering to his moods. She used to tell us we were lucky because at least we had a father. We never knew him well; his few words were issued as commands. My mother rarely stood up to him, but when she did, he bellowed.

I remember one time as a child when I heard my mother yelling through the closed door, "No, you're hurting me!" I remember really hating my father just that once. My mother, brothers, sister and I were all happier when my father was away.

When I first met Ray, I worshipped him. He seemed the kindest, most gentle man I had ever known. He said that he wanted to provide for me so that I could stay home and nurse and care for the children we planned to have. Ray often rubbed my neck or my feet and told me how much he loved me, that I was the only person in the world he could turn to. I thought that with Ray I'd finally have the family that I always wanted and that my children would have a father who cared.

After the children were born, Ray stayed away more frequently, became emotionally distant, and dictated decisions rather than discussing issues with me. Crying babies bothered Ray, so I often protected him by taking the children on car rides until they fell asleep or by keeping them in another room. Ray rarely talked with me and would sometimes sit for hours in front of the TV without getting up or changing the channel. I felt more and more isolated from Ray. I used to pray that the children wouldn't cry so I could sit near him.

One day I came home with my three-year-old daughter, Kristal, and found Ray sitting in a chair leaned against the wall. There was a bottle of bourbon on the counter. Ray asked me where I had been. When I told him that I had been swimming with Kristal, he accused me of seeing another man and threw a chair at my feet. Kristal woke up and started for the door, and Ray slammed the door in front of her so hard I was afraid it would slice her hand off. The whole house shook and echoed. I was so frightened that I grabbed Kristal and ran out the door. I didn't know where to go, so I drove around for hours and didn't return until I was sure that Ray was asleep. I had nightmares all that night. Ray didn't want to talk about the incident the next day. He rarely talked about problems we were having.

Ray had an almost uncontrollable jealously. He often told me that I had bad breath, so I was afraid of getting close to other people. When I talked on the phone with other young mothers that I had met through the Mother's Milk Drive, a local breast milk bank, Ray accused me of neglecting my own children and would yell at me to get off the phone. I felt embarrassed and isolated myself even more.

I became starved for conversation with another adult. In time, I developed a friendship with Leon, a friend of my brother's. Even though Leon was homosexual, we had a lot of interests in common. I believed that as long as I was monogamous, I was doing nothing wrong. But Ray was jealous and insisted that I stop visiting with Leon. The problem was greater because Leon lived part of that time in my mother's home. Ray tried to stop me from seeing Leon by threatening to kill himself, kill me, or never come home. I refused to give in. I loved talking with Leon, and often after putting the children to bed, Leon and I would discuss values, friends we had in common, or current problems we were having in our lives. Leon was like an oasis in my life. I discovered that the only time I felt I could breathe was when I was away from Ray. Leon was safe because he was gay.

Later, I fell in love with Jacques, who attended the same church that I did. Jacques shared many of the same beliefs that I had and had overcome many hardships in his own life. Jacques loved to talk, and was an accomplished artist as well as the most unselfish man that I had ever met. Jacques was paralyzed from the neck down but had learned to write, draw, paint, turn pages, guide an electric wheelchair, and do many other things using only a mouthstick and simple controls. Sometimes I drove Jacques to church or to special events or accompanied him to the local elementary school where he tutored fourth graders. I felt close to Jacques and asked his advice about problems I was having at home. I needed Jacques' friendship and wanted Ray to be friends with Jacques too. Once I went Christmas shopping with Jacques and he sped through the mall with me standing on the back of his electric wheelchair. We often had fun that way. Neither Leon nor Jacques ever asked me to do anything that would jeopardize my marriage to Ray. I appreciated their concern. As long as I had friends to turn to, I felt that I could endure my marriage. After all, marriage was for better or for worse, and now I had the children to consider.

Ray handled money poorly, and we were constantly borrowing from my mother. But the more I talked about going back to work, the more Ray put me down or would change his hours so I couldn't work outside the home. Eventually, we moved into a large home in a well-to-do neighborhood. We had a hot tub, a three-car garage, a live-in housekeeper, and all the other amenities that made us look successful on the outside. But inside, I knew something was wrong.

I didn't see the signs of drug abuse. I wanted to believe that Ray was a "good man," so I believed him when he said that the bank made errors in our statements and that he was taking care of the bills. Still, I felt guilty about the large sums of money that he was borrowing from my mother; we never seemed able to repay her. I must have been blind. When Ray started coming home with cut straws in his coat pockets, he told me he and friends at work were making straw animals with them just for fun. One day I discovered a vial of white powder on the bathroom counter. Ray admitted it was cocaine but said that he had only tried it once and he never wanted to do it again. I believed him.

As time went on, Ray became more violent; his moods were unpredictable. Sometimes Ray saw things that weren't there. Once Ray told me some invisible people had come into the room and they were there for me. Another night I heard a sound at the foot of the bed, and I reached over to wake up Ray. He wasn't there. I called out his name and still no answer. I heard the sound again and was overwhelmed with fear. I found Ray sitting on the floor at the foot of the bed with a shotgun across his lap. He told me that he had been sitting there for a while thinking about killing himself and he didn't know why he just didn't do it. I finally talked him into putting the gun down and climbing back into bed. I pleaded with Ray to get professional help, but he said that he was just under a lot of stress at work and that he could handle it, as long as he had me and the children to help him.

I tried my best to talk with Ray and help him through his depressions, but he was working a lot of overtime at this job. I rarely saw him anymore. I hated his coming home at five or six in the morning and wanting sex, but he would beg to show me how much he loved me. I always gave in. I felt that I had to since I was his wife and it was the only form of communication we had left. Once, when I refused, he yelled at me and slammed the bed so hard with his fist that my heart jumped and I froze with fright. Sometimes he would try to have sex with me while I was sleeping. That made me feel like I was nothing more than a receptacle, as though the rest of me didn't matter. I hated feeling like an object. When I tried to tell Ray how I felt, he got mad and stormed out.

About six months before I ran away, Ray and I had a violent argument. Ray threatened that if I said one more word, he would kill me. I told Ray that even if he killed me, he could never kill my spirit. That made Ray furious. He grabbed my neck in anger and held me until I could feel my life draining. Without air, I was powerless. I couldn't talk, breathe, or even find the strength to lift my arms in protest. All I could do was watch my life slipping away.

Then the world changed inside my head. I no longer saw Ray before me; instead, I saw the children. Somehow in my mind I went to them one at a time and reassured them that they would be all right. I told them my mother would raise them and see that they had everything they needed. She would tell them all about me and they would know that they were loved. Then I spoke to my mother and told her that I loved her and needed her help with my children. My mother and my children seemed to tell me that they understood; I assured them they could always find me in their hearts and I would help them. There was nothing else I could do. It was like watching a slow-motion picture passing before me. I thought I would never see my children again. I didn't want to leave them and I was sad, but I had no choice. I went over other details in my life and made sure that everything was in order; then I felt peace.

Ray let go. After that, I was more terrified of his anger. I froze when he got mad and cowered when he cornered me in the closet or pushed me to the floor. He even broke the shower door when he rammed his head into the glass in anger. I sometimes told Leon or Jacques, and they advised me to leave. But I knew if I left Ray would kill himself. I felt as though I were giving up my freedom so Ray could live, and I resented feeling responsible for his life. Ray seemed to own me with his love, and I couldn't get out.

In the summer of 1986, I hit bottom. My memory has blanked on many of the details, but time and healing are slowly bringing them back without the pain. That summer, as I had every summer, I took the children on vacation to our family's cabin in the mountains. This time I met Manuel, a man who lived near the natural hot springs in that part of New Mexico, and learned much from him about these mountains that now seemed like my second home. In time, he revealed that he was on parole for drug trafficking and that he believed that the local police were trying to plant drugs in his home so they could arrest him again. I knew he had recently argued with the police chief's son, so I invited him to stay in our log cabin until he could make sure he was not being framed. Drugs had never been a part of my life, but the feeling of being trapped was one I knew well and I felt sorry for him.

Manuel shared many stories about local customs and showed the children and me how to catch fish with our bare hands and where to find herbs for natural remedies. I felt privileged to be learning so much about the mountains where I had spent so many summers during my own childhood. I felt like a child again as I swam in swimming holes I never knew existed and hiked through ravines I'd never found before. Manuel introduced me to other families who lived in the mountains, and I took my children to visit and play with their children. I valued Manuel's friendship and was grateful for his knowledge.

Sometimes Manuel told me what his life was like in prison, and he told me he would do anything to keep from going to prison again. I listened to his stories of shootings and gang violence, but I never worried that Manuel would hurt me I was his friend. I knew he was becoming attracted to me, but I had always kept a distance, and I trusted him. I sensed no danger until the night Manuel didn't want to leave.

After putting the children to bed, I came back out and talked with Manuel in the living room. The police were no longer following him, and I thought it was safe for him to go back to his home. Manuel said that he loved me and that he wanted me. He pulled me towards him to kiss me. I tried to fight him off.

We struggled, and he tore my clothes. He kept insisting on his love for me. The children were asleep. I was frightened they would wake up and see what was happening to me. I remember beading with sweat as I tried to will him away because my arms weren't strong enough. I screamed silent screams in the back of my throat as Manuel raped me. I couldn't believe it was really happening. I couldn't stop him. He was too strong. My body was like a traitor to me, and I hated it because I couldn't get away. I had been faithful to my husband through eleven difficult years and now all that seemed as if for nothing.

I was ashamed and didn't want the children or anyone to know what had happened. I felt filthy and dirty. I had always prided myself on having high values and morals. Now I was afraid that if others knew they would turn against me because I wasn't any good any more—I was used and damaged.

I had learned in my marriage (and in my childhood) that when things get rough you just continue the next morning as though nothing happened. I didn't tell anyone. When I called Ray for money so I could come home, I got even worse news. Ray said not to come home. He told me that the electricity had been cut off, his car had been repossessed, the food had gone bad, and he hadn't eaten in four days. I panicked. I had nowhere to go, and Ray wanted to die. I pleaded with him not to kill himself. I called family members to help him with his car and food. I didn't tell anyone about myself. I was too ashamed.

I don't know how to explain what happened after that. Manuel raped me again and again and even more of me died. I felt trapped and couldn't find any way out. I eventually just gave up and gave in. I didn't know why I put my life in Manuel's hands. Being "loved" by Manuel felt familiar to me, like being in an invisible prison. I was drained: no food or money. My life seemed more and more closed in.

Even though Manuel hurt me, I was dependent on him to take care of me, too. Being dependent on Manuel justified the sex. I started feeling loyal to Manuel and no longer tried to get away. After a while I felt so destroyed that there was nothing more of me that Manuel could hurt. I don't know why but I developed a kind of love for Manuel, though it wasn't exactly love: I pretended to myself that I loved him so that I could endure the sex. Yet, I was scared of him and wanted him to go away. I don't remember how long Manuel stayed at the cabin before he went away.

When Manuel left, I felt empty. I didn't have a feeling to replace the shame and fear I'd felt when he was there. Two weeks later, he returned. Sex continued, and I would count backwards through the alphabet until it was over. Still, I missed him when he was gone. Without him I was nothing. I had no identity. Manuel said he loved me and he wanted me to have his baby. I felt paralyzed. I tried to separate my thoughts from my body so I wouldn't have to be there anymore. But I had so thoroughly lost control of my life that I could no longer grasp who I was. I wasn't anyone without Manuel; things were no longer real.

There was a stream that ran near the log cabin, and I often touched my legs or my hands to the cold mountain water. As a child, I often played in the stream, and I used to imagine that I was sitting in the hands of God. Clear blue skies, towering pines, and the fresh scents of mountain herbs, together with the clean air and the sounds of birds and other animals stirred my imagination—even the moss on the underside of rocks was perfection to me.

Now as I walked near the stream by myself, I tried to figure out what I felt. I tried every emotion I could think of but none of them seemed to fit. Did I feel sad? Lonely? Happy? I didn't feel anything. I couldn't tell the difference among those feelings. And yet I seemed fine on the outside. Nobody else noticed there was anything wrong with me. I could still do everything I needed to do. Therefore, I concluded, I must be okay; whatever the feeling was, I couldn't identify it.

Finally my mother gave me money to come home. Life at home was even more difficult than before. I was pregnant with Manuel's baby. Ray was moody. I never told him I was pregnant. I was too ashamed to tell anyone about that summer. I even lied to the doctor. I wanted to end the pregnancy as soon as possible, but I had to wait several more weeks to save enough money. I hated my body for being pregnant with Manuel's baby. I even hated myself for not wanting the baby, but I was afraid that if Manuel knew I was pregnant, he would come after me for the child.

In August of 1986, I went alone to have the abortion. I remember walking into the clinic alone. I had always dreamed of raising many children, but I couldn't love this one, not even the part that was me. I wanted the abortion more than anything else on earth, as though by getting rid of the baby, I could get rid of the shame that I carried inside me. When I got there, I couldn't afford the anaesthetic. I remember how much the procedure hurt, and I felt I deserved it. Afterwards, I doubled over in pain and just wanted to throw up. At least part of Manuel wasn't inside me anymore. I hated my body for making me feel like a criminal, lying and hiding from my family all day, spending money that should have gone for food. I was willing to do anything to make that summer go away, but I could not tell anyone that I had been raped. I was afraid they'd ask questions, and I couldn't handle that.

Several weeks later, Ray threw me across the room in anger, and something in me snapped. I remembered the TV commercial that showed criminals behind bars. The message was that when children see violence in their homes, they grow up to hurt others or to become victims of violence themselves. I realized that they were talking about Ray and me. I didn't want that for my children. I ordered Ray to go away. He refused. I knew that if I stayed, Ray would eventually kill me, and then he would be behind bars and the children would have no parents at all. I didn't have the strength to hold the family together anymore.

I was desperate to get away and to raise my family without any more pain. I didn't have enough money to move away; I had used food money for the abortion. I was no longer thinking straight. I knew that Ray had been a frequent customer at the Yellow Rose, a local topless bar. While driving around looking for work, I passed the Yellow Rose and pulled in. I leaned against a back wall and watched the dancers stripping on stage. A few months before I had felt frightened at the club's amateur night when

I danced as part of a dare between Ray and one of his friends. Now I felt comfortable in a place where people wouldn't care what kind of a person I was. I felt weak, dirty and incapable. I didn't think I deserved anyone's respect. I belonged in a topless bar.

Ray often told me that if I ever took the children from him we would never see him again. Since I was raised without a father, I wanted my own children to have a father at all costs. So I left the children with their father, in their own home near their school and friends. I thought I would only be away from them for a little while until I could come up with a joint custody agreement acceptable to Ray.

I had five dollars; I had sold my car to pay the mortgage and was now driving a car my mother gave me. So I rented a room on a pay-as-I-could basis from a friend at church who offered to help. I read books about divorce and sought counsel about joint custody. Ray and I finally met with a divorce mediator and filed papers, but negotiations stalled when Ray said there wasn't enough money. With the money that I earned dancing I paid a live-in housekeeper so she could watch the children until our divorce became final. I wanted a quick divorce, but events didn't happen that way.

The first month I danced, Ray tried to commit suicide. I arrived in time to stop him from pouring gasoline on himself. Two days later a hospital called requesting me to get Ray psychiatric help. By the time I got to the hospital, Ray had walked out against medical advice. I arrived at home in time to see Ray say his final goodbyes to the children before getting into his car. Ray told me he was going to drive off a bridge; I wanted desperately to stop him. I jumped into the passenger seat and refused to get out. I didn't think about danger for myself. As Ray pulled away and I saw the children playing, it struck me that this might be the last time I ever saw them. I suddenly wanted to claw my way out of the car. I cried inside, but the tears froze before they could fall. All I could think of now was staying alive. Once again, my life was in Ray's hands. Numb with fear, I managed to talk Ray into admitting himself to a psychiatric hospital. I moved back home with the children while Ray was away, and I continued to dance. I knew I never wanted to live with Ray again, so I moved back out when Ray checked himself out of the hospital before doctors dismissed him.

Moving away again was like leaving one nightmare and entering an even bigger one. When I went home to visit with the children, Ray often wanted to have sex with me. When I refused, Ray begged to express his love for me. Sex no longer meant love to me. Sex meant that I had to count backwards until it was all over. Ray said that when we had sex, he could feel my deep love for him. I didn't feel anything. I wanted to get away but didn't know how. So I got away in my own mind. I cried often, and my visits with the children became shorter.

Before the summer of '86, most of my friends knew me as a respectable schoolteacher who stayed home by choice to raise three beautiful children. I nursed each child beyond two years, made their clothes, helped found a local breast milk bank, and counseled new mothers on health and childcare issues. I later became involved with the home-school movement, even opened my own home school until the birth of my third child. Now my days had filled with invisible tears. I was stripping in a topless bar, and my husband was telling me that I wasn't good enough to be a mother.

The topless club felt safer than home to me. The club had a bouncer to protect the dancers. When I finished dancing on the top stage I moved to the second stage and then to the runway to dance until I was covered with sweat and ready to drop from exhaustion. I wore a lot of black in the early days. Dancing was my way of screaming from all the hurt and pain I held deep inside. I didn't trust men and kept my distance. We danced for tips only, and some days I made only seven dollars. Too often, I judged my worth by men's attention.

Dancing in a topless club was like swimming through every emotion in the world. The loud music helped to drown feelings, and the atmosphere set the stage for sexual games. Though I was unprepared, I adapted quickly. I watched the games that dancers and customers played, and I played my own. It took me months before I had the courage to dance close to a customer. I was inhibited, trying to deal with fear and discomfort. The only thing that felt natural was moving with the music. Music seemed to climb inside me, and I felt beautiful.

Though people I knew no longer respected me, I found other ways to build myself up. When customers complimented me, I asked them to give me their compliments in writing, on a drink coaster, so I could read their words later when I needed to feel better. In time, I began to like myself and the way I could move and control my body. I became good at my profession and earned the respect of the dancers and other people in the club. I grew to love being in a place where I was so easily accepted by other people. Eventually I built a wall of self-confidence that no one could enter. They didn't know anything about my private life. In this place with low expectations and no real intimacy, I began to explore who I was.

Dancing at the club was the turning point in my life. I felt at home with the other dancers, and some of them became my best friends. I didn't have to prove myself to them. At a time when I couldn't accept myself, the other dancers accepted me. The dancers seemed to know a lot about each other. They spoke openly about abuse in their lives, from incest to rape, and made it seem like "no big deal." One dancer in particular took me under her wing and told me I never had to compromise myself with the customers. I wanted to be like her. In time, I gave the same advice to other new dancers. We were like a family. We took care of each other.

When Ray told my parents that I was dancing, my father threatened to disown me, and my mother struggled to accept me. At my father's insistence, I met with a counselor. I told her I knew what I was doing. After all, the summer was over, I no longer lived with Ray, I was arranging a divorce through which the children would have both parents, and I had done it all on my own. Life was getting harder and harder, but I felt that if I were to quit struggling, I would be a failure. I had a new identity that grew out of my old pre-Manuel one: Jan can do it. Jan is strong. Jan can do anything. So I danced to exhaustion during the days and cried hysterically during the nights. I missed my children. But the price for going back to them was certain death, emotional and possibly physical.

My topless dancing shocked a lot of people, but I wasn't aware of how much they would hold it against me. Putting up a respectable front during my marriage had left me imprisoned. I didn't want any more to do with prisons. If society judged topless dancers as dirty, indecent and immoral, then perhaps I was in the right place. I had felt dirty, indecent and immoral—I felt like a topless dancer inside out. Ironically, even though life was hard, working at the club I began to feel honest and good. I didn't have to pretend to be someone I wasn't. It's as though I were saying, "Yes, I'm used and no good. This is who I really am. What do you think of me now?" It became a paradox: by living an identity that society judged as indecent and immoral, I began to feel honest.

As much as I learned from the dancers at the club, I still didn't know how to live on my own. I hated myself even more when a man pressured me into having sex with him when I didn't want to. I felt repulsed that my only role might be as someone's mistress. I didn't know how to push someone away when I so much needed to feel loved and cared for myself. It seemed that the only thing men wanted was my body, and I had already lost control over that.

I finally met Dan, a man who seemed to like me for my friendship, and I began to trust him. I felt safe with Dan. He was gentler than other men, almost like a female friend. Dan sometimes recommended songs for me to dance to at the club, and afterwards we would go out dancing or walking or we'd just sit and talk. Dan didn't like my working at the club, but he accepted what I was doing. Later, I told Dan that I had been raped. I told him in the same way that a person might relate what time she got up in the morning. I no longer felt emotional about it, and Dan didn't turn away. Though he was ten years younger than I, we moved in together.

When one of Dan's professors told him she was looking for someone to be a surrogate mother, I jumped at the chance. I had always felt beautiful when I was pregnant, and I felt cheated out of my last pregnancy. I wanted another chance to experience pregnancy so I could take it all the way through to delivery. I became friends with the professor and looked forward to delivering her baby. I saw it as a wonderful gift I could offer another woman. We talked about natural childbirth, midwives and the method of surrounding the baby with music—all the things that had been important to me while pregnant with my own three children. We had a lawyer write the contract, and I signed the papers. We planned to have the artificial insemination coincide with my return to teaching in the fall. We gathered the instruments, the semen, but circumstances changed.

My not living with the children had been hard on them. Whenever

I left after visiting, Jean would curl up in a ball, and Hunter would run after me crying at the top of his lungs for me to take him with me. Seeing the children hurt so much, I felt like someone was tearing my heart out of my body. But Ray wouldn't let the children go with me. I don't know why I always listened to Ray. When the house where they lived was foreclosed, he moved on to another house. He kept me from visiting this new home. When I tried, he threw me out. Ray said I had given up my parental rights when I moved out, but I was welcome to move back home again. I was afraid of him so I settled on seeing the children at weekend soccer games.

Ray became more and more possessive of the children. Since I was planning to get pregnant, I had already decided to stop dancing. I told Ray that I had arranged to teach three-year-olds in the fall so that Hunter could be in my class. Ray found another day-care center for him instead. I asked to take the children on vacation to the family cabin. Ray wouldn't let them go. I knew I was losing touch with them. My eldest daughter, Kristal, finally wrote a letter begging me to come home and help her. The housekeeper wasn't doing her job. Kristal was tired of playing the role of mother and maid. I was so torn; I felt helpless against their father.

Ray eventually agreed to let me take the children to the cabin, along with their grandmother, aunt and cousins. At the cabin, I saw how much my children had changed. They were like zombies—their eyes blank and expressionless; they rarely spoke. Hunter was terrified of bathrooms. Slowly, over the next few weeks, they opened up, but I knew they would close down if they went back to their father. This was the most time we had spent together since I moved away the year before. The children asked if they could stay with me. I put the surrogate pregnancy on hold so I could devote my time to my own children. Ray had shut me out of their lives; but I was determined to work my way back in. I called an attorney.

On his advice, I didn't return the children to Ray. Instead I went back to court. I thought the court would understand that Ray had been unfair and that I had tried my best to be a good mother. Ray's attorney presented me as a selfish topless dancer who had abandoned her family. The judge awarded custody to Ray. I couldn't believe it. I felt numb again. I had tried so hard that past year and now I was powerless again. I hated the smile on Ray's face when I returned the children. I hated the court for not seeing through him. I felt I couldn't do anything right in anyone else's eyes.

My life seemed unbearable. I screamed, yelled, cried. I didn't know how I could survive the pain this time. I didn't know how to apologize to my children for letting them down. How could they ever trust me again? What kind of mother cannot even protect her own children? I thought I would go crazy. All the hurt and pain of that previous summer in the mountains under Manuel's power came flooding back, and I felt dirty, filthy and no good. I had nothing to offer. I worked as a teacher for minimum wage; I wasn't worth more than that. I still taught three-year-olds, but Hunter was not in my class.

A friend I had known through the Mother's Milk Drive told me that in an unhealthy relationship one person's mental illness was equal to the other's. I knew how crazy Ray was, but I never thought that I was part of the problem. Now I was desperate for help. My father paid for counseling to help me adjust to losing the children. My problems were not over yet, but this time the court had guaranteed my visitation rights.

It was several months before I told my counselor, Carol, that I had been raped. That seemed so small compared to other issues; by now it seemed like only a bad dream. Counseling helped me through anxiety attacks when I would wake up screaming, beating my fists against the bed, my heart racing with fright. Carol asked me how I felt about different situations, and I tried to guess. I knew what people expected me to feel, but I just couldn't feel anything. Carol asked about my childhood and my relationship with my parents. She recommended a book about co-dependency and suggested a series of lectures for me to attend. She supported every decision I had made up to that point and helped me learn to believe in myself. I began to get flashes of awareness as to why I was drawn to men like Ray, why I trusted men who could hurt me.

I began to understand that when you give up self-will, you give up everything. It's as though someone else owns you. I gave away my self-will when I learned how to be a nice woman in our society. I was raised to put other people's welfare above my own. It was easy for Ray and others to control me—my own belief system was my jailer. I felt responsible for making Ray happy in the same way that my mother nursed my father through his depressions. I wore emotional blinders that kept me from seeing alternatives. I gave away my self-will many times. Manuel was only an extension of Ray. His raping me was no different from the way that Ray had abused me, and I developed the same sick kind of love for him. With Manuel, as with Ray, fear and pain defined my identity—and became my only experience of what it felt like to be loved.

Rape can happen in many ways. Rape is when one person's will controls another. It's like breaking in a horse to make it docile. Battered women are emotionally raped in many ways and have lost the drive and will to get away. Leaving Ray was never an option until the pain was so great that I could no longer survive. To me the only difference between a battered woman and a rape victim is that with battering the emotional scars are harder to heal because one cannot see where to take the stitches. Battering is a process rather than a single event.

Why didn't I leave if I wasn't happy? Pain is a powerful master. So is fear. Healthy people pull their hands out of the fire when they start to feel pain. I had learned to shut down my feelings so I could endure the pain. The more I hurt, the less I felt. I was like a leaf in the wind; whatever direction the wind was blowing I would go. When people asked me what I wanted I would say I don't know. Then I would cry. The limited awareness that resulted from abuse prevented me from seeing any other way to live. Victims are emotionally blinded as a result of their pain.

I underwent intensive therapy. I counseled with Carol twice a week and attended twelve-step groups four or five times a week. Later I began meeting with a group from the Rape Crisis Center. Even then I didn't tell them I had been repeatedly raped. I was still ashamed. I was afraid it might come up in court. I didn't understand why I hadn't tried to get away.

Through counseling I learned to put myself first. It took months before I could stop worrying about my children and start dealing with life without them. I had to accept that life is not always fair, but I am not a bad person, and I don't deserve to be hurt. It is up to me to see that no one hurts me again. I took a self-defense class and started lifting weights.

I quit worrying about how Ray would react to my choices.

But there is a difference between knowing something and feeling it inside. Though I no longer felt like a victim, I still had trouble asserting myself sexually. I became pregnant by Dan twice more that year. The third pregnancy made me think deeply. I had neither the time nor the resources for another baby. What I did have was a heightened sense of responsibility for the three children I already had. The nurse at the clinic told me that she often saw rape victims come in for abortions more than once. When you've lost control over your body, it takes a while to regain it. I received excellent counseling. I learned that I didn't have to have sex with my partner, even when he pressured me. I learned that it is my right to control my body and no one else's. I have the right to determine when I will or will not have sex, and I have the right to say NO. No one can take that from me.

Though I loved Dan deeply, I no longer wanted to feel dependent on anyone so I moved out. While with me, Dan read books about co-dependency and accompanied me to seminars and meetings. We frequently re-evaluated our relationship. I was afraid that since unhealthy people are attracted to one another, perhaps Dan was unhealthy. After all, he had been attracted to me at the lowest point in my life.

Accepting responsibility for my past gave me the power to change my future. I decided to rebuild my life. I listened to self-help tapes. I bought a cup warmer that says, "I'm excellent at everything I do." I taped affirmations on my mirror, on my steering wheel, wherever I was likely to see them. The affirmations said I was a powerful woman in charge of my own life. I wrote affirmations that said men can't hurt me, that I was a good mother, that I was a worthy person. Sometimes in anger I yelled them out loud as if I could convince the world they were true. Eventually I began to believe them myself.

Though I learned to live without the children, I still wanted to raise them. Reluctantly, I turned to my father again and asked him to hire a new attorney. He agreed. The attorney told me that I had a ninety-five percent chance of losing, but I didn't give up. I insisted the children be placed in professional counseling, and I set up contact with their school counselors as well.

There were lots of strikes against me: one psychiatrist's report said that

Ray would be a better parent. Another reported that I had a personality flaw that couldn't be cured: he said I had a difficult time accepting reality. Their reports scared me, but I knew I was getting better. By this time I was working in a psychiatric hospital as a teacher for emotionally, physically, or sexually abused children. Here, I learned about my own life and that my reactions to life events were normal for my experiences. But just like a broken bone has to be set to heal, so does a fractured identity.

I had been drawn to topless dancing as my way of dealing with sexuality in a place where men couldn't touch me. Now I wanted to learn a new way to live. I used my counselor and my attorneys as role models for how to behave and often asked myself what they would do in situations I faced. One night, I was awakened by a powerful dream. I was walking beside a large body of clear water when a stranger handed me a small piece of paper. I unfolded the paper and read: "Your mission in life is to write about experiences on the other side of the moon." At first I was confused. The other side of the moon is dark. Studying the dark side of the moon would require space travel, and I wasn't a scientist. Then it dawned on me that the moon symbolizes the emotions. I knew the dark side of emotions. I felt warm and peaceful inside. I no longer felt alone.

■■■

It was a year before we went back to trial. At the last minute, my attorneys advised me that I would have a better chance of winning if I just asked for joint custody. But I knew that joint custody would allow continued manipulation and threats. So I went for it all. Ray has always been a smooth liar, but this time on the stand he started contradicting himself. He could fool the court-appointed attorney and guardian for the children, but he couldn't fool an informed jury. The jury reversed custody to me, and the judge ordered Ray to attend counseling for one year as his stipulation for seeing the children.

Healing is never quick and easy. I was awarded the children and lost my job at the same time. I found a room with a kitchen on the side, and the three children and I lived in one room and slept in one bed, using boxes for our closets. I had trouble finding a job and received unemployment and food stamps off and on for a year. Then I went back to school to train for a career as a technical writer.

Experience can lead to wisdom. I now understand why people who live in fear make the decisions they make. People who live in fear face life as though they were wearing perceptual blinders. They cannot conceive of the options a healthy person might consider. With understanding and support, they can become aware of their emotional prisons and conceive an escape. There is one thing I wish all people knew about battered women. Battered women don't make wrong decisions. Their decisions are right for the awareness they have at the time. Awareness and self-understanding can set them free.

Today I raise my three children by myself, make my own decisions, and pay my own bills. I have goals, and I am achieving them. For the first time, I am in charge of my own future. I look at some events in my past as blessings in disguise; they gave me a chance to learn about myself. There are still scars on the inside. At times I catch myself in the shower defiantly saying to the ghosts of my past: "You may own my body but you cannot own me!" ■

## A Drop of Scarlet

Cynthia E. Matthews

The first thing that struck me about the defendant when the bailiffs brought her, shackled, into the courtroom was her eyes. Set in the soft and supple planes of a youthful face were shell-shocked orbs grown old from fear. I sat pondering the clammy feel of my hands folded in my lap while the judge ran through the preliminaries. By the time I was sworn in on the witness stand, my stomach was tied in knots of apprehension.

First to question me was Attorney Durst, counsel for the defendant, Angela Watts. "Ms. Hall, would you relate to the court the events you witnessed on the night of October 10, 1986?" I caught Angela's eyes and pushed down the fear constricting my throat. I knew I had to speak, for her.

"Yes, I can," I began. "I have been a volunteer for five years now with the Victim Assistance Program. One of my duties is to accompany police officers on domestic dispute calls. I was summoned to Ms. Watts' home after neighbors reported a violent disturbance at that address. When I came in the door behind Officers Hammond and Von Staten, we found Ms. Watts prone on the floor of the master bedroom. She appeared severely injured."

I had to pause for a moment before I could describe the sights that had assailed my eyes that evening. The recurring thought that kept haunting me was the sheer inhumanity of Frank Watts' unending pummeling of his wife's defeated body.

"Her hair and clothing were splattered with her blood," I continued, "and her face was almost unrecognizable underneath a mass of lacerations and bruises. There were deep gouges on her arms, apparently from attempting to block her husband's blows. Mr. Watts was straddling her body and slamming the butt of a handgun into her mouth. The officers shouted for him to stop, but . . . he wouldn't. He didn't even turn his head our way to acknowledge our presence; he just kept slamming, slamming the gun in her face. I wanted to help her, to stop him somehow . . . but I was terrified. His face was red and contorted with rage; his body was shaking uncontrollably. He seemed . . . crazed. He was screaming, calling her insulting names, and threatening, 'You're making me do this, bitch. This time I really am going to kill you!' The only way I could be sure she was even alive was that her body convulsed . . . her body shuddered each time the gun impacted."

The scenes rolled through my mind as I recounted the same images that had seemed suspended just above my face when I lurched, sweaty and breathless, from my dreams.

"Officer Hammond gave Frank Watts a warning, a warning that he was about to fire. In all the confusion, above the noise, each one of us heard the click of his hammer cocking. Frank Watts heard it, too. Only then did his fists stop driving into that shattered face, and he turned our way. As he did, he reached to shove the handgun into the waistband of his jeans. But . . . he missed. The gun fell to the floor. I saw her hand reach out for it.

"I remember being startled to see her move. She had lain so utterly still throughout the beating, almost acquiescent. It was as though she had quit struggling . . . to save her strength in hopes of finding a chance to save herself.

"Her fingers wrapped around the handle of the gun; she jerked it before her chest and fired. While he was still looking at the barrel of Officer Hammond's gun, the bullet entered just below his right eye.

"I could see in his eyes then that he knew she was the one who had fired. His features froze in utter amazement. I felt what he felt at that moment. And mingled with my disgust for the man, I had a brief twinge of pity. He couldn't believe she would hurt him, despite all the agony he'd inflicted on her. He just couldn't believe she would hurt him. I wondered if at that moment he felt regret, or empathy, for his victim, but before I could wrest an answer from his eyes, he was dead.

"The officers rolled his corpse off her, and as I kneeled beside her head, her fingers fluttered to his face and touched it gently. She pulled her hand away as her eyes focused on the blood glistening on her trembling fingertips. Her mouth opened and froze in unutterable pain for an agonizingly long moment before the dam inside her burst. She screamed," I concluded. The defense rested.

The silence hanging in the courtroom was broken by the staccato questions fired by the prosecuting attorney. "Ms. Hall, at the time Angela Watts shot and killed her husband, was he armed in any way?"

"Well, he had just dropped the gun a moment before . . ."

"Ms. Hall," he interrupted, "answer the question yes or no. Was Mr. Watts armed in any way when his wife took his life?"

Cornered, I answered the question the only way I could: "No."

"Immediately prior to his death," he stressed, "was Mr. Watts assaulting Angela Watts? Wasn't he, in fact, not even facing in her direction when she put a bullet through his brain? Answer the question, Ms. Hall."

Choking on resentment, I answered, "No."

"No further questions."

■■■

I didn't feel my legs move as the bailiff led me from the stand. I was totally unaware of the beating of my heart or the drawing of my breath as I passed Angela Watts. She looked so small, dark hair clinging to her damp cheeks. She never looked at the judge as he pronounced her guilty of second-degree murder and sentenced her to twenty-five years confinement in state prison. I tried to meet her eyes as she was led from the courtroom. I wanted to touch her with a comforting glance in this unflinching room that showed her no mercy. But, when I finally saw her eyes, I realized that she was no longer there; she had retreated somewhere deep inside herself where no one could follow.

Before the connecting doors between the courtroom and holding cells slammed irrevocably shut, I saw one last image of Angela Watts: a woman simultaneously a casualty and a survivor, a bowed dark head with eyes I didn't have to be looking at to see. From where I stood, I thought I saw on the tip of a trembling finger a glistening drop of scarlet. ■

## Section Five
## *Behind His Walls*

She sits still
    with no amnesty
in this square prison of a chair
    slouched
in make believe freedom
    figuring his words
won't hurt her
    his anger
will not surround her
    while she's stuck
inside her body
    bone chilled
unable to flee
    from its terror.
Later she'll grieve
    taste bitter
injustice, remember
    and cry again
'til she sheds
    one of her skins
growing lighter
    with less armor.
She'll hear him
    breathe
behind his walls
    his chest
heavy with stones
    his shoulders, old
fragile with sorrow
    his mouth shadowed

a cave of echoes
    repetitive, meaningless
no longer frightening
    nor cruel.

Manya Bean

"I am a prisoner here and the kids too. . . . Dad has had me like a prisoner. . . ." wrote forty-six-year-old Rebecca Simmons just four months before she died in a Christmas holiday massacre at the hands of her husband, Ronald Gene Simmons, forty-seven, a retired Air Force master sergeant. A total of sixteen people, fourteen of whom were family members, died with her; their deaths marked the worst family mass murder in the nation's history at that time.[1]

The words of Manya Bean's poem seem a memorial to Rebecca who, trapped "behind his walls," wrote: "Everytime. I think of freedom I want out as soon as possible." No longer willing to "make believe," Rebecca seemed to be planning an escape and a new life. The letter to her son, daughter-in-law, and grandson, also killed in the massacre, expresses her yearning to be able to have her children visit anytime, have access to a telephone, go shopping, go to church. Rebecca Simmons and her children were battered, tortured, and imprisoned in their own home.

All battered women are prisoners. Some are held hostage in their homes until they are killed, others in state and federal prisons for attaining their freedom the only way left—by killing their abusers. Images of imprisonment prevail in many of these writings; therefore I have juxtaposed stories that reflect feelings of imprisonment and entrapment alongside actual accounts of women in prison. Women don't usually kill; they commit fewer than fifteen percent of the homicides in the United States (Browne 1987, 10):

> Women charged in the death of a mate have the least extensive criminal records of any female offenders. However, they often face harsher penalties than men who kill their mates. FBI statistics indicate that

> fewer men are charged with first- or second-degree murder for killing a woman they have known than are women who kill a man they have known. And women convicted of these murders are frequently sentenced to longer prison terms than are men (Browne 1987, 11).[2]

Furthermore, the majority of women with a documented history of abuse by the men they killed—even with police photographs, x-rays, and hospital records—are charged with first-degree murder. Angela Browne's study indicates that when a battered woman kills, it is usually after years of violence that escalates to life-threatening levels and leave her hopeless and desperate. In most cases, the violence has begun to affect her children. The difference between the women in Browne's study who killed abusers and those who did not lies *not* in the personality of the abused but in that of her abuser.

Men who were killed by their women drank more alcohol, used drugs more frequently, made more threats, and committed assaults more frequently. More of them abused children, as well as their women; the "abuse of their mates was more frequent, more injurious, and more likely to include sexual assault" (Browne 1987, 181–182). In short, battered women who kill are just like those who don't, and all of them are "just like you and me," according to both Angela Browne and Lenore Walker (Walker 1989).

Women who have been subjected to a high level of pornographic sexual abuse often find being held in prison an escape from being held as a hostage at home. As Walker explains: "Some have been raped with such force that their genitals and internal organs have been torn or irreparably damaged. As a result, many have had to have hysterectomies when still very young. . . ." (Walker 1989, 124). Brenda Whitmire was twenty-seven when she had her hysterectomy. During the same operation, she had to have her bladder "reattached." While still recovering from that surgery, she was beaten so severely by [her husband] Jimmy the night that she shot him that she has no recollection of the shooting.[3] Whitmire's testimony, written from her cell at Gatesville (Texas) prison, is followed with a letter by her mother, Cyntha Fregia, which illuminates our understanding of intergenerational violence and the effect of a violent marriage on members of the extended family.[4]

"Studies show that only a small percentage of women accused of killing their abusive partners are actually acquitted at trials. Rather, the vast majority (seventy-two to eighty percent) are convicted or accept a plea, and many receive long, harsh sentences. . . ." (*Double-Time* 1991). In 1991, 2,000 battered women in America were serving prison time for defending their lives against their batterers.[5]

Reports dated 1991 cited thirty-three women on death row; of these, fourteen were condemned for the murder of a husband or lover. In twelve of these thirty-three cases, there was evidence of "significant physical, sexual and/or emotional abuse" and evidence of battering was documented in every case. Yet, "almost no jury in the trials of the fourteen women who murdered husbands or lovers heard expert testimony on the psychological effects of battering . . . nor on the question of self-defense (*Double-Time* 1991, 3). As of 1997, forty-four women, averaging twenty-eight years in age, were incarcerated in fifteen states under a sentence of death. Women testifying before the Committee on Domestic Violence and Incarcerated Women were serving average sentences of fifteen years.[6] The extremely long and severe sentences women serve raise serious questions about the fairness of our criminal justice system.

Clemency efforts in behalf of women in prison vary from state to state and are usually initiated by grass-roots organizations. In December 1990, Governor Richard F. Celeste of Ohio granted clemency to twenty-six women; in February 1991, Governor William Donald Schaefer of Maryland granted clemency to eight women. Advocates in New York and Texas have been organizing for years trying to determine the best strategy for instituting a "mass clemency" campaign in their respective states. On May 16, 1991, Governor Ann Richards of Texas signed a resolution directing the Board of Pardons and Paroles to investigate the cases of all persons convicted of crimes related to domestic violence. Brenda Whitmire, who began her twenty-five-year stentence for "murder with a deadly weapon" on October 7, 1988, was one of the approximately one hundred women in Texas prisons whose cases were reconsidered as a result of this legislation

(*Double-Time* 1991, 2). Whitmire was released "on mandatory supervision" on May 8, 1997 after serving nine years of a twenty-five-year sentence.[7]

Unfortunately for Debbie Furlough, Tennessee is not one of the states where legislative changes are in progress, according to information received at the National Clearinghouse for the Defense of Battered Women in Philadelphia. Debbie Furlough, who was given a life sentence for murder in the first degree on August 18, 1988, will not be eligible for review until September 15, 2014.[8] Furlough seems to whisper her story, "Betrayal," from her Tennessee prison cell. Ruth Peachey, a psychiatrist who testified as an expert witness at Furlough's appeal, calls the detachment evident in her tone a symptom of post-traumatic stress disorder (PTSD) of which battered women syndrome is a subcategory. While the lay use of PTSD has been trivialized through indiscriminate application, the term provides an accurate description of the victim's state of mind at the time of the murder, and usually by the time of the trial as well, and is an essential element in the legal defense of victims who kill their abusers.

"Judge," by Carolyn Page, is a warning of what women can expect when they enter the judicial system. "Married Lies," by Diana Hannon, is a warning of what men can expect from tough women who see through their claims of contrition, know it will happen again, and take strong measures—if violent—to protect themselves. Answering violence with violence may not be the solution of choice; however, here we celebrate the heroism it takes to stop being a victim.

Beverly Hirsch's "Free at Last" was written long before she knew freedom. Although the violence perpetrated by her abusive husband is part of the story, the excerpts included here focus primarily on the negligence and brutality of the criminal justice system. The first excerpt describes a glitch in prison security that leaves Hirsch unprotected from her abuser even while behind walls. The second covers the times Hirsch "blew the whistle" on prison corruption—on two separate occasions at two different federal penitentiaries (1987–1989)—and the retribution she suffered at the hands of prison and government officials. The two letters from Latricia T. Brown, incarcerated at Arizona State Prison–Flamenco Mental Health Center, amplify our insights into institutional abuse described by Hirsch.

Judith Strasser's "Escape from a Gilded Cage" demonstrates that even when there is substantial economic privilege, marriage as an institution can become a prison where love can become a form of confinement. The two poems that close this section dramatize that moment when, in retrospect, a woman realizes that she had seen an early sign of her abusive partner's potential violence, a sign she ignored. Victoria McCabe's "What the Bride Saw" and Janet Jonathon's "A Bar Scene" discover the connection between actual prison bars and the invisible bars constructed by society that obstruct a woman's vision and obscure the signals that threaten doom. Such doom begins and ends behind his walls. ■

**We Just Played War All The Time**
Brenda Whitmire

I guess I knew of Jimmie for several years just never had met him until November of '81. By May of '82, Jimmie had me involved in illegal things that at the time I was not sure of them really being illegal and how far it would go. Jimmie had worked for these people for eleven years and they were very well known in our town. Little did I know he was setting me up for a trap. By June of '83 I was divorced from my husband and Jimmie so call own me.

During this time I saw things that would scare anyone to death. From beating up people, having people put in jail to killing people or having someone killed. I tried getting out of his trap and games, but it just made things worse on me. I was too scared to tell my family in fear of what might happen to them. I couldn't involve the cops because he was doing favors for them on the side. I begged him to please let me go and I would never say a word to anyone of what I saw or done. He just laugh and said go ahead and go and live your life in jail because I'll tell them you did everything and it will fall all back on you. I was too scared to take my chance because I had saw what happen to other who cross him.

I was abuse during this time trying to get away from him so I gave up that idea and except [accept] that I had to stay no matter what to save my family and myself. I can't tell you how many times I was beat crazy to where I didn't know who I was or where I was. I was locked in rooms for days with nothing to eat. Raped by him and others, and things that he would find to use. Took out in the woods to show where I was going to die and be put so no one would ever know what happen to me. Our lives were lived military style all the way. He was always going to kill someone, and always made sure he kept a gun by his side. In fact we even had to sleep like military. My house was even camouflaged in colors everything dark colors. We just played war all the time.

In October of '84 we were married in a graveyard no less. Why? Because he wanted to make sure I understood I was his forever and if I ever tried leaving I'd end up where I started our marriage. I was so scared and upset over this I stay away from my family for a month so I wouldn't have to face them. When I did see my mother she knew something was wrong. She ask me why didn't I leave and come back home, but I was too scared to tell her why. At first I tried hidding my beating from my family, but my mother found out. From that day on she always worried about me if I was ok or even alive. There would be months between me seeing my family because Jimmie wouldn't let me see them. I always had to sneak behind his back to see my family. That hurt very much because I was always a family type person. He hated my children because it remind him of my first husband someone he hated and wanted died. In fact he would always ask my little boy what he was going to do without a daddy. I can remember to this day my little boy saying, "I'll always have a daddy." But Jimmie would come back with, "Not if I kill him."

I guess you could say it was the mental abuse that was getting to me, by black eyes and bruises and other parts of my body would heal, but my mine was falling apart little by little. To keep from losing it I turn to drugs it would take my pain away. I would lay awake at night think when was all of this ever going to end. I learn to stay awake and not move all night so that I wouldn't wake Jimmie. Once my problems started with my bladder it was very hard for me at night to get out of bed to use the rest room. I always had a fight getting out of bed. He even went to the rest room with me to make sure thats what I was really doing. It get to where I'd hold it all night so I'd not wake him up.

In February of '85 Jimmie lost his job with the company he had worked for and just worked with the illegal things he was involved in. Jimmy never worked another day until August of '86 when I finally got him a job. In March of '85 I went to work at a video store and by June I was managing it and making good money. By Christmas I was spending at least seventy-two hours in the store to stay away from Jimmie. It didn't take him long to figure out what I was up to, and that's when he started calling every fifteen minutes, and going to work with me at times. It got to the point that when I went to the rest room I had to call him and tell him and call back when I got out. If for some reason it took me a little longer than what he thought, he would call. His reason for all of this to people was because he loved me so much he couldn't stand to be away from me. When comming to the store he was always in a rage and it started to scare the girls who worked for me. I even had one girl quit.

Jimmie was a time person, always timing me on things like how long it would take me to get home at night from the store. It would take seventeen min. if I didn't caught a red light or a train. There were a many of nights I went home scared and sick to my stomach because it had taken me more than my seventeen min. I would drive in our drive way and see the lights off and know that he was somewhere hidding in the house waiting for me so he could jump me. I caught myself speeding everywhere I went and if I saw myself being late I would get real upset and would lash out at people.

I caught myself trying to figure out how I was going to stay out of trouble with him. So I did everything he said to do. I was told what to wear and how to fix my hair and makeup. I went as far as when I had trouble with the store alarm I got the police dept. to call him to tell him I was running late. He accused me of playing games with the police to trap him. This went on until the end of our relationship.

It was told to me to find him a job that it just might keep him busy and off of me. I begged everyone I saw to please hire him he need a job bad. Now keep in mind Jimmie never wanted to work a real job it took up too much of his time on the things he was involved with besides he couldn't keep his finger on me at all times. Boy was I wrong! He would call from his job every chance he got, and I'd better be there. In being the manager I had to make bank deposits, have meetings in Liberty at another store which was six miles away, plus going into Houston once a week to pick up videos. That was just half of it. That alone was a pressure on me because of the way he was treating me. Every afternoon when Jimmie would get off work he would stop by the store and expect me to go home with him then and if I didn't once I got home I'd get the hell beat out of me.

In the back of my mind I'd ask myself what was I to do. I needed my job to get away from him before he really drove me crazy or killed me. Before I knew it I was going home at 4:30 in the afternoon with him and letting one of the girls cover me. When I say cover for me I mean to my boss, really doing my job for me. I couldn't even make a bank deposit out right by then. I was making all kinds of mistakes in money, movies, you name it.

My last six months with Jimmie was a living nightmare. He told me: it was my fault he had a job, I loved my family and children not him, I was out to get him, over and over, you name it. He started having real bad dreams at night and would wake up hitting me, so I stop sleeping nights and I started taking naps at the store. I really don't know what was bothering him, but he had change a lot, gotten real jumpy. He had a gun for every room in the house, started making traps to trap people if they came up in our yard, he would even look at the tire track and foot prints in the yard. At times he would set and look out the window with his gun wishing for someone to drive up so he could kill them.

His abuse was even different no more black eyes if he was careful. He started doing body punches in the kidneys you name it, he didn't want anyone to see my bruises so thats what I thought. He started raping me with things like flashlights, you name it. By January I had to have bladder surgery and a hysterectomy because of the things he had done to me. I was very upset just living the life I was living and then to go and have surgery on top of it all. What hurt me the most was that he set down some rules with this surgery. I could never see my family and children again and I would do what ever he said. That was when I just wanted to die. What was next!

I agreed with him and set it up to have surgery at the end of January. I stayed one week in the hospital and so did he. I almost went crazy he didn't want anyone to see me at all when he was at work during the day he would call to make sure the line wasn't busy he even told the nurse not to let anyone see me. After the third day my mother was allowed to see me so she could bring me home, but that was it. Within thirty days I had surgery my family and children taken from me that would mean I could never sneak again to see them.

A week after I was at home he beat the hell out of me and raped me. I wanted to die! During the time I was with Jimmie he had come to me and ask if I would let him shot me and then he would shot hisself and we would die together. At that point I was ready for it. I lost weight and didn't want to live any longer. I couldn't even look out a window without getting in trouble. There would be days that he wouldn't speak to me. My second week home Jimmie came home and started drinking and beat the hell out of me. My face was black and blue one eye closed, all that day he drinked.

He put me in one of our bedrooms for the weekend I was left there 'til Monday morning when my daddy come to check on me because my neighbor had call my family and said they hear a lot of racket over at my house. So he waited for Jimmie to leave to check on me. Opening up that door was the hardest thing I had to do. For my daddy to see me in the shape I was in knowing I just had a major surgery and couldn't even get help for myself. It upset my dad very much and he went to get my mother crying to come take care of me. She came over knowing we were taking a big chance for them being there. I had not eat since Friday and I need a shower. Before I could get out of the shower I past out. My mother doctor me and fed me while I explain what had happen to me. That day Jimmie called at least twelve times to make sure I was there and no one was with me. Of course I lied and said no.

When he arrived home that afternoon he found footprints in the yard so that cause me a ass beating. Once I was able to drive I went back to work. I had to figure out how I was going to get away from Jimmie. During this time I never saw my children and I had to sneak to see my mother. Jimmie told me if he found out that I saw my children or family he would kill them all starting with my kids and ending with my dad, and then me.

So I went to making phone calls. I called the police dept., sheriff's dept. even tried to put him away. Each time I got nowhere. The sheriffs dept. said now Brenda you know Jimmie that's just going to make him worse besides you don't really want to do that to him he'll just get out of it. They were right. See Jimmie had rape and abused his step daughter and nothing ever happen to him. The school had push this and the welfare had even taken her away. So I went to a lawyer for help he was also a friend of our family and knew my problems. He told me he would file for a divorce if that's what I wanted. But if Jimmie wanted me he would find me and hurt me worse. At that time I said fine I'd ask him to leave and take my chance. I felt I would be better off dead. No more beatings and I wouldn't have to live knowing I couldn't be with my children and family.

From the day I ask Jimmie to leave until his death he was very different in lots of ways. In the past he had shot up our T.V., deep freeze, the inside of his truck. He always keep his gun off of safety. The last few weeks before his death he target practice with all of his guns, clean them, slept with them, took them to work with him knowing it was allowed at work. We even talk about letting him shot me and then he would shot hisself. We went as far as going to the place he had pick out for us, but said it wasn't time yet. Things were different like if we were going to war at least that was the way he acted.

The morning that all this happen he woke up drinking and in a bad mood. He accuse me of looking out the window at my father and slapped me. I went to the store that morning and when I got back we got into a fight. All that day we fought all day long. I don't remember very much, but I remember begging for help and for him to please not hurt me anymore.

The night this happen I was put in the hospital and about two wks later I woke up and realize I was in the hospital thinked I was there from my surgery. It was told to me that Jimmie was dead, and that was the first I knew of it. I stayed in the hospital for nine weeks, and saw a doctor up until I was locked up last year. I was release from the hospital and right after that the grand jury indict me for murder. I was out on bond for a year and a half.

My lawyer kept telling me I'd never go to trial, but with the help from Jimmie's mother I had a trial. She wanted justice and would not leave town without it. The day of my trial my lawyer told me the DA said he would plea for five years. My lawyer laugh and said we'll beat this one. The public said my trial was like a three ring circus people comming going the jury spending most of their time outside of the court room. For two weeks this went on I was so confused about things I didn't know if I was comming or going. I never slept during my trial I was running in the back of mine [mind] and reliving my life with Jimmie.

There were so many lies told at that trial I didn't know what really was going on. Everything was very upsetting and not to remember anything that really happen that night really confused me. In fact the people who testified against me knew more about my life and what happen than I did, all hear say! That's what put me here there was no evidence on me at all. They refuse to let my medical reports and doctors in to testify for me. They were more concerned in my money and where I got it. If I had another lover or if I was gay none of it was ever prove. After two weeks I was sentence to twenty five years in prison with a deadly weapon which means I'll spend eight and a half years here without my children and life. I've got my case on appeal but those things could take forever.

In comming to prison it was hard I wanted to die at first. Then I thought I wouldn't let these people beat me. Jimmie had beat me, but not killed me and I made it this far so I could do it. My first three days in prison I couldn't talk at all. I had to write thing down just to let people know what I need. Once on the unit I started group and realized I was also sick in the relationship. Group has help me a lot. I know the difference in a sick relationship now. I've learn how to cry tears not to be scared to cry and that its normal to love your family and yourself. I've got a lot of growing to do in life! To deal with the guilt, hurt, and pain I still have. At times I still feel like giving up, but a part of me wont let me.

Being in prison reminds me of my life with Jimmie in a lot of ways. It's like he's right here with me. I still have trouble sleeping at nights and often talk to myself. Why did he do all of that to me. What really happen that night. I guess that's what bothers me the most. The unknown of it all. I've even begged him [in her prayers] to please tell me what really happen.

I'm writing a journal for my children to read once they're old enough so maybe they'll understand what really happen in my life. My little girl doesnt remember much but my little boy does and he has trouble dealing with things now. I know one day soon my nightmare will end for me and I'll put all this in the past, but until then I'll live one day at a time. ■

**On the Outside Looking In—**
**A Letter from Brenda Whitmire's Mother**
Cyntha Fregia

Anna Belle Burleson was chair of the Formerly Battered Women's Task Force in Austin, Texas, and editor of their newsletter *Heartland*, where different versions of these two pieces appeared. Burleson and her advocacy group have worked for the release of Brenda and other abused women in prison. A heroine in her own right, Burleson uses her personal history of abuse to empower other survivors, to fight for changes in the law and for improvements in the social service system. In 1996, Burleson co-founded the National Domestic Violation Hotline (800-799-SAFE). Recently she established Heartwings, a personal development program that sponsors retreats for women who have survived abuse.

October 4, 1989

Dear Anna Belle:

Brenda told me on our weekend visit about writing her story for you. I told her I was glad she could share her experience of being battered and sexually abused. It is still not always easy for her to open up with her life as I know you know how she feels. Brenda has come a long way with group therapy and counseling in the last eight months. As she said, this counseling is for a cycle of sickness that she probably would never have realized and accepted or seek help for herself in the free world. But now, because of the counseling she has received, she will be able to pick and choose good people to associate with and avoid the sickness that is always lurking around to attack weak people.

I want you to know that through Brenda's counseling and help and her discussions and letters with her Daddy and myself, we now realize the part we played in Brenda's life, the cycle of abuse she thought was right—because as a small child Brenda witnessed her Daddy abusing me. It is sad to look back now recalling the times she remembered from her childhood. Not until she was in first grade did I take a stand against her Daddy because Brenda had spoken to her teacher about being worried about her mother because her Daddy came home from work and was mad and yelling and cursing. She told the teacher she hoped her Daddy wouldn't hurt her Mama because he always hit her. The teacher was kind about trying to let me know—Brenda was upset and crying in class.

Needless to say when I talked to Chester, my husband, about this, he was furious that Brenda had said this. At that time I told Chester his hitting me had to stop. Not only had I never before known that men would hit women, but there was also the shock and hurt for him to hit me and the embarrassment of trying to hide the bruises. The cries of my children, the hysterical spasms my one-year-old little girl would have at the loud roar of her Daddy's voice, made her fear all men at that time. All these years since then I felt I had a good marriage and life; no more physical abuse. But God, did I realize the verbal abuse I took and my children witnessed? Not until I'd been made aware through Brenda did I see the abuse was still there—just in a new form. It is still here between me and Chester. I love him and I know he loves me; he is trying real hard to not make me the victim of his temperament. I told him he can overcome this because he quit hitting me years ago. He still attacks me verbally when things don't go right for him, but he will quit. I feel this.

On our way home from our visit with Brenda and, as she and I called it "our family group session," Chester said to me:

"It's hell our baby has to be in a place like that after all she's gone through in her life, and the vicious beatings she took off of Jimmy to be locked up still being hurt like that."

I said, "It is sad."

He said, "It's hell when you sit and listen that you're to blame for all of her problems."

I told him, "Like she said, she didn't blame us. She just wanted to share her realizations of the sick cycle she has been in. She wants our help to stop this cycle because her two kids are living in this same cycle of sickness." The day she walked away from her children, she put them in another cycle of abuse because their Daddy constantly reminds Josh and Jenny of their mother's leaving them and how bad she is that she's in prison.

Brenda's goal is to walk free to help other victims of abuse and with God's help get professional help for her children so they can be free of this cycle. She has these two beautiful children who so badly need their mother's love and help.

My grandson, Josh, eleven, told me several months ago when I picked him and Jenny, eight, up for a visit: "Mim-maw, I'm so glad you came to get us. I like to go to your house so I can feel free. It's the only time I'm free from being told how bad my Mama is. Mim-maw, that hurts me. I love my Mommy. They don't know how mean Jimmy was to Mommy and us. They don't know what happened but I know Mommy's not mean and she loves us a lot." With tears in his eyes, he said, "Mommy needs to be home so I can live with her. I love her and she loves me."

Jenny said. "Yeah, Mim-maw. We love her and we need to be with her. Can we come stay with you until she comes home; at least you love us like Mommy does."

Dear God, that tore my heart up. I had to pull over to the roadside to hold these babies, they hurt so bad. I talked to their Daddy and stepmother about this and asked if I could take them for counseling and he refused saying that they'll be all right; he's bringing them up right. Can you believe this? Probably so.

I want to share this with you and your newsletter: Brenda says, "No one knows until they've walked in your shoes the life of fear you live. Fear of your life, your families' lives, the living hell you live in, unless you've been there. No one knows the hell you live in prison after years of being the victim until you have been here."

If only we had known where to turn for help.

No one knows the living hell parents go through knowing their child is being battered and sexually abused, not knowing how to help her, without more harm coming to her. And then to still be abused by our legal system and have to be taken away and put in prison. It's a never resting mental hell. Thank you Texas Council on Family Violence for caring. Thank you Anna Belle for the newsletter.

Your friend,

*Cynthia Fregia* ■

**Judge**
Carolyn Page

Raw wind sweeps me up the stone steps
to the court house where I sit with my
Legal Aid attorney.

Faces gawk as the complaint is read,
as he whispers to the judge, bringing
my dainty, flowered diary
to His Honor's attention.
A recess of good reading is followed by:
"Bailiff, clear the courtroom."
My lawyer says it's going well.
"What's going well?"
"It appears he likes the way
you've, uh, documented the . . . .
Oh, here he comes."

"Meet with me in chambers?"
He smiles benignly and motions.
I wonder what he wears beneath those robes,

which description of prolonged
conjugal cruelty he's savored most.

"It seems he threatened you
if you didn't give him . . . ."
"Yes!"
"And how long on your knees?"
"An hour or two, usually."
"If you don't mind my asking,
how did he manage to . . ."
"But I do mind, Your Honor."

An hour later my witness verifies
my estrangement, that I've lived alone,
and finally . . . I have my decree.
Next day my diary is returned to me.

Two weeks later, ten at night His Honor
calls expressing his concern,
suggests we meet for drinks
at his house, but I wriggle free,
still wondering what he wears beneath. ■

**Married Lies**

Diana Hannon

The first time he hit me, I cried.
Worse than the slap
was the thought that
somehow
I deserved it.

The next time he hit me, I left.
Bundled up the kids
went home to mother.
Oh
How he wept and pleaded.

Sugar, Sweetie-pie, Darling, Baby
Forgive me. It'll never happen again.
I gave in.

The last time he hit me,
I didn't cry
didn't leave
didn't give in.

I shot him
quickly, deliberately
Bending down with anguished face I pleaded,

Sugar, Sweetie-pie, Darling, Baby
Forgive me. It'll never happen again.
And once more I pulled the trigger. ■

**Betrayal**

Debbie Mae Furlough

I was twenty-two when I met Tim, the man who became my batterer. I had just left my first husband when our marriage fell apart after the crib death of our only child.

Tim was easy to talk to and very understanding. He helped me to heal and get stronger. We lived together for several months. We had to struggle just to get by financially. One day he demanded all my money and got very angry. I decided to leave. I moved to another town and got a job.

Everything was fine until I found out I was pregnant. I knew I should let him know and I did. Before I knew what was happening we were back together, living at my parents. I thought we should get married but he refused.

I lost my job when I moved home. He worked for a couple of months until he hurt his back. Things were good between us then. We were both anxious about the upcoming birth of our child. Then one morning he argued with me. I don't remember what it was about. He turned over a bookcase in my mom's living room, hit me, called mom and me names, and shoved a chair into me.

He apologized afterwards and promised to never do it again. I believed him and Mom and I forgave him. I never realized that this would set the pace of my life for the next couple of years.

Things were good for the first couple months after our daughter was born. It didn't last though. I thought things would be better if we had an income and a place of our own. I got a job a little over a year after giving birth. I started saving up money to rent us a place. He wanted a motor cycle. We argued and he knocked me down on the bedroom floor, twisted my arm and told me to give him the money or he'd break it.

I gave him the money and started saving again. He started taking me back and forth to work when I went on night-shift, sometimes sitting in the car all night to make sure I didn't try to leave. I found a place to rent. It was close to my parents' house but it would be our own. We had to wait a couple of weeks to move in. Now he insisted that we get married. I didn't want to, but after being slapped and knocked around so much I was desperate. I thought if I do everything he wants he won't hit me anymore.

After our marriage and move, things just got worse. The violence that I had been victim of increased and also turned onto our daughter.

He told me that he'd asked my eleven year old sister to have sex with him and that he had thought of having our two year old daughter first. I was so shocked I didn't know whether to believe him or not.

I got my sister alone and questioned her. I then knew it was true. I went to the Police Department. I explained that I was being beaten regularly and that my sister felt threatened by him. They said there was nothing they could do until he actually did something. I felt helpless and scared.

He threatened to hit me with a hammer one night if I didn't have sex with him. I struggled and broke free from him. I ran out the back door and tripped off of the back porch. I remember the sharp burning pain when he rammed the hammer handle into my vagina. I must have blacked out because the next thing I remember I was sitting up on the side of the porch. He was holding me and apologized, crying. I felt numb.

One night he held me out over a bridge railing and threatened to throw me off. Another night he put a knife to my throat and said he was going to kill me. I told him to go ahead.

Our daughter was sitting in the corner of the room crying. He went over to her and put a cigarette out on her head. He told her, "There, now you have something to cry about."

He would watch me as I slept. He'd wake me up by slapping, pinching or burning me. He tried to suffocate me with a pillow once until I passed out. It was a living nightmare.

One morning I woke up to the sight of him, pants down, penis erect. Our daughter lay before him diaperless, legs spread. I don't know if I gasped, screamed or if he just sensed I was awake. Next thing I knew he had knocked me back onto my bed. He asked me if I wanted to live or die. Then he laughed and said for me not to worry, he hadn't done anything.

The next day he was supposed to go to another town to look for work and stay with family. He was going to send back money for our daughter and me to come join him. My cousin was going to drive him there. As we rode he turned to me and whispered, "You wouldn't go to the police or anything stupid like that would you?" I told him, "No."

He had my cousin stop for some beer. He ordered me to get out and get it for him. When I got back in the truck he was telling her he had changed his mind about going that day. As we drove back toward home he whispered to me over and over, "What you accused me of, I'm going to do." I knew he was talking about what I had seen the day before when I awoke to see him with our daughter.

He asked my cousin to pull off the road at a remote creek where he had been fishing. We got out there and sat on the water's edge. He kept whispering, "What you accused me of, I'm going to do." I was scared.

When he said he was going to do it tonight, I got a gun out of the truck and shot him. The gun wouldn't fire again. I jumped up and grabbed another gun from the truck and shot again. It's a nightmare I'll never fully wake up from.

At trial I was convicted of first degree murder. I am now waiting on a retrial, which I was granted through Appeal.

■■■

January 1991
Comment on Debbie's Story

Ruth Peachey, M.D.
Consultant in Research and Social Psychiatry

Three years ago when I was asked to "examine" Debbie in preparation for testifying as an expert witness at her trial for first-degree murder, she was overwhelmed with deep feelings of pain, guilt, grief, loss, and confusion. She was suffering from both physical and psychological symptoms that are characteristic of Battered Woman Syndrome, a subcategory of Post-Traumatic Stress Disorder.

After two years of incarceration she has worked through her dreadful experiences and healed herself to the point where she has made sense of the senseless and has regained a solid self-worth, despite her "nightmare" from which she "will never fully awake."

Retelling her story now, in a matter-of-fact way as though detached from the horrendous past, illustrates what battered women call "numbing out," as one way of dealing with what is intolerable. Numbing out is a way of defending against and enduring severe abuse without losing one's sanity. Technically, it is called "dissociation."

Most victims of abuse who heal and become survivors nevertheless bear scars, one of which is reluctance to relive the trauma and a tendency to "numb out" if forced to revive painful memories, as is inevitable for Debbie as she prepares for re-trial.

■■■

*Update from Debbie on her Case*

On Monday, April 15, 1991, I was reconvicted of First Degree Murder. My lawyers are starting the appeal process over for me.

My sister, who was allowed to testify at the second trial, has finally been freed from him. She feels no more shame or pain.

I live free even from inside the razor wire. I take my memories and emotions from that time of abuse in my life and stick them away from me like old boots in the back of the closet. My prayers are that someday we can all live in love, peace and harmony.

Deb ■
July 1991

## Free at Last: From a Prison in Colorado

Beverly Hirsch

*Editor's Note:*

In 1984, Beverly Hirsch was sentenced to Federal Correctional Institution, Lexington, Kentucky, on federal welfare fraud charges. In May 1985, she was transferred to the Cope House, a half-way house in Dayton, Ohio, from which her (then) ex-husband Sam McKamey kidnapped her and held her hostage. Hirsch's current interment is the result of a 1987 crime spree that followed that kidnapping. Though it must be noted that Hirsch had prior convictions for bad checks and welfare fraud dating back to 1976, McKamey cut a deal with the Jefferson County District Attorney whereby he would go free in return for statements placing all the blame on her. McKamey was never prosecuted. Hirsch plead guilty and received a sentence of forty years from Judge Gaspar Perricone.

Subsequent to his August 1986 statement, McKamey wrote two letters, one dated November 20, 1986, and one dated March 3, 1987, to United States District Court Magistrate Michael R. Merz, in Dayton. He confessed that he had kidnapped Hirsch from the half-way house and forced her to commit the crimes, asking for reconsideration of her case.

Rather than including most of the violence Beverly suffered at Sam's hands (though some is described), these excerpts focus on Hirsch's experiences within the walls of the prison system.

My file on Beverly Hirsch includes her eighty-one-page autobiography, several legal documents associated with her case, a psychological report written by Lenore Walker, which evaluates her as a victim of battered woman syndrome, numerous articles she wrote while in prison for *Jubilee*, a Christian newsletter, and copies of articles about her in *New Directions for Women*, *Time*, and several newspapers.

■■■

*June 10, 1984: FCI, Lexington, Kentucky*

I arrived at the Federal Prison escorted by two U. S. Marshals on a hot day in June. Never being involved with the Government before I was, needless to say, scared to death. We came in the door to a large reception area, our names were taken and then we were told to go to R&D, short for receiving and discharge. We walked down the two flights of stairs, me in shackles, belly chain and handcuffs, [walking between] the two aloof Marshals. I entered the door to a dimly lit dungeon that badly needed paint, with a number of weather-beaten tables. The Marshals took the chains off, and said, "This is it, good luck" and with that they both walked out, leaving me behind.

I brought a huge suitcase of clothes and items that I thought I would need, only to discover I was not going to get a thing! The suitcase was addressed back home and that was the end of that. I was allowed to keep the clothes I wore in, and that was all.

The next several hours were filled with the processing of my body into the Bureau of Prisons (BOP) computer system. It was late that evening before I got out, but no matter when it would have been, I was not prepared for what I was walking into.

My first step into prison had to be equivalent to how Alice must have felt when she stepped through the looking glass. The courtyard was beautifully landscaped, men and women were strolling around the walk, holding hands. I just stared, because I couldn't believe this prison was "co-ed."

After the first shock wore off, I became fluent with what was expected of me, [what] was and was not allowed. The basics with the men was "just don't get caught." A rule book was handed out and if you followed it, I doubted one would have much trouble. I didn't intend to have any problems while I was there. I just wanted to do my time [three years], and get back to my family.

I phoned home to reassure Sam and the boys that everything was all right. I gave them the visiting hours and they said they would see me that weekend, but I left out one fact, it was co-ed. I knew when Sam found this out, there was going to be hell to pay! And boy was I ever right!

It didn't take long for Sam to start the same old jealousy crap. He moved to Lexington so he would be able to come every day. He told me if he came everyday, I wouldn't have a chance to be with anyone else. The fact that there were men there put extreme pressure on me. Before long Sam began accusing me of being with the men. How could I tell him I worked, ate and participated in programs and recreation with them, but that I did not have the popular "walkie" relationship with any of them. Sure I had friends, but I was not with anyone, and really didn't intend to get involved in that scene.

Sam's abuse of me continued even while I was locked up. Five months after I was there I had come out of the visiting room on more than one occasion with bruises from Sam grabbing me. Would I never be free of this? Rusty [her fifteen-year-old son] was living with Sam and I felt I could not jeopardize that, at least not right then because I had no one to take care of him. So for now I felt I had to play his game with his rules. I did, until . . .

Rusty phoned the institution saying it was an emergency. Phone calls are not allowed and messages are rarely given, but my counselor, Ms. Christianson, just happened to be there to take the call. My son was hysterical; Sam had phoned from work saying he was going to kill him when he got home. Evidently what had been going on was Sam was supplying my son with pot and other drugs. I didn't even know Sam did drugs. Rusty left a plastic glass on the stove and it melted, causing a great deal of smoke and the fire department was called. When they came in, there was pot laying on the end table. Sam was afraid they'd be back with a search warrant, thus his remedy was to threaten a fifteen-year-old child with murder. . . . I was in prison, my hands were tied as to what I could do. But with the help of my counselor we got Rusty on a bus to Dayton where my mother met him taking him home to live with them.

The following evening, Sam came to the prison. He already knew I had helped Rusty leave Lexington, but I would not tell him where Rusty was. I was standing at my usual spot behind the glass entrance doors in the courtyard, watching for him. He walked in, all 285 pounds of him, took his green army jacket off, setting it beside the metal detector, walked through it himself, picking up the coat on his way up the ramp to the visiting area. I went to the door in back. I was anxious and scared of what kind of a scene he was going to make tonight because of Rusty, but I knew I had to face him. Now that I had Rusty out of Sam's care I felt I could make a move on getting Sam out of my life too.

I feel reasonably sure that Sam must have realized this because that night he came prepared. He was nice at first, then he became more difficult. Everything I said he acted like I didn't know what I was talking about, that I just fell off a turnip truck and how could I even think about managing my life without him? What I didn't realize was that on the Saturday visit he had seen me walk across the walkway with a male staff member who just happened to be leaving, a coincidence, nothing more. He didn't even mention it then, but today, Wednesday, he decided to pick a fight about it, swearing I must be getting it on with him because we looked too chummy. If I'd just admit it, he would understand, but at least I should tell him the truth. My insistence of innocence only made him more furious, until finally he grabbed me, holding me hard, putting his coat between us and near my hip.

Then he reached into his pocket, jabbed me and I froze, my blood turned to ice when he said, "How fast do you think they can get to me after I blow you away?"

This man, the one who said he loved me, couldn't live without me, the same one who made those promises of getting help and never hurting me ever again, now had a gun pointed at me from within his coat pocket. I knew better than to move. I remembered well the other incidents and I was not going to risk being killed by this crazy man. I realized too when he came in that night that he had been drinking, he reeked of booze and his eyes were bloodshot. I was a little surprised they even allowed him to come in that kind of condition.

Anyway, the fact remained he was here and I was here and the gun was between us and he did have his finger on the trigger. How I ever got out of this one I will never know. But I calmly told him how much I loved him, how much I needed him, that my life depended on him. He didn't see through it, all he had to do was pull the trigger, I couldn't risk that, so I lied, told him everything I thought he wanted to hear and it worked, he put his coat back on the floor, then laid his head on my shoulder and told me he just couldn't live without me and he was so afraid of losing me. Shortly after this encounter, I went to the rest room and talked with the guard and asked her if she would ask Sam to leave, as there were too many people visiting that night and the locals would have to go so the others could come in. He left and I nearly collapsed with relief that he was finally gone.

The following day I had a session with my psychologist. I told him what had happened the evening before in the visiting room, not realizing he was allowed to void our confidentiality if he felt there was a security breach or a danger of that happening. Later that day I was summoned to the warden's office. There were a number of people sitting in there and after a short discussion I was given the choice of discontinuing his visiting privileges or they would do it for me. I chose to take him off my visiting list. I felt like the whole world's burdens were lifted from my shoulders. I was very happy about the turn of events and not unhappy at all that Mr. Simpson had discussed with others what I had told him in confidence.

I did not phone, write or have any further contact with Sam. I assumed he would probably move back home, but I didn't want to know. In March of 1985 I was going to take a five-day furlough to my parents' house. I intended to stay with them, file for divorce, sign up for college and interview for a job I'd been offered at Wright Patterson Air Force Base.

■■■

Only one of my friends knew I would be coming home, a previous co-worker and a very good friend. What I didn't know was that she had become close to Sam in my absence and that she was going to tell Sam I was going to be at my parents' house. Why she chose to violate my trust in her, I don't know, but to make a long story short, Sam found out I was home.

Phoning me at my parents, a shock to me and them both, he threatened to sell all my things in storage, to smash what he couldn't sell and then come looking for my parents, my kids and don't forget the dog. My god, I was panic stricken! What was I going to do? My mother flat refused to allow me to go anywhere near him so I told him to come up and we would talk. He did, his trusty gun with him. I was standing outside. He was in the car and my mother came out. She told Sam to give her his gun if he wanted to talk to me. He told her to go to hell, grabbed me through his open door and sped off down the lane, the door flying and me hanging on for dear life. My mother, screaming hysterically for my father, began running after the car. Needless to say that was hopeless. Sam took me about a mile from their house and beat the crap out of me. Then he left me lying there torn cloths, battered and bloody.

By the time I reached my parents' house they were near frantic with worry. The sheriff was there. They all stared at me when I came through the door. I must have been a sight. My mother was never one to handle blood well, but she was pretty good that night. Hugging me she helped me into the bathroom. I couldn't tell her that Sam had raped me, that just wasn't something you talked about. I think she knew but I also think she didn't want me to say it.

After I was cleaned up, I had to face the now impatient sheriff deputies. I refused to discuss anything with them and would not press charges. My mother was furious with me, she thought that Sam should be put behind bars. I was too scared of him to feel safe in doing anything. I just wanted to be left alone.

Before I left my parents I had to go get my things from his parents' house. My father took me. I picked up things without incident and Dad and I went over to my sister's house where my car was parked. I had planned to take it up to the farm so they could put it in the barn.

Dad had just left when Sam pulled into my sister's driveway. I was scared to death because he had been drinking. My sister took off for the house to call the Trotwood police. They got there in only seconds to find me flat against my car trying to get away. As the officers detained him with questions I sped away. That didn't stop him, he came to my parents house that night around 11:00 P.M., scaring the heck out of all of us by throwing a beer bottle through my parents picture window. Again the sheriff was called, but by the time they got there this time, Sam was long gone. Again no charges were pressed.

The following day my mother took me to the attorney's office where I gave him $400 to start the divorce. I was being released to a half-way house in May, just eight weeks away and I wanted that divorce hearing as soon as I got back to Dayton. My mother drove me to the bus terminal in downtown Dayton where I boarded the Greyhound back to the walls that would hold me for eight more weeks in safety, or at least I thought, if only temporary.

■■■

*1987-1989: FCI, Lexington, Kentucky*

Since I had been at Lex before, I had no real problem with being there. This was a co-ed facility, and I knew if I had to do time, this is the icing on the cake. I immediately went to work in automated data processing (ADP) as that is where I worked when I was there before.

A lot had changed in three years, including all the supervisors. Two months after I was there, one of the programmers came to me with the prototype of the new program going to be run for HUD. We had become pretty good friends, and we were both in for hot checks and fraud type crimes. What she showed me was copies of people's credit history, social security number, employment, income, credit rating, bank balances in both checking and savings account, with the account numbers, including credit card numbers. I was amazed at this information, and could not believe a job like this was intended to come into a prison. I became angry at the fact I'd just gotten forty years for getting this information on the street, and using it to commit fraud, and the government was going to hand it to me on a silver platter and not expect anyone to use it. They had to be crazy!

I went to [my supervisor] and told him how I felt about this new contract. He explained to me they had not been awarded the contract yet, but they were bidding on it, and that is why the prototype was made. It was a million-dollar contract, and we had lost so much work over the past year, the contract was needed to keep the ADP factory open. He assured me that information would not be on the actual entry program, but these were just samples of the "type" data that would need to be keyed.

That kept me quiet for a while. Then two months after this conversation, we were awarded the contract. Again I went to [my supervisor] and questioned whether or not the same information I saw on the other sheets would be sent in. He again assured me that it would not be.

In came the contract, and low and behold, identical sheets just like the ones I'd seen just months prior to the awarding of the contract. I was furious. How could the government justify putting inmates in a situation where they could use the information to conduct further crime? I was already aware this was in process as I had been asked how they [inmates] could scam the info since this was my type of crime. After receiving forty years for this, I intended to stop the government any way I could, and be damned if I would stop at nothing. The stupidest thing in the world is to think you can take on the government single handed. I'm here to verify that only a fool does this, and you cannot win. But I sure gave them a run for their money.

The first letter I wrote was to a friend that writes for the *National Enquirer*. He picked up on it right away, but every time he called to verify my story he was told that it wasn't true, and I quote his words, "They said there would never be any thing sent into the prison like that." I wasn't going to give up, somehow I was going to get someone's attention.

I went to [my supervisor] again, telling him how wrong I thought this contract was. He told me, "If you don't like it, get a job change." That just added fuel to the fire. But, he already had a plan for me! That evening I was called into the Lt.'s office at which time I was informed an incident report had been written on me by [him]. I couldn't believe it, [he] had written me up on some bogus charge to get me sent to segregation, and of course lose my job. Well, that worked, but I'm sure he was not ready for the consequences of his act either. I wrote five BP 9s, contacted a local reporter, and declared war! I was found not guilty of the alleged charge and released from segregation two days later.

I went back to work in ADP. [My supervisor] was dead set on getting me out of ADP though. He told me to sign a job-change. When I refused and told him to fire me, I could do something about that since I was his third best "keyer." And that's exactly what he did, fired me.

I got on the typewriter and proceeded to type letters to Senator Ted Kennedy, the US Attorney General, HUD in Washington, D.C., and a few others. The letters were posted on a Monday, and by Friday, at 7:00 P.M., I was summoned to the Warden's office. While being escorted by two Lts., I asked if I was going back to segregation, and to my surprise the one stated "right now the warden would like to bury you under segregation."

Awaiting me in the office was Patrick Kane, Warden, Capt. Davis, Harry Coleman, Superintendent of UNICOR, the U.S. Attorney, and one

Secret Service Agent. It was quite obvious that none of them believed what I'd claimed, and they were not in the best of humor that they were sitting in the warden's office on a Friday evening. I stated the facts, and it wasn't until 11 P.M. I was allowed to return to my room.

They were now going to go to the ADP office and see if I was telling the truth. The one comment made to me that I will never forget is this: Mr. Coleman was defending his ADP supervisor . . . they are not there and they would never be as the material would be far too sensitive to sent into a prison.

At 7 the next morning, Saturday, there was a U-Haul van that pulled into the back loading area of UNICOR, out got two armed U.S. Marshals. Already there were the secret service agent from the evening before, Kane, Coleman, five officials flown in from D.C. and of course the U.S. Attorney. They proceeded to remove every sheet of paper from the ADP factory.

On Christmas day, 1988 the front page read, "Inmates have access to Credit Cards and much more." On December 30, the headlines read, "HUD contract canceled at the FCI in Lexington, KY after inmate 'blew the whistle.'" *Time* magazine contacted me to do an article. The January issue read: "Criminal Charges?" and a photo accompanied the article. The magazine (January 9, 1989) was released at noon on January 2, and by 2 P.M. I found myself again in lock down. Now they claimed it was for my own protection. Who from? The administration? Those that were going to lose their jobs? Who? Didn't matter, I knew I would never get back out, and I was going to be shipped.

On January 17th I was taken from segregation and packed out, then sent on my way to another facility. I was soon to learn I was being shipped to Pleasanton, a facility in the Bay area of California. This is what is known to the federal inmates as "Diesel Therapy." This means an inmate has caused trouble at one facility, and he/she is transferred to another. Five days a week, two DC-10s do nothing but fly inmates across the country. The waste of tax payers' money is absolutely not a consideration as they plain don't know. This is not an ordinary trip. As you board, there is a four point U.S. Marshal rifle team, you are shackled and belly chained with cuffs attached to the waist. You board from the steps, which are extremely difficult with chains on, if you stumble or make any fast moves you are likely to look down the barrel of a rifle, so you make an attempt to not make any unexpected moves. Once seated, there are five Marshals and a P.A. (physician assistant) on board, the two pilots are part of the U.S. Marshals also. Washington D.C. schedules the flights, and we're off to wherever, but you can bet, it will be days before you get to your destination. When an inmate is put into "Diesel Therapy," he/she is aware it could take months to get to the next facility. That evening we got into Birmingham, AL where we stayed for two days.

I want to explain the conditions one has to deal with. No comb, no toothbrush, no toothpaste, no deodorant, no soap, no clean clothes. Birmingham to me was the worse place we stopped, although many will disagree and say it was Norman, OK. In Birmingham, you are placed in a double cell. At 5:00 A.M. you are woke up and forced to go to the day room, where breakfast is served at 5:30. A normal menu would be cold grits, green scrambled eggs, and dry soggy toast. No milk, sugar, salt or butter. And black coffee. There is no choice of getting up to eat, everyone must leave their room. The inmate is not allowed to return to his/her room until 10:30 P.M. In the meantime you have a TV. No laying on the floor, you must sit at the picnic-like table for eighteen and a half hours. We were given no towels, so taking a shower was difficult too when you have to dry yourself with a wash cloth, and then put back on the same clothes as before your showered.

Our next stop was Norman, OK. I found this much more tolerable. The food is good and at least you can take a cold shower (there is no hot water). Again no personal hygiene items are given but sometimes a comb can be borrowed from one of the other inmates. The bad part of course is trying to put four in a cell made for two. Going to the toilet is hazardous for the persons laying on the floor, of course there is no room to walk anyway, so it's not easy to avoid stepping on them. I was there for ten days, the usual stay is three, then we were off to Hunting Beach, CA; same day back to Phoenix, AZ. Then to Denver, this is one day flying and I'm not counting all the little stops in between. When we arrive in Denver, I'm removed from the plane. I couldn't believe it because our next stop was Sacramento, which was my stop. Two Marshals were waiting for me and proceeded to head towards Wyoming. I couldn't believe this but of course nothing should surprise any federal inmate when they already knew the horror stories of these trips from others. The date was January 28, 1989, eleven days after leaving Kentucky. I was bounced like a ball all over the great state of Wyoming, only to be brought back to Denver on May 3rd, headed west one more time on the "air-lift." Of course by now I have learned the lesson being taught quite well, this is their way of saying, don't "blow the whistle" or this could happen all over. I'm a quick learner, but not intimidated easy either.

*Editor's Note:*

[Beverly goes on to describe the dehumanizing experience of the rest of the "air-lift," including one incident where they "sat in 100° F weather for five hours, no supper, no water, no bathroom, no moving, no standing, no anything!" She arrived in Pleasanton, California, on May 5, 1989, a facility she "liked," though she describes "doing co-ed time" as "difficult." Her account of her time there includes her involvement with an abusive fellow inmate.]

One would think that after the "diesel therapy" I received for blowing the whistle in Lexington I would not get myself further involved in fighting the BOP. As I said, I can not easily be intimidated anymore. One of the things that came out of the trouble in Lex was that I'd begun writing for a Christian magazine in California. My topic was always the abuse of taxpayers' money by the government.

Shortly after arriving in Pleasanton I exposed the UNICOR sewing factory for exposing inmates to hazardous material, formaldehyde. But the best one was when I busted the Captain helping his self to hunting rifles that the government footed the bill to the tune of $42,000 plus. He was transferred the day after the story hit the stands.

A counselor, not even mine, gave me a direct order that I could not write about any other inmates, the staff or any event in the prison. By giving me that direct order in front of witnesses, I knew I had her.

Within twenty-four hours my attorney, Deborah Levy, filed in the Federal Court a civil rights suite against the BOP and Ms. Williams, alleging a violation of my First Amendment rights—the freedom of speech. Within days of the filing, the direct order was unofficially rescinded, and I was unofficially told I could send any newspaper clipping I wanted out of the paper. Part of the direct order was that I could not clip and send out of the institution any controversial articles. When it went to court, I was to be given an apology and the BOP was told to formally take the direct order back. Two months later and four letters from my attorney to the U. S. Attorney's office the order was taken back.

In the meantime Senator Alan Cranston was contacted and if it had not been for his office's intervention, I would have been shipped again, another "Diesel Therapy" trip. Somehow I survived the nine months at Pleasanton. I was then illegally transported to the state of Colorado to finish their sentence, which I am currently doing (court action pending). I arrived (here) at the Canon City [Colorado] Woman's Correctional Facility, where I am told my parole eligibility date is February 5, 1995. On June 22, 1990, I appeared before Judge Gasper Perricone in Jefferson County District Court. . . . Dr. Lenore E. Walker, who had testified at a hearing in Ft. Collins the previous March, testified. Perricone was so adamant about the term, he stated that he didn't care how good I had been in the federal prison, he felt society needed to be protected from me. In 1988 he had reduced my term to sixteen years to be served concurrently to the federal term, and he would not reduce it further. My mother drove to Denver from Dayton, Ohio, with my sister and brother-in-law. The judge still would not budge. I had to prepare my mother for Dr. Walker's testimony, because she was not aware of the [extent of] abuse or cruelty Sam put me through. I was really worried she would not be able to handle it, but she did and she was strong for me, as it was very difficult for me to hear.

Where does it all stand now? I am currently on appeal on the Jefferson County June 22nd hearing. It could be years before I hear anything and the likely hood of winning is almost non-existent. . . . Sam? Well, he's still out there, enjoying his freedom, most likely unchanged, free to torture or kill another woman. I once sent him a Birthday card. It read: Have a nice day from the wife you put away.

**Glossary**

*Walkie* —prison lingo for male/female pair that walk around holding hands.

*BP-9* is an administrative remedy for the inmate to address a problem with the staff. Normal procedure is for a staff member to investigate the alleged issue and then forward it to the warden for him to review, make a decision, sign and return the answer to the inmate.

*UNICOR* is prison industries inside the federal prison, a privately owned government company.

*Comment:*

Dr. Lenore Walker concludes in her nine-page report, filed with the court on March 28, 1990, that:

> Beverly Hirsch was a battered woman in her relationship with Sam McKamey, that she had developed Battered Woman Syndrome, a subcategory of Post Traumatic Stress Disorder, and that there is still some evidence of the PTSD today. Further she committed the check cashing in Jefferson County under the duress of Sam McKamey and accepted a plea in Larimer County without fully understanding the implications of such an act, due to the Battered Woman Syndrome, one result of which is a strong denial of the seriousness of the abuse to others and minimization and repression of the potential and actual abuse.

■■■

*Editor's Note:*

At the conclusion of the hearing, Judge Perricone rejected Hirsch's motion and Dr. Walker's evaluation. The judge found her to deserve no mercy and sentenced her to forty years. This same Judge Perricone sentenced Floyd A. Flore, who pleaded guilty for criminally negligent child abuse, to four years imprisonment. Six-month-old infant Alicia Nicole Hurtado died on October 22, 1989, as a result of brain injury caused by

Flore's in repeatedly shaking the crying baby. According to a newspaper article by Marlys Duran, a *Rocky Mountain News* staff writer, Judge Perricone could have sentenced Flore to up to sixteen years in prison but chose the lesser penalty because "shaking wasn't as violent as the abuse some children suffer." ■

**Letters from an Arizona Prison**
Latricia T. Brown

Jan. 23, 1992
Dear Miriam Harris,

I am a female inmate at the A.S.P.C. (Arizona State Prison Complex) serving thirteen years, no parole for second degree murder. My release date is Aug. 16, 2002. My defense was temporary insanity (self-defense).

I had been in a religiously oriented business relationship for less than one year. This relationship turned into a very possessive controlling and adulterous nightmare. I was trapped in an abusive relationship, both mentally and physically. The day of the incident was Aug. 16, 1989. Earlier in that day I had an abortion. While I was asleep in my bed, Melvin Wilson raped me from my anus. Wilsons body was found naked in the driveway by the paperboy. He had been shot, and he was dead. It's been three years, and I still do not remember everything that happen that terrible night. I remember the rape and screaming to him to get out, "I'm not a DOG," and he ran out the door. I didn't know that I shot him. I remember closing my eyes and pulling the trigger, but I didn't know that I had hit him. I [was] just wanting him to leave me alone. My psychologist says I had a "Brief Reaction Psychosis." The same diagnosis as a Mark Austin of Arizona. He was the man who in 1989 stabbed his estranged wife to death. He was found innocent by reason of insanity and spent six months at the Arizona State Hospital. I am presently at the Flamenco Mental Health Center, which is on the Arizona State Hospital Grounds. I've been under psychiatric care since 1970, as well as taking psychiatric medications. In 1970, I was raped by two men at gunpoint. (There is a police report on file in Indiana to prove this.) My current diagnosis is, "Brief Reaction Psychosis in the context of a chronic bipolar disorder, mixed personality disorder, with marked histrionic and compulsive traits." In 1970 I had a mental breakdown and I was committed to a psychiatric hospital for six months. Since then I've been hospitalized three other times for manic depression.

If I'm not mistaken, Mark Austin had not been under any psychiatric care. When a woman is mentally and physically abused there are no words to describe the suffering, pain, and humiliation. And because of this humiliation and fear, thousands of cases are never reported, and nothing is done until the abuser dies and the abused woman is sent to prison for murder. This is not Justice. Women are being put aside as they have been for centuries. We are left with mental and physical scars for the rest of our lives. The courts are not sensitive to our human sufferings. When I read about Mark Austin, I could only breakdown and cry. I thank God for governors like Gov. Richard Celeste of Ohio, who granted clemency to twenty-five women prisoners who he said committed crimes because they were victims of battering or other forms of physical or emotional abuse. Yet here in the State of Arizona our rights as women are being violated. Arizona does not support a self-defense law.

Since I have no family or friends in Arizona, I've submitted paperwork for a Correctional Interstate Transfer. I have been waiting for two yrs, when it only takes 90 days to process. They first told me I would have to pay $1800 for the transfer. Now it's $3,250. They are trying their best to screw me with discouragement.

Ms. Harris, enclosed is my manuscript. I know you said no more than (25 pages max) I hope that the 28 pages will be exceptable. I must explain that I wrote this to all churches, because of the position they have in our society, and because of what I experienced before my incarceration. As you read it you will understand.

I have been raised-up in the Pentecostal Church, with moral views on life. And this was the main issue during my trial. (My character). . . .

Sincerely
Latricia T. Brown #80226

Arizona State Prison Complex

April 6, 1992

Dear Miriam,

Thank you for writing. Your letter was very much appreciated. It so happens that I had been told by officers that my "religious tapes" will be confiscated, and I'm being denied "Quiet Time" in one of the isolation cells ("The Hole").

Of course I've been praying every day in private, but because I "pray" it's forbidden. I've talked to the clergy and he mumbles, jumbles. So I've written to the "Civil Rights Division," and "The Civil Liberties Union."

The system is designed to take your hope away. I feel that being incarcerated is more than enough punishment. I am not in prison to be punished and no prison system is legally authorized to inflict additional punishment.

They are pushing inmates to "suicide." We are still confronted with a more humiliating harassment, which results in rape. We're told to seek out "Justice," but that same "Justice" puts us into a bottomless pit of more shame, fear, and humiliation.

Law Prof. Anita Hill stands in my mind as a woman of outstanding courage and dignity. I believe that God used her as the instrument which made it possible for sexual harassment to come out of the closet, but there are still a lot of women who are not coming forward.

It's time for us to band together and form a strong women's movement. I believe that such a movement will reflect the views of all women.

For centuries women tend not to share information with one another, and this is the reason why men have been so successful, they believe in helping each other.

Thank you again for reading my manuscript. I had an article in the "Religious Column" of the *Phoenix Gazette*, and I'm working on another project. I would be honored if you use quotes from my letter.

Please send me a copy of your book. It's so good to know that women like you are around helping us fight for our "human rights."

I have a burden for women in prison, there are so many injustices we experience. All programs are geared to helping the male inmates. Women in prison are a forgotten lot.

I'm presently organizing, "Adopt A Prison For Christ Ministries." This program is geared to helping women in prison and the ex-offender.

I pray that your writings will open up Societies eyes to the sufferings of women.

You will be remembered in my prayers. May God continue to bless you and your loved ones.

Sincerely,

Patricia T. Brown #80226 ■

**Escaping A Gilded Cage**

Judith Strasser

*Spring 1990: A Prologue, in Retrospect*

The classified ad in *Poets and Writers* requests first-person stories from battered women. "Women in prison, especially" the ad encourages to write. But all battered women live in prisons; I think that is the point.

I lived in a prison for years, until the early morning of December 5, 1986, when Michael, my husband, punched me in the eye, and I decided at long last to break out. No matter that he had an Ivy League education and a Ph.D. in chemistry. No matter that I had a master's degree in "communications research." No matter that we had plenty of money, a house on a lake, a sailboat, that our children attended private school. My prison—our prison, really, although I don't think Michael knew it—simply had gilded bars.

Through the end of that December and into January, I sported an impressive black eye. I went to work, drove carpools, shopped for Christmas presents and groceries, talked with sales clerks and moving men without trying to hide it. The men who saw me—friends and strangers—

asked, "What happened to you?"

"My husband punched me," I told them, and they were visibly shocked, terribly upset. More than one man hugged me tight, tears brimming in his eyes.

The women who saw me didn't need to ask. They understood right away, whether they knew me or not.

*Looking Backward: 1985*

I made my first run at the prison bars just after my forty-first birthday, September 30, 1985. It was a glorious fall day, sunny and blue, the air spiked with a hint of cold coming down from Canada. Mike was out of town, racing his sailboat at a weekend regatta. I drove to an old house near the state capitol, a center for the prevention of drug and alcohol abuse. I hoped the people at the center could answer some questions for me. Does social drinking include four or five double shots of Jack Daniels on the rocks? Can someone be an alcoholic if he only drinks after 6 P.M.? Do alcoholics pass out on the couch after dinner every night? Is my husband an alcoholic? How can I stop him from drinking? I desperately needed to know.

But I didn't want to go in. Someone might see me. I might get answers I didn't like. I gathered my courage and opened the door, looked around, embarrassed and confused. The room was small, full of chairs, an old couch, a battered reception desk. I approached the receptionist.

"Uh, do you have any information about alcoholism?" It seemed a stupid question, but it was all I could think to say.

"The library's in there." The receptionist pointed me toward the next room, floor to ceiling books. Several shelves displayed stacks of pamphlets for sale: "Facts about Alcohol and Alcoholism," "Alcoholic in the Family?" "Crossing the Thin Line Between Social Drinking and Alcoholism" "Alcohol: Simple Facts About Combinations with Other Drugs," I browsed for a few minutes, grabbed up twenty dollars' worth of pamphlets, and rushed home to read in privacy.

I called my close friend Sara, the adult child of an alcoholic father. "I think Mike's an alcoholic," I said.

"So what's new?" she responded. "You told me that at least a year ago."

*The Early Years: 1972–1982*

In fact, I had been battling denial for a very long time. Michael and I had married in 1972, after living together for three years. Our first child was born in 1975; our second, in 1978. Three years later, in 1981—when our children were three and six years old—I learned I had Hodgkin's Disease, a curable cancer. I was treated for more than a year with surgery, radiation, and chemotherapy. I felt very strongly that I had somehow made myself sick: something—I wasn't sure what—was terribly wrong with the way I was living. I felt exhausted and bored by the responsibilities of caring for two children and a large house. I wished I had a respected career instead of a rag-tag assortment of free-lance jobs and volunteer work. Mike said I could do whatever I liked outside the house, but every time I asked him to help with the shopping, the cooking, the cleaning, our sons, I got an argument. We didn't need the money, and I didn't want to take a full-time job on top of what I was doing at home.

In the early mornings, when the children woke up, Michael pulled a pillow over his head so he could sleep. Most evenings, he stretched out on the couch and napped for an hour or two after dinner while I gave the kids baths and put them to bed. Then he complained because I didn't want to stay up as late as he, because I sometimes "acted" tired rather than enthusiastic when he wanted to make love. He bought sexy toys and fancy lingerie to make our sex life more exciting; somehow they weren't enough to lift the pall of exhaustion and growing resentment. I remember thinking, before I got cancer, that the only way to get him more involved with the children and the house was to get very sick, so sick that he could not expect me to do everything myself. But even while I was undergoing chemotherapy, Michael resisted helping out.

I began to read about the links between mind and body: articles about depression and cancer, Norman Cousin's *Anatomy of an Illness*, Dr. Ernest H. Rosenbaum's humanitarian guide to *Living with Cancer,* Dr. Larry Dossy's startling "New Age" speculations on space, time and medicine. Finally I told Michael that I thought I had made myself sick; unless I could somehow change my life, I would probably get sick again.

Michael criticized my "superstitious," unscientific attitude and continued to argue with me about what he would and wouldn't do around the house. He also sought solace for his tragedy (sick wife, young children) in other women's arms. I felt as though he was looking for my replacement while he waited for me to die. Michael explained that I should not be jealous: he could not provide proper emotional support for me unless he got support from others. That seemed reasonable. I re-read the last three volumes of Simone de Beauvoir's autobiography—*The Prime of Life, Force of Circumstance, All Said and Done*—and a long interview someone had done with her regarding her relationship with Jean-Paul Sartre. DeBeauvoir and Sartre each had other lovers. I thought I might find in their example a cure for my jealousy.

*The Build-up: 1983–1985*

Shortly after my chemotherapy and radiation treatments ended, in early 1983, Michael's boss fired him for reasons Mike could not—or would not—explain. Michael said it was a blessing in disguise. We could live on money he had inherited while he set up a consulting business. He didn't want to work for other people any more. He printed up letterhead and bought an expensive computer but made little effort to seek out clients for his consulting work. For the next three years, Mike programmed his computer, sailed, smoked dope, and drank. I took a part-time job so we would have health insurance and tried to figure out why my life wasn't happier.

By 1985, I thought I had the answer: the problem was my work life. I had been working as a free-lance radio producer, part-time grant writer, volunteer administrator for a non-profit organization. Now both children were in elementary school and I wanted to create a full-time challenging, satisfying career for myself out of my spotty work history and scattered skills. A week or two after I decided Michael was an alcoholic, I applied for the job of managing a new public radio station in Alaska. I wasn't sure I had a real chance for the job, but I felt I had to try. Within a few weeks, it became clear that I was the leading candidate.

Mike was happy to let me move to Alaska to take the new job; as he said, he'd always encouraged me to have a career. But—although he wasn't working—he refused to go with me and he would not let me take the children. "It would be too disruptive," he explained. "It might not work out after all." (The job started with a six-month probationary appointment.) Our sons, Eli and David, were seven and ten. I had no interest in abandoning them to take a job, however wonderful it might be.

The problem, I finally realized, was not my career. Living with Michael was making me miserable. In fact, applying for a job in Alaska had been my desperate attempt to escape. But it was not so easy. I didn't want to leave without the children. And I didn't want to stay with the husband who forced such choices on me. I turned down the job and found a psychiatrist to help me figure out what I really wanted to do.

*The End: 1986*

Michael had hit me only a few times in our sixteen years together, but he became increasingly violent as I, through therapy, gained the sense that I was entitled to have my own feelings—and sometimes even my own way!—and gathered the moral and psychological strength to stand up for myself. One evening in June, as we ate dinner on the deck overlooking the lake, Mike announced, "We're going to get a video camera." Eli and David were surprised and delighted. David asked why.

"So we can show your mother how ugly she looks when she's mad," Michael answered. He's drunk, I thought, and didn't respond.

The kids finished eating, left the table, and ran out onto the pier. I stayed on the deck with Mike, not saying anything, looking out at the lake. Without warning, Michael slapped my face, hard.

I was stunned and scared. He's out of control, dangerous, I thought. It's time to take the kids and leave. I walked out to the pier where Eli and David were playing. They hadn't seen Michael hit me. "Let's go get ice cream," I said. But Michael had followed me. Now he blocked the end of the pier, taunting me, bullying us, so we could not get to the car. The neighbors had gone down to the lake to see the sun set; they watched us from their backyard swing. Eventually Michael allowed us back on land. We went out for our ice cream cones; when we returned Michael was gone. I found the note of apology he left. He'd gone to a movie. I put the kids to bed and decided it was safe to stay after all.

But the slap was a turning point. Michael's apologetic mood didn't last very long. I thought constantly about leaving. In late June, Michael—very reluctantly—agreed to see a marriage counselor, but he clearly didn't respect the process, or the man we were seeing. He continued to drink heavily, to communicate primarily with his computer, to insist there was nothing wrong with him. He urged me to move out, to rent an apartment nearby. "The kids can go back and forth; they'll hardly notice anything's different," he said. "If you don't want to rent, we can buy you a house."

I talked to a lawyer, a realtor, friends and relatives. On the Fourth of July, I made an offer on a house I wanted to buy. I had a week to find financing and remove all the contingencies. During this week, Michael seemed to fall apart. He bought me expensive jewelry; pleaded with me to stay; apologized for his "male chauvinism" in selecting sex toys and gave me a blank check made out to a catalog company so I could choose my own "sexual aids."

Although Michael had told me to move out and had suggested we buy a second house together, he now refused to make money available for a down payment. His behavior was so bizarre that I was afraid, if I left, he would take some sort of violent action against me—or against himself. I talked with my psychiatrist, with the marriage counselor.

I talked with Michael. "Living with you is like living with two different people, or two different parts of one person," I said. "There's the Mike who is thoughtful, gentle and kind. And there's the brutal and hostile Michael. I never know whom I'm dealing with. It's like Dr. Jekyll and Mr. Hyde. I can't live with the brutal and hostile Michael, and I can't live with the uncertainty."

"Don't call me schizophrenic," he said. He seemed scared.

"I'm not. I'm saying that there's the Michael I want to stay with and the Michael I want to leave. I need to know I can say 'Enough of this' to the brutal Michael and he will stop bullying me."

Finally, Michael seemed to understand. I thought—or maybe I just wanted very much to think—that he recognized that he needed help. I withdrew my offer on the house. We worked out a set of conditions necessary for me to stay: vacations we would take, a car we would buy, an agreement to continue marriage counseling. He said that his highest priority was improving our sex life. "Everything else will follow."

I disagreed. "Our sex life will improve when things are better between us. When I'm not tired all the time from the tension of living with you. When I'm not afraid of you."

I told him I would leave if he ever hit me again. He refused to make any promises.

*The Bitter End—Saturday night, 6 December 1986*

Incredible, ugly twenty-four hours just past—and it's all over now, baby blue.

I spent yesterday at work. On the way home I stopped to pick up items for pizza. Mark and Ellen Lange came for dinner and dominoes and stayed until 11. Michael was incredibly uptight, especially when the turntable didn't work. Mark commented later on how tense David was and aware of Michael's every move.

Before the Langes arrived, Michael told me that David's sixth-grade teacher had called again about David's difficulties at school and had suggested getting "help" for David—he had traced the veins on his arm in ink again. During the domino game, Michael said something very depressed and fatalistic about being tired of life, and David said, "That's what people say who are thinking about suicide."

After the Langes left, Mike seemed willing to talk and hadn't had much to drink (I thought). We didn't get very far. "I can't live with the kind of hostile frigidity I've been getting from you," I said. (In the past couple of days, in fact, I've been having bad breathing problems caused by anxiety.)

"You can warm me up if you try," he said. "Just love me up a little. Come on, you can do it."

"I can't warm you up when you're encased in ice. I do love you, but you need to get some help. You need to talk to me, to reach out to people, not close yourself off like this."

He got very upset. "I don't need any help but your love. I'll change my will and commit suicide before I see some shrink."

About 12:30 A.M. or so, I said I thought he needed to find something really productive to do.

"You want me to be like Oliver North? There's someone really productive." (He despises Oliver North.) Then, after innumerable repetitions of how I had to show that I love him by making love in mid-day, he told me that all I did during the day was "occupy my time" so I could avoid him.

I said that I work during the day. (I was still doing grant-writing and free-lance writing, editing, etc.)

He sneered. "You're not working all the time. You take time out to write poetry." He compared writing poetry to the kind of "productive" work that Oliver North does.

I went up to the third floor to avoid further conversation with Michael.

He followed me upstairs, basically to say that he'd been thinking that we should rent an apartment for me to live in for two or three months or so. I said I didn't want to leave. "If I do leave, it won't be temporary. It will be for good, and I'll take the kids with me."

"Won't they have some say in where they go?"

"The courts will decide."

He punched me in the face three times. I got away from him and cowered near the dormer window on the lakeside of the house. (Bad move!) He became very contrite, almost immediately—began begging me to hit him, wanting to hold me, calling me "melodramatic" and telling me to "stop acting" when I said I didn't want him to touch me or to go and get ice for me. I just wanted him to leave the room, but he wouldn't. And he wouldn't let me leave, either.

Finally, he agreed to let me go downstairs to get ice for my eye. But as soon as I came back up, he was all over me wanting me to let him hold me, to go to bed with him, to let him hold the ice pack—and again trapping me in the dormer when I tried to get away.

After about twenty minutes of this I said I had to pee. He laughed and said he did too. He went to the third floor bathroom. I grabbed my purse from my desk chair and ran downstairs and out of the house, but I didn't get out of the driveway before he came out the kitchen door, in shirtsleeves, and blocked the driveway with his hands on the hood of the car. It was very cold, but we had a standoff for about ten minutes—I in the locked car, prepared to sleep there if necessary.

At last he gave up and went inside, and I drove to the Spence Motel, checked in about 2 A.M. and slept until 8.

In the morning I drove to University Hospital and had my face checked. I was pretty sure nothing was wrong, other than the swelling and black and blue, but I wanted an official record of the battering. The resident encouraged me to call the police. At first I was reluctant and just left a message for Alice, my lawyer. Then I agreed, but the police wouldn't take a report on the phone. They said I should go to the police station to report and have a photo taken.

Then I went to Michael's mother, Peg, to tell her that I was going to try to get Mike out of the house and was going to file for divorce. By this time, my face really looked awful, and Peggy was, of course, terribly upset. Alice called me back while I was at Peg's and strongly recommended that I not go home without a friend along. Alice said I had two alternatives. I could move out. Or I could get a temporary restraining order and have the police show up to get Michael out of the house. This seemed too awful for Mike not to mention the kids.

I called the Langes and asked them to come home with me—even to offer Mike a place to stay. They decided they couldn't do that; it would make them "accomplices" in "evicting" Michael from his own house, when they are about the only people he might feel he can turn to. They also encouraged me to move out, arguing that would be safer, if less convenient, and less likely to arouse Michael's anger. If it were only me, that would be easier to do, but Alice said I should not leave David and Eli at home with Mike for any length of time. So they would have to move out, too—and it seems truly unfair to make them leave their toys and their rooms.

While I was at Peg's trying to figure out what to do, Mike showed up, cool as a cucumber, with the kids—apologized—they all asked me when I was coming home and would I go to the Y with them this afternoon. David was very remote, Eli very warm but tentative. Mike apparently told them as they were going out to the garage that I wasn't around (in case they hadn't noticed!) and that he hit me "accidentally" because I said that they would have to live with me. Eli especially wanted me to know that they wanted to live with us both, even if we were in different houses. He looked so serious.

I decided that what triggered Mike last night was my threatening to leave. I thought that I could probably go home and stay neutral enough about my plans to make it through the weekend without him getting violent—giving me some time to think about options. Mike and the kids left after I said I'd be back in an hour or two.

I went to the police station and after a long wait to get into the building and for a squad car to show up, gave a full account, had my picture taken, and refused their offer to accompany me home so I could get my clothes and leave again. They were concerned about *their* liability, returning me to a known unsafe place, as well as about my safety. But I insisted that I knew what I was doing, and they eventually let me go.

I got home about 1:30 this afternoon—Mike was still very apologetic, wanting me to forgive him, kiss and make up. I tried to remain noncommittal. He made a big show of planning the rest of the day for the family. First he said we would all go to the Y to swim. Then he scratched that plan. Instead we hung around the house all afternoon, spending some of the time in bed. Michael wanted us to nap together; I lay down with him, but I was much too tense to sleep. Michael had gotten TV dinners for the kids and wanted to take me out to eat. I made it clear that I did not want to go to a fancy restaurant with my black eye, but I agreed to a movie where it would be dark. We went to the 5:00 show of *Star Trek IV* and came home to eat TV dinners and Chinese take-out.

During dinner, Michael said he wanted to talk after the kids were in bed. I warned him that I didn't have anything to say, but I'd listen. I wondered if he would say he's decided to get help for his drinking, or whatever—though he had a drink with dinner, which surprised me. I could tell, from his breath, that he had a lot to drink last night—perhaps after I left? I didn't think he was especially drunk when we were talking but perhaps I was too tense and tired to pick up on it.

After the kids went to bed, Michael put his arms around me. I tensed and said, "It will be a long time before I can relax when you touch me."

"Don't be ridiculous. Just shake it off. You've done it before, you can do it again. Just make yourself get over it." Then he told me what he wanted to say: that I was right, last night, when I said he had to tell me what was bothering him; that he'd eaten too much anger over the past six months, but that I had to listen to his complaints (for example, about my exercising in the mornings or leaving pots in the sink) and accept them. "A lot of good came out of our conversation last night," he said. "We made progress, even though there were some bad points to the evening."

I almost threw up.

Now I am faced with figuring out how to proceed. I haven't much time, since I figure that Mike will lose control when he realizes I am leaving him and the police said that the DA [district attorney] will probably get around to pressing charges of battery on Michael on Monday or Tuesday.

So I have to decide whether to get an injunction against Mike and kick him out—or to find some place for David, Eli and me to go, probably on Monday evening after I tell Michael what's happening. And I have to find a friend to be with me when I tell him.

*Monday morning, December 8*

I am sick with fear, anger, sadness—and YET in a tiny corner of my brain, where the long-term planning goes on—optimism and relief.

Yesterday morning I woke up determined to take David and Eli and leave on Tuesday evening, while Mike is bowling. But the plan didn't feel right. I imagined Michael coming home at midnight to no one; I tried to imagine how I could come back to get my things, if we left with just clothes, sleeping bags, Legos and a few papers; I imagined the way adventure would quickly pale in an unfurnished house on G Street that is available to rent.

I called Alice, who said I had only two legal alternatives: to leave (but Michael would have to know the whereabouts of David and Eli anyway) or to kick Mike out with a temporary injunction and restraining order.

I called Peggy and said I had decided not to sneak out with the kids (I also imagined how terrible and uncomfortable that would be for them) and she agreed that, however awful this is for Michael, it is more "dignified" for me to stay in the house.

I can't sneak out. It would just show David and Eli that the physically strong one gets away with whatever bullying behavior he chooses.

We played happy family again yesterday (Sunday)—going to the Y, Michael doing laundry, and Eli, David and Michael cooking dinner for Peggy and me. I became terrified when Mike started to insist that I act less cold to him—"Why can't you get over it?"—and teary when I talked to friends. Ellen said, "How sad for you all." Lydia said she was crying to know this was happening to a friend of hers.

And then in the evening, I began to imagine the process-server coming to the door, and I began to feel very sorry for Mike, and upset that I'm making his life hell (I'm making his life hell!?) so I called Rachel who I knew would strengthen my resolve because she is a psychiatrist and she has known Michael for a long time and understands his behavior.

And finally I went to bed about 12 and was able to sleep, mostly, until about 6:30 A.M. or so, I'd guess, when Mike curled around me like a spoon, and I became terrified again.

On Monday, December 8, I left. After conversations with my lawyer, I picked up the children at school and took them to a restaurant to explain what was happening. None of us could eat. We spent that night at a motel. The next evening, December 9, we stayed with friends while a sheriff's deputy served a temporary restraining order on Michael. Michael refused to leave the house.

On Wednesday morning, December 10, I had to call the police and stand in the kitchen watching as a rookie officer evicted my husband from our house. As he took box after box of clothes out to his car, Mike continued to argue that it was his house and he didn't have to leave. A police investigator told me later that Mike would probably have been thrown in jail for resisting arrest if he had not been an obviously intelligent white man living in a large, expensive house. On his last trip through the kitchen door, he said, "I'll be at Peggy's. Give me a call and let's have lunch."

I moved back in after he left, had the locks changed, and stayed in the house until I was able to find a smaller, less expensive place to rent for myself and my sons.

*Tuesday night, December 16*

I've made considerable progress on moving: set up the 23rd as the moving date, agreed with Irene, our cleaning lady, that when she comes on the 20th we'll do some packing—the kids will be gone. And I got my new phone number.

Picked David up after school, with Eli in the car, and we went to get boxes. We also went to Northwest Fabrics where the woman who was measuring the fabric looked at me and said, "Oh, you look like you were in an accident."

I said, "No, someone hit me."

And she said, "My second husband did that to me," and then described lying on the table getting stitched up while the doctor asked whether she was going to report it to the police. She didn't, because she was scared, but later she did leave her husband. She said, "And here I am, ten years later, and everybody's fine." Her son is an Eagle Scout and her children make all As. I felt this tremendous sisterhood, camaraderie.

It sort of fit into a conversation I had with Mark Lange, who came by for lunch. Mark was encouraging me to write an article—just a little article—about the differences between the way men and women have reacted to my black eye. I said, "Michael would have a fit."

Mark answered: "You're not associated with him anymore, remember. You'll get used to that." ■

## What the Bride Saw

Victoria McCabe

The hottest afternoon in August,
Three gilts nosed under the fence,
Rooted up the garden until the man
Raged out of the house, swearing
And running

For fifty minutes he chased to get them in.
One snorted its pure
Defiance, would not be guided
To the hoglot, wore the man
To a humid frazzle. He'd had all
He would take; found a two-by-four
Near the shed; swung it, for practice
In mid-air.

He would never talk, later, of how
He clubbed the pig in a corner, chopping
At its hide until it collapsed, grunting
And snorting, the bright blood splotching
Up the fence they'd painted "Barnyard
White" the week before. He couldn't
Stop chopping.

No one now would believe it, she often
Thought, after the years of his deep
Silence, after seeing him walk away
From a fight or two. But she knew
The fury in him, and worked to keep
On his good side. ■

## A Bar Scene

Jan Jonathon

The "books" say that before a woman enters into an abusive relationship, she sees a sign—at least one sign—of what is to come. This was my sign:

When we were dating, I thought Tim was kind. He seemed quiet and laid back. I saw him angry only once. We were in a bar. He wanted to go somewhere else and I didn't. He slapped me across the face. I was totally shocked. No one had ever slapped my face before! I remember thinking that if I had an engagement ring, I would have taken pleasure in throwing it back at him. But my parents were in the middle of wedding plans, so I convinced myself that this was an isolated incident. I denied my feelings. An isolated incident . . . .

I was wrong; he wasn't kind. ■

# Section Six
## *Regeneration*

### There Is Such Strength Within the Beauty and Fragility of a Rose Otherwise How Could It Return Summer after Summer?

Marilyn Elain Carmen/Aisha Eshe

Marilyn Elain Carmen/Aisha Eshe posits the rose as a universal symbol of eternal return—the repetitous cycles of death and rebirth that accompany all of our life journeys. "Maybe That's Why," her autobiography of regeneration, explores her need to name and rename herself and demonstrates the paradoxical nature of intergenerational violence: while her choice in violent and abusive husbands echoes her childhood experience, with her own children, she is calm, loving and patient.[1]

The letter inside the envelope marked "Confidential" expressed a fear that was almost palpable, fiercely demanding that "Pearl's" true identity and location be closely guarded because her life and her daughter's were in grave danger. Exhaustive and exhausting, the story is marked by Pearl's attention to detail that maps the labyrinthine confusion one often confronts when seeking help from counselors, lawyers, psychiatrists, and pastors. Learned helplessness shapes this woman's struggle toward freedom and demonstrates how ambivalence retards the process of escape.

Liz Marshall's "Letter to Friends" and Brenda C's letters to her family capture the process of transcendence through writing. Lynch's prose contrasts public image with private truth, while Brenda C's confrontation with her guilt for "breaking up the family" fosters an acknowledgment of her own survival skills.

In her essay, "The Abuse of Forgiveness," Nina Silver confronts the attitude in society, and now in social services, that punishes women who, victimized as children by rape/incest/abuse, fail to "get past" their anger, fail to forgive their offender, fail—after a "decent" period of time—to "shut up" about it all. "By calling anger a 'stage,' they have you nailed as surely as mental institutions have you nailed until you confess your illness . . . say what they want to hear" (Armstrong 1990, 4). For Silver, anger is no stage. Forgiveness affronts her integrity; an alternate healing process must be invented in order to transcend her history of abuse.

An Alice Walker poem that opens "Letting go in order to hold on/ I finally understand how poems are made," offers a possible method for achieving such healing (Walker 1984, 17-18). Part of the writing process, no matter what we write, involves "letting go" of something we hold deep within our unconscious minds and this is the first step in "holding on"—to sanity, to self-esteem, to the strength built from reaching for inner knowledge and validation.

Many who have tried to forgive find that it is not possible, leaving us to wonder if perhaps it is enough to forgive oneself for being unable to forgive. Perhaps there is no resolution, no closure, no happy ending. Nevertheless there can be transcendence, there can be inner peace.

Shirley W. Jones' "Stepfather" expresses anger in simple terms. Jones' catharsis is not a whole piece but a fragment, a beginning, an unsilencing that is, in Myrna Sharpe's words, a "detoxification"—spitting out the poison. In Edith Riley's "Sanctuary," the unnameable is tucked into a private, hidden room of the self; pain is expelled through words while the secret remains guarded, under wraps. The author controls the poison—by keeping it enclosed, it cannot spread—but by writing about it, she discloses its existence, discharges her secret.

Just as anger cannot always be eliminated by forgiveness, so pain cannot always be spit out to be transcended. This section gives credence to the individual nature of the process of growth and renewal, toward a new way of being in the world. There are as many approaches to healing as there are stories. For most of us, the process cycles back on itself—healing blooms eternal. ■

## Maybe That's Why

Marilyn Elain Carmen/Aisha Eshe

The presence of violence, abuse, battering has been such a central part of my life until the last five years that I am sometimes amazed and always relieved that my life is now free of this horror. I am forty-eight years old, and as I look back over the years I realize that the torture I endured and accepted did not start with any of my three husbands nor the other men in my life. Rather, these years of abuse provided me with a link to my battered childhood. I was "at home." I was "comfortable."

My childhood memories are sketchy. I have many blank spots, and many of the memories I do have are without feelings, just pictures, almost as though they happened to someone else, like watching a movie screen. I do know, however, that my aunt and mother were extremely abusive toward me. The least little thing I did, or did not do, such as walk into a room too slowly or maybe stumble, I would be called dumb, stupid, nigger, or ugly, big-lipped, flat-nose nigger.

The issue of color was always present in our home. We were a Black family, but my mother and aunt were very close to having white skin, "high high yella" as it was, and still is, called. Recently I discovered that our family's racial heritage is African, American Indian, English and Chinese, which explains my mother's and aunt's light complexion. Me—well I'm more red than yellow, so it became easy for my mother and aunt to look at me and call me a "nigger."

I was the dumb one. I was the stupid one. I was the one who would never amount to anything but a slut, a whore. If something was missing in the house, it was assumed that I stole it. I can remember vividly being thrashed with a large leather belt with a gold buckle for many hours into the night. My mother and aunt took turns. I can see the welts now as my hands race across these typewriter keys. If my brother, who was three years younger than I, misbehaved, it was assumed that I was his instructor. If I sang, or looked the wrong way at my aunt, she'd slap my face.

My mother and aunt were both diagnosed as suffering from paranoid schizophrenia. It is clear to me now that they acted out many of their hostile feelings on me. Many nights I had to sleep in a bed with my mother between my brother and me. I was not allowed to move at all during the night. If I moved, Momma would slap me. I would lie there stiff and very still, almost afraid to breathe. On nights when I'd suffer one of my many asthma attacks, she'd just lie there and listen to my struggles for breath. One night I was praying to God to let me breathe when my brother asked Momma what was wrong with me. She said, "Oh, Marilyn is just asking God to help make her a good girl."

My father was present at least physically until I was about eight or nine at which time he walked out of the house after a huge fight with my mother and my aunt. I realize now that after such an upbringing, it was only "natural" for me to "seek out" a man who would continue the abuse that was my way of life. I always found one. It wasn't difficult, almost like I wore a sign that read, "kick me—I'm available."

The first man was Peter. I was eighteen. A virgin. He convinced me not long after we met to have sex with him. He would say, ever so sweetly, "don't worry about getting pregnant. My mother will love you. She will help with the baby." That was just what I wanted to hear. I was so hungry for a mother, a kind loving mother, one who wouldn't have minded that I moved around in bed, one who I didn't have to sleep with every night, especially when she was crazy, mean. I so wanted a family. A little baby. Someone to love. Someone to love me.

I was thrilled when the doctor, after getting an extra feel and commenting on how soft and juicy I felt, told me I was pregnant. (The dirty ol' bastard!) Peter and I were together off and on for the next four years. I conceived four times. Three children. One miscarriage.

Peter's abuse started before my first child, Michele, was born. I was about five months pregnant when, as I moved to get out of a car, I felt a sharp sting across my face. I don't remember the incident that led up to Peter smacking me, but I know I was shocked and humiliated. I was hurt.

The fights continued. He stayed out for days at a time, and when he did come home, there would be no paycheck. No money. Many were the times when I'd go to his job to get some money before it evaporated, only to have him tell me that the checks didn't come in that day or that the boss died before he signed them.

Of course, when he got home, I'd be upset. An argument would occur, and I'd end up with a black eye, or perhaps he'd knock me to the floor, bruising my back that is constantly sore from open-heart surgery when I was seventeen. My surgery was extremely successful, but I had the procedure in the days before it was perfected. As a result, I have a huge scar across my chest and up the middle of my back. This entire side reacts painfully to cold or pressure. Peter, of course, knew this, which is probably one reason why he seemed to enjoy pushing me or punching me on my back.

I'll never forget the time when I was eight months pregnant with my second child. Peter and I were in the bedroom. Again, we were arguing about something. I don't remember what, probably money or his women. He told me that he used "Stay Long" for his women. I asked him what it was and he said, "It keeps me from coming so fast when I'm screwing. I don't need to use it for you though."

That day in the bedroom with my belly almost to the floor, he slapped me so hard in the back that I fell down. Right after that, I had to be rushed to the hospital. John, my first son, was born one month early. He weighed 4 pounds and 13 ounces. He is now twenty-seven.

After another child was born, I finally left Peter for good. But, you know, it really did not make that much difference. I continued to seek out man after man who would abuse me in one form or the other. I was looking desperately for a father, a mother, for someone to love me.

Peter's mother—you remember, the one who would love me so much and help with the baby—turned out not even to be a friend let alone a "mother." She was one to smile in front of my face, but Lord, when I turned my back! She thought I was awful for pursuing Peter for the many hundreds of dollars he owed me for child support. I finally agreed to sign it away in order to have Peter take our daughter to live with him because I could not control her behavior when she was in her middle teens. She stayed with him for a year.

Many of the post-Peter relationships and one-night stands are nothing but a blur to me now. I was in a constant state of search. What I continually found was someone to treat me as I had been treated as a child. A horrible circle.

I was also in a constant state of being high. I abused prescription and over-the-counter drugs and alcohol for over fifteen years. On weekends, sometimes even during the week, I'd go from bar to bar, leaving my babies with almost anybody. Even at times, leaving them alone. Always searching.

In all fairness to myself, I should mention that there were many times during this period of my life when I had to work two, even three jobs to hold things together. Once I was a waitress in a bar, my favorite place, or so I thought. Only God took care of my babies in those days. I worked every weekend, three nights for fifteen dollars plus tips. I got very small tips because I was always too tired, after working at a typewriter all week, to smile. Tired and in constant pain. The cold air in the bar caused my back to ache. The men did not tip or ask to take you home if you didn't smile.

I did find another husband in a bar, though. My third. He, too, was nice at first, especially when he found out that I was buying the brand new house that I lived in with my three children. He thought I had money when actually I was able to purchase my home through HUD with no down payment because the apartment that my children and I had been living in was condemned. What a joke! But of course, the joke was really on me.

Lawrence moved in about a week after we met. How foolish of me to think that this smiling, curly haired man would provide my children with a father and me with the comfort that I thought I needed to make my life bearable. Lawrence was deceitful from top to bottom: I discovered that he wore a wig when I noticed that his sideburns were lopsided.

I soon found out he was even more psychologically and physically abusive than the other men in my life. We had enormous fights every weekend. I'd end up with black eyes, skinned knees, bruised shoulders, a sore back, swollen lips. There were always marks on my body: it was a natural state. Some of the scars are still visible after over fifteen years. They fade more in the summer as my skin is coated from the glorious healing sun.

Oh, I wouldn't just stand there and let Lawrence hit me. I'd fight back. But I could never win. How in the Hell could I? I wasn't strong enough. And it would always end up with me abusing myself some more with drugs and alcohol. In those days I turned everything in on myself. I punished myself for everything. I was the guilty one, so I made sure that I found someone to make me pay for my guilt.

He wasn't the type to smack me in the face when I first walked in the door. My black eyes, swollen lips, and gashed knees never came as a surprise. He was too smart for that. Something always preceded his wife-beating, which as I think about it now, let him off the hook, so to speak. In fact, he assured me, "everyone knew I was crazy anyway." Yes, that was one of his favorite things to say to me, especially when I was upset about something. And I did get upset—he made sure that I would.

Like the time he refused to drive me and our sick baby to the hospital because he was busy in the basement—drinking whiskey and watching football. Crystall, my youngest child, was just a few weeks old, and she had been running a fever off and on all that previous night. I was worried. I knew that she needed medical attention. I would have taken her to the hospital myself, but I do not drive. I have never learned to drive, nor will I ever. I have been affected by the many times my mother and my aunt in their insanity would put my brother and I into the family car and drive across town, threatening to run the car off the bridge and into the Susquehanna River or off the side of a steep hill if I did not tell them who told me to be bad.

Finally, after I threatened to call a cab, Lawrence did manage to come up from the basement and take Crystall and me to the hospital. Of course, he found some way to turn his daughter's sickness into being my fault, saying that if I had taken better care of her she would not have gotten pneumonia.

Lawrence was masterful at initiating events that would leave me lying in bed crying, having swallowed tranquilizers chased with wine. As I said before, these were regular occurrences, practically every weekend. One Saturday in particular, he walked in the door and asked my youngest son, Michael, where he got the large toy that he was playing with on the living room floor. It was Michael's eleventh birthday, and I had shopped that morning for a gift I knew he wanted.

For some reason, Lawrence did not like the idea of his stepson enjoying himself on his birthday, so he started yelling at me for spending a lot of money on a foolish birthday gift. Mind you now, I had a full-time job with the government at that time, one I had for years.

Lawrence grabbed the toy from my son. Then he turned toward me and started going through his usual repertoire of name calling: "you nappy-headed nigger." The odd thing about that is Lawrence is darker than I but he felt himself superior to me and my older children because his mother was West Indian. Another of his favorite things to yell was, "the only Carmens in this house are me and Crystall. Those ugly nigga brats of yours ain't Carmens. You ain't no Carmen either, and I don't want you using that name."

He had a way of getting things going in our household—like pushing me. Now, hey if someone pushes me, I'm sure gonna push them back. He knew that. And the fight was on. I'd always end up the loser with a bruised eye or blood dripping from my mouth, or maybe sitting on the steps unable to move because he punched me in the back.

The police were regular visitors to our home. Sometimes I'd call them. Most times one of my older children called them. By the time they arrived, the fight would be over. I'd be sitting on a chair in the living room, strewn with furniture, broken glass, a turned over pot that once held a plant trying hard to survive amidst our confusion. Lawrence would be seated calmly on another side of the room. As the police asked questions, I'd be completely irrational, even incoherent at times due to the previous fight and my lack of control over the situation. Lawrence, on the other hand, would sound completely rational saying things like, "she's crazy, and she just starts tearing up the house. I had to do something to stop her so she wouldn't hurt the kids or wake up the baby."

The cops would take out their little pads and make some notes. One of them would usually say, as I sat crying asking them for help, "We really can't get involved in domestic matters." Then they'd leave.

After the police left, there was nothing for me to do but to go upstairs to look for the pills that I stashed all over, swallow them with wine and go to sleep. I really didn't want to wake up, but I always did. Usually the first thing I'd see when I awakened was Lawrence standing beside the bed with a tray of food for me.

I have learned to analyze my life now using my own self-help techniques such as meditation, prayer, and yoga, reading and writing, along with conversations with a counselor/friend. I have come to find, through many of these moments, a certain inner peace, a calmness. There is always a prayer in my heart asking God to give me strength to find my peace. I am learning that I can control certain aspects of my life, that there are certain decisions that I must allow myself to make. I no longer search for that person who will make my life bearable. I have found that person. Me.

This realization gives me space in which to breathe. I no longer feel that I have to sleep with the first person that looks kind. Looks, smiles, can be deceiving. I have not had a relationship in over five years. I know now that I deserve to be treated like the special human being that I am, that we all are. This time, I intend to wait until that person, who recognizes me as special, finds me or at least until we bump into each other.

I do not want to give the impression that I have let my abusers off the hook. This certainly is not the case. They were at fault and I hate the things they did to me. I hate the things I allowed them to do to me. But I am learning to give up my role as victim. I am learning to build on my own inner strengths and leave bitterness, remorse and recriminations behind me.

As I think about it now, it occurs to me that my father's presence in the household, during my early years, was not one of strength. I loved him very much as a child. One of the most beautiful memories I have of him was the morning that I snuggled up close to him in bed. I must have been about six years old. I felt safe and secure. I am sure that it was a very spiritual feeling—one that I have spent all of my life trying to relocate. Several months ago, a friend whom I respect a great deal hugged me. It was weeks after that hug that I realized that in his hug I felt the safety and warmth that surpasses even sexual feelings and moves toward spirituality with another human being. I know this friend is not my father, but I realize I have been looking for that feeling all of my life, and I am very fortunate to have found it again. It's like that search is over. My father is now about seventy-five and he lives in Florida with his third wife. We keep in touch with a rather surface relationship.

My brother is forty-five now. He is an engineer for a company overseas where he lives with his second wife and two children. We see each other once a year when he comes to the states. We have always kept in touch and it seems that over the last few years, we are becoming closer. We were very close as young children even though my aunt and mother tried to make a great difference between us. I was always very protective of him. When I stole from a store because we were hungry, I always took something for my brother to eat as well—two cakes, two bags of potato chips.

My older children are now grown with families of their own. While I do see them regularly, I do not feel as close to them as I do to my youngest child. One of the reasons is that they seem to be stuck in the past. They continue to see me as the person I was instead of as the person I am today. Crystall is sixteen and she lives with me. She has always been very supportive of me. Actually she is my very best friend, one of the two people on this earth with whom I feel completely safe and with whom I can talk to about anything. Crystall has been a published poet since she was five and she is also an actress.

My mother died when I was eleven. My mother, my brother and I were asleep on a mattress on the floor. When I woke up my mother was dead from—as I have figured out through the years—an epileptic seizure.

My aunt is about seventy-six and she lives with her second husband in a large house and is very lonely, I'm sure. I have tried over the years to come to terms with her but I have decided that since she continues to accuse me of stealing such things as her soap, her apple corer, pictures, I can no longer bear or accept these accusations. Just recently, I put an end to her abuse. In the last three months; I have not visited her. Because I feel very sorry for her, I would visit her if she were ill and asked for me but otherwise I have broken this very destructive tie.

Lately, I have begun to look at myself intently in the mirror, not to see how attractive I am, but to try to see what is really inside, behind, within the image I see. Something occurred to me the other day. I realized that I look very fragile, gentle, almost like I'll break in half if someone slams a door around me. When I discovered that, I went into the kitchen and discussed it with my youngest daughter, Crystall. She said, "Yes, Mommy, you do look fragile. Very fragile." As she said those words, I began to think of roses and how much I look forward to their beauty that returns every summer.

I know that I must continue to realize the power and strength within myself, within my soul. It comes to me as I write this that I have given up looking for the abuse I endured as a child. What happened to me as a child was wrong, and I no longer need to live that way. I also know that it will be a daily struggle to maintain my sense of power and to render powerless the memory of the abuse I suffered.

About 10 years ago, while searching for an understanding of my African heritage, I adopted the name Aisha Eshe. Last year, with the assistance of my counselor and reaching toward my soul, I decided that I wanted to reconcile with Marilyn, that I wanted to call myself by the name that my mother named me, that I wanted to be more in touch with the child inside me named Marilyn. So now Aisha joins hands with Marilyn so that we can walk stronger. Together we wrote this poem.

*Maybe That's Why*

Yet when I was a child
Whatever my mother thought would mean survival
Made her try to beat me whiter everyday.

from Audre Lorde, "Prologue,"- *From a Land WhereOther People Live*

Momma and Aunt Marge
Lashed that Brown leather belt
Across my back my legs my shoulders
Maybe they wanted to lift
Some of that color off my skin
Maybe they wanted to pull
Some of those kinks outta my hair
Maybe they thought if they beat me long enough
My nose would rise up to meet
The lash of that brown leather belt. ■

**Ascent From A Ring of Fire**
Pearl

**Prologue**

Once I saw that a wedding ring was in my reach, I drove blindly toward it with no thought of the price I'd pay to claim it. It took over four years from our first meeting to secure that "band of gold." It's been ten years now since the wedding. My custom-made dress is wrapped in blue tissue, boxed and stored for my seven-year-old daughter. Even if she's not the superstitious type like I am, she may want to wear it someday. The engraved rings, my gold band and diamond, are in the bottom of a locked metal box deep in my hope chest. My ex-husband threw his away. The metal box contains many such momentos. It is a time capsule for my daughter and me to exhume when we are ready to examine a searing piece of our history that choked our spirit and scorched our souls, jarred our peace of mind and nearly ended our lives. This is our story.

**Binding Courtship**

I assumed early in my adolescence that a stable and successful marriage was the only reason to be dating. The fairy tale "happily ever after" world would follow, translated into modern terms—terms I defined by my strict Catholic upbringing and by my impressions of ideal family life I observed in TV sitcoms. I fervently pursued my goal, until each new relationship would fail to meet my acid test, or my would-be true love became fed up with my ideas. I even acquired a few proposals along the way in my search for what I considered the "right type."

He had to be college educated and liberated, an intellectual but not a "nerd" who was too stuffy to make me laugh. I wanted someone who could understand and discuss basic liberal arts theories, but not someone who would be too unmaterialistic to value hard work. I wanted a man who valued and respected loyalty, the "golden rule," and earning one's keep. He had to be black, or at least part black, because I am, and he had to be stable in his cultural and ethnic identity because I was not. And I was searching for a soul mate.

I met this "right type" at a party neither of us planned to attend. He fit my criteria well: a three-sport varsity athlete with a 3.1 grade point average in the academically challenging field of communications. He was on scholarship and exhibited the best combination of Nubian beauty and Caucasian features I'd ever seen. He, like I, had avoided dating and alcohol deliberately so as not to be distracted from his studies or sports by someone who was looking for a future meal ticket. Within a month, he would describe me to friends as his "dream girl." We became inseparable and basked in one another's affection that spring season.

It was the second semester of my senior year at a prominent East Coast university, a time when I decided to enjoy myself. After three and a half years of a grueling schedule—maintaining a 3.8 GPA, commuting one hour each way from my mother's house, working twenty hours a week and full time in summer to supplement my scholarships and financial aid—I felt I deserved some fun. I was the first person in my family (both sides) to complete college right after high school; however, a few of my relatives who held formal education in high regard were also completing degree programs at this time.

After graduation, I moved five hundred miles away to accept a scholarship. We struggled to perpetuate the relationship during the two years of my graduate studies in analytical public management. Then we decided to live together as the best way to revitalize our romance and prepare us for marriage, with careers first and then kids.

During this same time, I rebuffed my mother's disapproval of our forthcoming union. My only sibling, a brother fourteen months younger and recently enlisted in the army, often defended my choice. I did not know this, and found out too late to thank him. In the second year of my graduate studies, I was called home to make funeral arrangements when my brother was killed in a freak motorcycle accident. My mother was too devastated to direct these activities, and she threatened suicide for months afterwards. Meanwhile. I hardened, focusing on my day-to-day obligations and efforts toward the realization of my own dreams.

**Trappings**

When it was time to marry, I intended that our ceremony and reception would showcase such style and sophistication that our friends and relatives would be talking about it for years to come. We had a story book wedding—on an island, at the height of the social season, followed by a Caribbean honeymoon, all of which we paid for ourselves. Oh, did they talk about it and drag out pictures. Our relatives' recollections of the wedding outlasted the marriage itself. Keeping those vows we made so extravagantly sent each of us to a separate hell, a hell we endured for the following four years.

But first came the good life. In our late twenties, we had surpassed all of our family members with our education, career opportunities, homes, furnishings, and impressive annual income. We fit the mold for the contemporary term "yuppies." Living seven-hundred-and-fifty miles away from our families was a mixed blessing: from the time we began living together, we were close enough to visit quarterly, bragging of our accomplishments and high lifestyle, but far enough away to maintain our separateness. When my husband suddenly became ill three years later, the distance became a source of loneliness and isolation, and allowed us to conceal from our loved ones the "bad times."

As the eldest of two in a single-parent family, a "latchkey" child, the interracial daughter of a "feminist," growing up during the years before these terms even existed, society looked down on our lifestyle as deviant. Under these circumstances I had limited exposure to normal adult male behavior and healthy marital relationships.

Consequently, I learned to accept it when my future husband vented his frustration. He would scatter items from a tabletop with a backhand sweep, punch his fist through a door, bang his head on the wall. These incidents occurred rarely, at first—at the end of a stressful day at work, or over an argument about whose turn it was to do dishes—but when they did they were intense.

Before we were married, I called a marriage counseling service. They told me that they only met with married couples who had serious problems, and my descriptions didn't sound that bad. Later, after marriage,

I consulted with priests who advised me to be more patient, to pray more, and to see if I could irritate him less. The priests would remind me that I'd married "for better or for worse." The background music of my life taught me to "stand by my man." I believed with all my soul that I should "rather be with him in his world than be without him in mine." Each time I questioned his behavior I received answers that placed the responsibility for my oppression back on me, and I would resolve to do a better job as a wife and as one of the faithful.

I learned early to keep out of the path of his explosions, to act "normally" afterwards, as if nothing unusual had occurred, even though the outbursts frightened me. Most of the time he apologized and soothed my frazzled nerves with techniques he'd used during our courtship. That made it easy for me to forgive and forget.

Once after we were married, I helped him reconstruct a bedroom door he demolished in an apartment we rented. We bought the plywood and paint, smuggled it into the building at night and borrowed some tools. Using the new wood and paint along with the old door hinges and knob assembly, we made and hung a new door within a few hours. By this time I was growing accustomed to his rages, and he began to apologize less.

That band of gold on my finger frequently reminded me of days spent in my girlhood dreaming about future womanhood and married life, the life I was now living. With that perspective, I justified my acceptance of his lashing out as a small installment on the expected payoff in security, stability, warmth, and a cozy home life. I assumed that these occasional flare-ups of "temper" were just a passing phase, while he adjusted to our being together after so long a separation.

I honestly don't think any of us had a good idea about handling this situation. Except my mother. She knew, and I avoided her. We had a track record of disagreeing on certain topics. I just added my marriage problems to the list. If one of my relatives had told me to "get out while you're still alive," I must have laughed it off, missed it, or deliberately ignored it.

I attributed my husband's lack of coping skills to his macho upbringing by his single-parent father and to his numerous years in sports, an outlet, which he no longer had. I figured that my job as a wife who "keeps the home fires burning" was to control my behavior and his so we could avoid an explosion, even a little one. Unconsciously after each incident I withdrew a bit. Later, I'd forget the incident.

**Flickering Dreams**

In our third year of marriage we bought a home and had our first child. We would have done so sooner, but two years earlier we were caught up with his sinus infection which grew so serious in two short months it destroyed his optic nerve and permanently blinded him in one eye.

His partial vision loss, change in facial appearance and confrontation with mortality slowly affected his self-image and outlook on his life, despite his rigid self-prescribed physical recovery program. "What might have been" became his topic of choice. I coached him through each bout of depression to try to help him see that our lives weren't over and that we could and should still pursue home ownership and children. "We have each other to be thankful for!" I'd plead, as I watched the fire and spirit in his eyes drain away. I knew that if I didn't keep our dreams uppermost in my mind that I'd lose all I'd worked for as well.

**Sparked Contacts**

My first recollection of physical violence directed at me (rather than near me or at an object) was of being pushed backwards over a low upholstered lounge chair during a late-night argument. I was four months pregnant and we were within one month of moving into our home. He stood over me shouting, "You better hope that baby is a boy, because if it's a bitch like you I'll kill you both."

He later cried and called his mother. She told him that all couples go through these times, but he should try not to hurt me again. She suggested that he not force himself on me sexually because that's what contributed to their (his parents') divorce. This advice saved me from future marital rapes. She never spoke to me directly, even to ask if I was all right. Her words were repeated when he promised never to hurt me again. I believed him—like I never wanted to believe in anything more desperately.

**Recharged Circuits**

The baby and the house were our way of reclaiming what was ours, and with a vengeance. At first he was very involved in preparations for both. Though there were times he would withdraw and sulk and I'd leave him alone, we began to have fun and there was genuine warmth between us. He cared for and played with the baby despite her gender and earlier threats. He turned out to be an OK parent/home owner, nothing special. Once the realities of yard mowing, low cash flow, and baby feeding set in, we began to quarrel again. To ease the tension, I took on some of his share of chores.

Just about the time I succeeded in losing the excess weight of pregnancy, my career blossomed. I had less time to give to him or to the chores. I met the baby's needs first, then my own. My time juggling just added to our growing list of disagreements and I had to learn how to steer our conversations to avoid his anger. But, I kept telling myself, this time there were "good reasons" for my flexibility: his medical condition and his "natural" jealousy of our new family member made it difficult for him to cope.

Things settled down for a few months. Then his checkup was due. Just after our daughter had her first birthday, he had another surgery to remove growths, after which he announced that no matter what the doctors told him, he was not having any more surgeries. Three months later, when a fourth operation was recommended, we began to argue. He decided I was setting him up for failure in his life and that I was working with the doctors to turn him into a human guinea pig.

I sought the advice of our priest and a minister. They encouraged us to work together, reminding him of his obligation to his family and reminding me of my obligation to let my husband lead the family decisions. Quite ironically, his own religious fervor emerged, a much more conservative view than mine, delivered with a radical intensity. He quoted passages from the Testaments to me, carried rosary beads, and became a Eucharistic minister in our church which included giving sacrament to shut-ins.

I also called a new hotline that advertised phone counseling for men's anger management problems. I was so involved in helping my husband get through his bad days that I probably didn't hear discussion focused on my needs. Besides, he walked in and I hung up, afraid I'd be punished for discussing "our business" with "strangers." This was his response to my occasional suggestion that we seek advice from a marriage and family therapist.

**Fanning the Camp Fire**

He began to complain about my being in his life and hinted at a divorce. I didn't plan on leaving because I felt I'd made a commitment to him for life, our life. I actively avoided any talk and thought of divorce, convinced we'd succeed against all odds, never realizing it would be our very union that would become our greatest enemy. But because of his repertoire of frightening behaviors and his refusal to have surgery, I began to see the child and I as one unit and him as separate.

By the time my daughter was eighteen months old, threats of violence, sometimes carried out, became his first response to most problems. His frustration and anger were a constant part of our lives, initially focused on his illness and its effects. Soon any topic that we had previously argued about also sparked conflict.

Sometimes I lived for days waiting, trying to "read" him, wanting just to get his outburst over, so I could rest easy, sleep. I hoped the rage would blaze like a pile of ignited autumn leaves whose vivid plume dissolves into a dark smoky cloud, which fills the air and then evaporates with hardly a trace. Instead he'd just hiss at me continuously like the old-time steam radiators that never run out of steam.

During this same period, he began to rely on chemicals—alcohol, pot, and pot laced with PCP. His drug dependency was accompanied by either excessive, vegetative television watching or Olympic sexual needs, with or without me, to relieve his "anxiety attacks." At first he indulged occasionally on weekends, then all weekend, then after work, then before and after work, then constantly.

Often, I welcomed his excess television watching and unexplained absences, which I knew were drug- and sex-related. I felt lucky he didn't bring home diseases! His absences gave me a chance to sleep, breathe deeply, play with the baby, listen to music, play racquetball, or run errands without his accusations of my doing it all wrong or having affairs. I was spared duties involving heavy housework, thanks to my mother's form of support: she hired a maid service after the baby was born. We talked on the phone, though infrequently, and when we did, we avoided talking of marital problems. She respected my need for her not to pry.

He didn't see the contradiction in his life—physical workouts and getting high on drugs all in the same day. He would advocate lessons of scripture and lash out against me with equal devotion. Once, I pointed these contradictions out to him and he reminded me of that "transgression" for two days. I spent much of my time making explanations for his behavior and for mine which increasingly became an attempt to mask my dissatisfaction and eventual horror of the prison I'd created for myself and my child. "Family life" became a matter of steeling myself for his brooding, hissing retorts, followed by noisy sudden exits. His behavior patterns shattered the tranquility of mealtimes and playtimes with my toddler.

**Raking the Coals**

When he was angry with me for something I did, often for no reason, he would terrorize me. I knew I was in trouble when his entire body would stiffen, his eyes would turn a cold, dark color I called "shark-eye" black. He would reel around and glare at me. It was like watching a transformation from Jekyll to Hyde. After a while I was not sure for which offense I was being punished. Fortunately I learned to read his face and actions and could anticipate a blow about three seconds before it hit. Our life together became a bed of hot coals I walked across daily, hopping from one delicate topic to another, balancing precariously over the white hot ones, blistering when I'd land on a gray one. As time went on, there were fewer and fewer gray areas; everything in our life burned with white heat.

The ways he terrorized me included driving very fast or close to another car then stopping so suddenly we nearly tipped over or caused other cars to skid and screech. If I protested or showed fear, all his features would beam in pleasure. He would chuckle at my terror and then call me a "cry baby" in disgust. He would come up right in my face, nose to nose, and shout commands like a drill sergeant.

In the last few months we lived together, he began to fling glasses and plates, still filled with warm food, at me with the same ease he used to fling insults like "bitch, get out of my face." He would grab my wrist or forearm in a vise-like grip with such force I couldn't use the limb for days after, and the marks of his nails scratched my skin. He would raise a clenched fist, swing his arm, pause, just an inch short of my face or back, then resume and let go of the blow in full force on furniture near me, shouting, "That could have been your head!"

**Kindling**

He began to involve our daughter in his threats, and we had our most violent incident at home. In later years, my daughter would describe parts of this scene, which I never described to her, but which occurred when she was less than two years old and barely talking. We had come home from dinner at a neighbor's where he'd been drinking heavily during the visit. Our child had trouble settling to sleep, so I went to rock her. He burst into the room yelling at me to "make that brat quiet." He picked both of us up while we were rocking in the chair, and yelling the entire time, dropped us from a height of three feet mid air. He grabbed the child, twisted my arm when I tried to retrieve her and pushed me out of the room and slammed the door.

I pounded on the door, pleading with him to let me in, to be careful he didn't hurt the baby. She was crying hysterically as he smashed the chair repeatedly against the wall and the floor, breaking large sections off the rocker. He passed out on the bed with the terrified child in his arms and me sitting by the door in tears. In the morning, he said he didn't remember the incident, despite the debris.

How did I allow such behavior to continue? Why did I risk the life of my daughter whom I loved so dearly? Why did I risk my own life? Looking back now I see that I rationalized: maybe he did black out; maybe he really couldn't remember doing these things. And if so, maybe he didn't mean to hurt us and deserved another chance. Perhaps, I reasoned, the debris would scare him enough that he'd work harder at maintaining sobriety and composure. Maybe it wouldn't happen again. Maybe . . .

Later that summer, when we were on vacation visiting a friend of my family, I struggled to conceal the tension. But she could see it and offered to take care of my daughter while he and I spent the night in a hotel in a nearby resort town. We did but just fought and had a few ugly street scenes while window-shopping. When we came back, the friend tried to get me to talk about our problems. I declined but she persisted.

She surprised me by confiding two very unusual incidents concerning my husband. First, he had made obvious and vulgar overtures to her niece, ten years his junior, to the point where she was frightened to be alone with him. Second, this friend had observed that he would bounce our daughter on his lap with such regularity that he maintained an erection, which strained his zipper and spotted his pants. I was so embarrassed, I shortened the visit on the pretense of needing to finish a project at home, but really I just wanted to return to our privacy.

Again, I rationalized that his lack of "social skills" had to do with a "mental health problem," depression, due to his "cheated life." If he was sick, he wasn't responsible for his actions and it was my "duty" as his wife to "save him"—to get him to a therapist. But first we had to get back home where he could feel safe and where, I believed, he would not "act out" his frustrations.

Back at home, I discovered I could no longer control him with pleading, placating, errand running, money spending, agreements to start over, or sexual obedience. He seemed caught in a quickening spiral of violence where more violence and more extreme subordinate behavior on my part were needed for each incident to stabilize him. I thought that's what a wife should do—forget my own needs for emotional and material recovery from the damage he'd done to date!

### Counting Seconds between Lightning and Thunder

I sought the aid of a family therapist without his permission but with his knowledge. My excuse, which he accepted, was that I felt like I was losing my mind and needed help. This he could accept because it fed his projection of my maladjustment. I never thought that the lie would reveal the truth.

In the first session I asked her to help me help my husband get through his bad days. There were so many for such different reasons. I also told her how he frightened me, what my friend had witnessed, and that our marital relations, though frequent, satisfied only him. Although he never forced himself on me, I began to use my sexual compliance as a sedative to minimize his' rages. I described our tragedy, compromised dreams, his illness, depression, drug use, refusal to get physical or mental help. She asked me if I could remember the last time he had two good days in a row and I couldn't. Then she suggested that I invite him to join us.

He stood us up. The therapist described manic depression and asked me what I would do and where I would go if I had to leave my house suddenly. I shrugged. She suggested that I store some of the baby's and my clothing at a friend's house, one whom he didn't know. This suggestion, which shocked me at first, within three weeks would germinate into an escape plan. Our third session took place two months later when I was in hiding and engaged in a custody battle.

Meanwhile, I had moved my daughter to a new day care center to socialize with more children and have more fun in her day. When I brought my husband to meet the director and teacher, he was so high he didn't remember the meeting or the route. This would prove to be a blessing in the near future.

**Shocked**

That weekend we had another argument, this one over child-care since I had some errands and projects at home. He said he was going to his boat and taking the baby with him. Before I could recover from this threat, he snatched her from the floor where she was playing. He began walking the distance of two miles to the train, in glaring sun, holding our two-year-old who had no sun protection or even clean diapers. I ran after them, with two diapers and a bottle, yanked the scarf off my head full of rollers and tied it around her head, forcing back the wave of horror welling up inside me. I couldn't protect my child from the sun; and worse, I couldn't protect her from her own father. She naively, innocently smiled as he cooed at her. Then he tugged her away from me and told me not to follow. I sobbed as I watched her little legs try to keep up with his. Then, he put her on his shoulders and they faded out of sight.

I waited the interval needed for them to reach their destination and then drove down to the pier. Many people were boating leisurely having a fine time. I was a wreck and looked it. Many of those same people watched as I tried to pull her away from him, out of the boat, a small rowboat built for one person. But he pushed me back, hurting my forearm and keeping my child just out of reach. She didn't even have a life jacket on!

I pleaded in a low voice, "Please come back. Give her to me, she can't take this sun and heat."

"Oh shut up, you pussy," he blurted, glaring at me, then nodding politely to the onlookers.

I crumbled inside, looked around at the observers, walked back to my car and returned home so stunned that I don't remember the drive. My imagination began to work, and I envisioned everything from sunstroke to sexual abuse and drowning. I spent the next six hours tormented, crying and praying. At dusk I called the boathouse. His slip was still empty but no boats had been found in distress by the regular patrol. I asked the boat master to advise the patrol boats of my concern. In the back of my mind was the nagging question whether to run away with my child, followed by the inevitable concern: to where?

Then I called Mom who had recently moved across country. We both cried for fear of my daughter's fate. She told me to take hold of this tremendous fear and reshape it into anger at my husband, to hold on to that anger and devise a plan of prompt and legal escape. I told her I was going to continue to see the therapist and together we would devise a safe escape plan and possible destination. There were no shelters that I knew of at this time.

In retrospect, that conversation with my mother marked a moment when my mother's and my own perception of the reality of my situation became one. There was no "I told you so" in word or tone. Within three days, a second critical conversation with my Jesuit-trained pastor sealed my psychic freedom.

**Singed Ties and Live Wires**

Yes! She made it home, her diapers soaked with river water and urine. I stripped her and bathed her to warm her chilled body and, more importantly, to inspect her for damage. Relieved to see she was fine, I said a novena. The next day we returned to the security of work/school routines, allowing me a respite to review my plan and prepare for action.

My husband went into a world of his own. He seemed very close to doom. He moved into the basement, a part of the house I didn't venture into; it was as if the devil-incarnate lived there. When he emerged, he would quote scripture passages to me as if he were conducting an exorcism. My own frequency of praying increased, usually when I couldn't sleep. He removed the knob on the front door—the only one I could have sneaked out of—and hung rosary beads in its place. Once I saw him kneeling in front of this would-be altar, talking to himself. At night, when the baby and I went to bed on the second floor, we could hear him three floors down, through the air ducts, talking to himself, listening to music or TV. At one point he packed and unpacked his duffel bag while I begged God to make him leave.

To make him leave: herein lies another clue to my immobility. I saw the solution to my problems as him leaving. I had selected and furnished this home, I had more things to move, more to lose than he. Why should I go? I just wanted for my child and me to get on with our lives. He was the stranger in our home; he was the menace to our safety. We needed to be rid of him like a body needs the amputation of a diseased limb. It was just too inconvenient to imagine trying to maintain a semblance of pride, family life, and financial stability, and to continue to pursue my career if I had to relocate.

My lawyer later told me it was just as well that I tried to remain in my home. The prevailing state law punished a woman who left her husband whether or not she took the children with her. Abandonment by the wife, regardless of reason, usually resulted in the husband's award of all marital property and the full custody of the children should a divorce petition by either party result. And of course, the same law and judicial response did not apply to the abandoning husband.

**Seizing the Moment**

A day later, my husband had an ordeal at work. He shook up his employer so much that the security guard spent the majority of the day watching him. The employer called me that night and suggested I get some mental health help for my husband. Then he suggested that we begin paper work for a medical disability. The next day, my husband quit his job (and ruined his career), accusing his supervisor of conspiring with me and the devil to drive him crazy, but the voices in his head told him not to worry. He told us he was receiving his guidance and we were not to disturb him. I talked to him on the phone and he asked me if I could hear the voices in the phone wires that were speaking to him.

Later that day, he wandered into the walk-in psychiatric clinic at the hospital where we had spent so much time. He was seen by one of his former doctors as well as a psychiatrist; but they released him because of the liberal laws concerning involuntary committals. The doctor explained to me that my husband would not freely admit himself for help. I knew by now that my daughter and I had to get away from him but in a way where he could not find us and punish us further. Leaving was our only choice. Anything less was certain death.

The very next day, his first out of work, I couldn't talk him out of driving my daughter to her day care center and then me to work so he could have the car. So while he was in the shower, I kept the conversation going, as I lined up my workbag and set it next to my daughter on the floor near the back door. Just then I heard him shut off the water and realized I'd run out of time. I dashed past the bathroom and was halfway down the stairs when he realized I was running out. Since he was dripping naked, he tugged a pair of pants over his wet skin and bounded after me. In one movement, that seemed to pass in slow motion, I scooped up my baby in one hand and my purse in the other and got out the back door, through the gate and leapt into the car. Just as I slammed the door and reached to jam the locks, he grabbed the handle.

Then he stopped, caught his breath, smiled, looked around as if to make himself look respectable to any eye witnesses. With all his might, he lifted the front of my car about four feet off the ground and told me to get out. Then he set it down. A neighbor walked by. I rolled down the window about an inch and shouted as loud as I could, "Call the police." Unaffected, he stopped, said "Good morning" to each of us, and continued on his stroll, adding that he didn't want to take sides in one of our squabbles.

I pulled out of the driveway before my husband could block me and took the baby to the day care center. I told them what was going on. At that point I realized my hair was barely combed, I had no make up on, my skirt was unzipped, and I had forgotten to brush my teeth. The director was very understanding and we discussed how to handle a possible abduction scenario. On the way home—I'm not sure why I went back to the house—I flagged down a police car and asked for an escort to get a few things out or to fix myself up for work. I told them I was afraid "my husband would hurt me." They reluctantly followed me home, parked in front and explained that unless there was a crime in progress, they could not enter the premises. Basically they agreed to watch me go into the house, wait a minute or so and then leave!

My husband came out of the house, as if auditioning for the good citizenship award, telling the police that I'd been seeing a therapist. But he showed them a pitcher filled with milk and a sugar bowl filled with sugar and stated that I was trying to poison him. The officers suggested that he return these items to the house. While he did they spoke with me, not sure whom to believe. They suggested that I not go into the house, and that I get my husband some mental health help and then drove away!

So I got in the car and applied my cosmetics so I could go straight to work. Why, I don't know, but I let my husband drive me to work, a distance of five miles during which I kept my hand on the door ready to make a quick exit. All the while I was talking as calmly and as lovingly as I could, promising him sex and drugs later on. I knew when I got out of the car that I would never let myself ride in a car with him again, or in any confined space within grabbing distance for that matter.

**Burnt Offering**

I closed the door to my private office, which had a large window view overlooking the river—the one he had rowed down with my daughter in tow—I called the doctors at the clinic. I asked how we could work together to get him to a hospital. My boss came in only once. I told him I had a serious personal problem, needed to use the office and would take a sick day. I guess I'd been showing signs of stress or had been such a good worker, or both, that he left me alone. For myself, I could no longer conceal "our problem" no, "his problem," from our priest, co-workers, friends, neighbors or long-distance relatives. My mask was disintegrating. It was time for me to wake myself from this nightmare and my darkest fears, to end the masquerade of my marriage once and for all.

Many calls later, I still had no offer of real assistance or a clear idea of what I should do next. But I realized I had to do this alone. Neither doctors nor lawyers could initiate the action. I was talking about involuntary committal to a mental institution and the local laws were very cautious about this "powerful taking of one's civil rights," as our priest, the same one who warned me to get help earlier in the week, would explain later that same day.

Our priest suggested that I consider taking my child and leaving my husband for a while because he feared for our well-being and physical safety. When I reminded him of my wedding vows, he reminded me that a primary precept of the Church is the preservation of life, above all else. He went on to say that in cases where the physical or emotional life of most or all family members is seriously threatened by continued union with one member, the Church advocates separation, with the preservation of life as paramount over the preservation of the union. Religious marriage counselors apply this principle most often in cases of a hardened alcoholic who beats his wife and children when drunk. He then added that he saw no difference between that same hardened alcoholic and my violent spouse who was rejecting therapy, a subject I had discussed with the pastor before he saw for himself the danger I lived with.

As an afterthought, my pastor said that this view, this translation of Church precepts for family problems, alcoholic or otherwise, is not held by all priests. I may run into opposition from other church officials, especially if I divorce. But I should not let that opposition discourage me or let it become an obstacle in my relationship with God.

This conversation, along with the one with my mother during the boating incident, procured emotional passage for what I had left to accomplish in the days and months ahead and directed me with a sudden urgency and righteousness I had been unable to conjure on my own. I sensed that the moment for escape was very near. I felt confident that I would instinctively recognize and seize the moment when it arrived. That confidence came from feeling waves of psychic and physical energy in the last few days and hours before, finally, taking action.

By early afternoon, I was talking to the county mental health officials, having given up on receiving help from the private hospital. The county had recently begun a crisis intervention program that worked with local police to respond to "domestic violence" problems. That was the first time I heard the term "domestic violence." I'd never heard those words—that terminology before. It sounded like a contradiction in terms. But surely, "domestic violence" was an accurate description of my reality. The program worker began her shift in two hours. I waited, concerned that I was running out of time. He was due to pick me up at work in four and one-half hours.

Two hours later, after confiding in a co-worker, I borrowed her car and met the crisis intervention counselor. With her help, and with my priest as my reluctant witness, I sobbed and trembled uncontrollably while I signed involuntary committal papers.

Then I gave the police instructions about how to get into my house, how to find him in the basement den, and what behaviors to expect from him. I asked for extra police to restrain him. In broad daylight, less than an hour later, about fifteen minutes before he was to have departed to pick me up from work, I watched from the borrowed car parked a block away, as four large officers positioned themselves at the doors, knocked, entered, and later emerged with him from our home. He was escorted to a wagon, handcuffed, and loaded, relatively peacefully. I sobbed with pity both for him and for myself.

My empty house seemed haunted and we stayed with friends who later told me I was in a daze most of that first weekend. They let me sleep, talk, eat as I wished, while they took care of my daughter. During this time

I called the mental hospital to check on my husband's progress; the doctor and staff described his "manic" behavior. I didn't care what they called it as long as it kept him away. When I drifted in and out of sleep I had nightmares of him breaking out and coming to kill me even though he didn't know where I was. These nightmares would follow me for years.

**Synergy/Gathering Strength**

Three days later, after the police removed him from our home, we all met face to face in a committal hearing. He was across the table from me and I was terrified. I avoided eye contact imagining that should he even gaze at me, he could conjure up enough evil to burn holes in my flesh. With great effort and the assistance of a few witnesses, who struggled with the idea of helping me even then, I succeeded in proving he was volatile, a danger to himself and to others.

His legal defense at the involuntary commitment hearing argued to excuse his drug use as attempts to self-medicate, in his last-ditch attempt to protect himself and his family from his violent tendencies. They discussed his history of splintered parent and sibling relationships, his lonely and unloving childhood, the effect of racial discrimination on his psyche, and his family history of manic depression as well as the effect of his continuing medical problem, which had settled in his brain. They didn't discuss enough, I thought, his years of athletic and "macho" training which encouraged physical outlets for stress and aggression without regard for injuries to others.

He was committed to a state mental institution for thirty days, but with many day passes and phone privileges. I was told to be thankful for such a speedy and generous detention. Later I learned I had set precedents in the county with my case regarding the rights of wives to exercise authority over their husband's property—meaning me, our child whose life he had threatened, and the house and furnishings I bought! I was warned to keep up my guard at all times. And my well-seasoned lawyer was right! Fortunately, before things between my husband and me got out of hand legally, she assisted me with obtaining a "power of attorney" that I would use to sell our home at a loss, just before it was repossessed.

**On a Wing and a Prayer**

He moved back into the house after his release. My daughter and I went into hiding for good. I found myself terrified and, at the same time, grieving for my lost dreams for a life with him. My mother's friend took us in. Fortunately, I had packed and stored the majority of the furnishings from our three-story home, which were mine, before leaving. On one of his day passes he came by while the storage company was working. The workers sensed the danger and none of them left me alone with him. He gave me a few instructions along with some insults. I left behind a few things he wanted—like framed pictures and our bed, which I found in pieces months later.

Because of the divorce and the financial and custodial battles we had to conduct, I was within his grabbing distance on several occasions. I cleverly found ways to move us from a secluded spot back into the public view, even though it meant other people would hear "our business." During these times I tried to maintain a nonchalant attitude when in his presence. But I sensed that to be in his presence constituted serious danger to my life and well-being; so I would walk very slowly past him and keep objects between us just in case he attempted to mutilate me with one well-timed blow.

In a brief meeting at a friend's home, just before he left the state, he reinforced my instinctive fear. Passing me in a room, he smiled through his teeth and hissed, "I should have really hurt you when I had the chance. Next time we're alone, I'm going to rip your arms out of their sockets and smash your skull to bits in the palm of my hands. Don't forget it!" Then he looked over his shoulder and winked.

I took each action one step at a time, to extricate myself from the grip he had on my life, child, finances, mind, career and material goods, never knowing what challenge would lie ahead, only knowing it was better than lying in bed at night worrying what he'd do next to me or my child. I'd be breathing rapidly, shaking uncontrollably, and trying to cover that up too, while I disconnected my life from his in slow, almost silent steps, while he stayed absorbed in his anger and shock about my new behavior: going into hiding; arranging for his detentions and succeeding.

**Out of the Ashes**

With the help of a clergyman, a county mental health worker, a new family therapist, a very savvy lawyer, many relatives who provided whatever financial assistance they could afford, and friends who offered timely support, I separated from and eventually divorced him. I likened my choice to one of a burning house—I with my child, had to be the first to seize the only ladder to the ground without letting him realize it or catch up to me. That's the only defense a woman really has—to be faster and smarter, because she's usually not physically stronger.

My final divorce settlement, obtained twelve months after separation, gave me the right to privacy I requested for my well-being and protection from his violence. In my divorce petition, I explicitly stated that I did not want to have any further direct contact with him, nor did I want alimony. That would be too high a price to pay for having him in my life. It also gave me full custody of my daughter without visitation rights for him. This victory was due in part to my mother's friend serving as a witness, corroborating my allegations of indirect sexual abuse of our daughter.

During the separation period, we grimly arranged a court-ordered supervised visitation, which upset everyone but him. He forgot the scheduled visit and went out of town for a boat race. (A stroke of luck? I'll take it!) That oversight enabled me to tighten my custodial petition, removing the visitation option and refusing any offer of child support because I proved I could easily support both of us. This, combined with his emphatic denial of his mental health problems and his refusal to seek help, confirmed my sense of justification for this divorce. After my lawyer explained the legal criteria for marital as well as parental abandonment, I ceased to have any feelings of guilt about severing the relationship between my daughter and her natural father. In later years, I learned my instincts about protecting her from him had probably freed my descendents from the chain of abuse—the learned behavior patterns passed down from one generation to another through experiences such as we had endured.

I resolved to forge a new life alone and to look over my shoulder in case he was on my trail. My only motive was my desire for my child and I to live like "normal people," to exercise our civil rights, to define a life of our own rather than living as prisoners of his anger and violence.

A year later, I heard rumors that he became engaged and his fiancée had a temporary restraining order placed against him. I don't know what became of his life-threatening medical problems, abandoned career, or bankrupt finances. I do know many of his creditors tried to find him through me. I had placed an ad in the newspapers, however, warning them that as of the separation date, I was no longer liable for him.

Now I am thousands of miles away. I haven't seen him in over five years. I had to disconnect from an entire lifestyle, career, a network of friends, even a few nice in-laws, and start over from "scratch."

How humbling, especially after having become accustomed to our affluence. For the past few years, I have struggled hard to rebuild each piece of my life; no one is handing it to me. I legally changed my name and my daughter's. I pushed myself to build new friendships with neighbors, day care providers, and merchants. I was careful not to draw attention to myself, but eventually became known for my frequent inquiries about security measures with day care providers. I realized after a while that building a better life is more the result of planning than of chance. Mostly it's struggling with small accomplishments, day after day, until one day you notice you've taken another giant step forward. Victory comes in small ways, like getting a job or seeing a new neighbor wave hello.

I continue to take precautions; I always will. I have advised a few friends to alert me if anyone makes inquiries about me. I have written this essay using a pseudonym. I keep my phone number unlisted, hesitate to give my address to old friends, keep my home and car doors locked at all times, feel anxiety when phone calls are the wrong number, and still examine people in the street who resemble my ex-husband or his friends or relatives.

Unlike so many women in my situation, I have obtained needed resources and encouragement at critical times. I also have new husband (yes! I still believe in marriage) and a second child, to ease and celebrate the transition.

My new husband was a longtime friend from my late teens. Ironically, he was a former boyfriend who once proposed. When we accidentally reacquainted after nine years, it was awkward for us both. He had heard rumors of my troubles and offered to help me move simply because I needed help and he could spare it. He had matured, was unattached after his own recent divorce, had a few weeks of leave from his military career, and had been intending to make a cross-country trip but lacked a companion. It was sheer luck for us both.

Within a year after I settled in a new job, placed my daughter in a new day care center, and reestablished myself as "head of household," my friend and I were married. As a wedding gift to my new husband, I promised not to discuss my past life so that we could focus on the life we are creating together. I also obtained a church annulment from my first marriage after three years and tremendous efforts.

In fact, as evidence of my former husband's non-status, we don't speak his name even when he and that life do come up. We refer to him as "what's-his-name." That was my idea; it's both therapeutic and superstitious. If I don't say his name, I can keep him out of my present and in some spiritual way maybe I won't contribute to whatever vitality he has left. It has been said that the dead are truly gone when they are no longer remembered. Not speaking his name is a step in that direction.

About a year after I remarried, my nightmares stopped. At first, we kept guns in the house and had a plan for using them. My new husband had his own nightmares about being able to protect us. When I dream of my ex-husband, my new husband and I talk about it briefly, as any other news item of any other day. In the same way my daughter has become our daughter.

In fact, we chuckle as we observe preferences and habits of my new husband becoming part of our daughter's definition of father. They share mutual interests; he established himself in her life on his own terms. Their bond is one that I missed as a child and envy from afar. As they say, "anyone can be a father but it takes someone special to be a dad." Both my husband and my daughter know this difference.

My ex-husband's effect on my new life comes in subtle reminders—some good, some bad. I see his face and physique in miniature in my daughter, and I see people in her that resemble his family. I hear songs that revive a time and place in my mind's eye, and I recall specific events as I participate in certain cultural/ethnic activities familiar to times passed.

Sharing the birth of my second child, a son, with my new husband, and adjusting to that event, created deja vu experiences.

But fortunately the similarities between my former and current life are few. While our new family also has arguments and one near-violent incident, we deliberately work to create a warm and loving environment without violence. When we get angry we take timeouts as adults and use this same technique with our children for discipline. We resolve our problems thoroughly as they occur and so that everyone wins. We try to balance the needs of the situation with roles at hand, but do not necessarily affix firm roles or rely on the images of authority solely to accomplish a goal. For example both my husband and I are partners in the nurture and discipline of our children, supporting each other in their eyes while doing so. And whoever gets home first fixes dinner.

The signs and memories of my former life have become like the gray hairs beginning to poke out at the crown of my sable mane. I don't pluck them out. I just notice them at the moment and comb over them. But I let the ones at my temple show, reminding me that I've earned each one and lived to tell the tale.

**Ascent of the Phoenix**

I do volunteer crisis work in a women's shelter and on a twenty-four-hour hotline for domestic violence intervention. Assisting residents to continue life while in hiding, talking to first-time and repeat callers struggling to examine or cope with family violence, or chauffeuring a woman and child to the shelter after participating in a police escort to retrieve a few of their belongings, I see myself in their place. I provide information and encouragement or just listen. It's difficult because I can't force my views or sense of timing on them. Teaching these women how to make choices and live with the consequences is basic to the counseling itself.

I try to be that spare hand for someone else like the ones who reached out to me when I faced a deep dark abyss and realized I'd somehow lost my direction and was in danger of losing my last shred of self-esteem, my confidence as a good mother, my skill and discipline as a worker, even my physical life. Without the assistance I received from so many when

I was needy I never would have escaped or found the courage to begin again or the sense of reality and hope to continue. I can not and will not forget those debts. Maybe I'm superstitious, or aware of my vulnerability, but my involvement with other abused women and their plight gives me strength and keeps me ever-ready for the possible return of my own abuser. Though I've planned how to handle the dim but real chance of another confrontation, I never forget the extent of his rage and the fact that if he got close enough he could release it on me for one last time in full force.

I've risen above that former life like a phoenix from the ashes. I've settled on a plateau of confidence and inner strength that replaces the need to cling to old myths. What hell it was to be rejected yet bound to a destructive and dangerous life in the name of honor, duty, and the traditional American and Judeo-Christian way.

No training ever prepared me for that lesson. I was taught that there was nothing that hard work and dedicated love wouldn't remedy. Charred remains of my former life remind me that sometimes you have to run for your life. Or retreat and sever ties drastically, the way firemen dig trenches to prevent the spread of a massive, raging blaze across a virgin meadow.

I will never again relinquish control of my life to anyone so completely that I feel the only means to living life as I've fashioned it is through the demands of another. I've drawn the line in my mind, my spirit, and in my marriage between what I will and will not exchange for that "band of gold." I suppose I've replaced notions of "happily ever after" with "that's just how life works." For a few of us lucky ones the way life works out after all is how we've dreamed for it to be in spite of ourselves. ■

## Letter to My Friends

Liz Marshall

When you walked into my home, you would be surprised at how big it was. From the outside it looked small. Inside was a living and dining room filled with antiques, a bright kitchen with rainbow wallpaper and white tile. The family room was sunny with lots of plants and toys scattered on the floor. When you came over—only when he wasn't there—you liked what I had done to fix up an old house. But you didn't see what I saw.

I saw the white tile on the kitchen floor that my husband and I put down. I can still hear him say, "Amelia, can't you do better than that?" I saw the rainbow wallpaper, a bargain I found at the local hardware store, and remembered him yelling at me, "When are you going to get this stupid room back together again? It's a mess." I saw him standing in that kitchen saying, "I wish I had a gun. I'd blow your brains out."

People walked into the living room and exclaimed over the beauty of the Victorian couch and carved sideboard. I saw hours of trying to get the dirt out of those carvings because he would point with an accusing finger, "Can't you be a little more clean? You're a slob and it's disgusting. I can't live this way."

All of you saw a pretty family room, and I saw him putting his hand around my throat, pulling his fist back and saying, "Please hit me so I have an excuse to hit you back."

You saw the nice office with the cast-iron-and-wood library table and lace curtains I bought at a rummage sale. I saw the ice bucket flying through the air and shattering the lead-paned window. The glass lay there for weeks because I refused to clean it up. I left.

You saw clean windows. I saw the bars of a prison I had made for myself. ■

## Woman with Two Children: From the Letters and Diary of a "Formerly Battered Woman"

Brenda C.

*Editor's Note:*

On November 5, 1989, Brenda C. left her husband, because, as she writes in her diary, "He was really drunk and he threatened to . . . kill me." When he packed to leave her and the children that night, he included two shotguns. "I still don't know if they were loaded but . . . any man who could sit at the dinner table and tell you that he could kill a human being before he could kill an animal makes a believer out of me." She called the police, who took her to a shelter where she went into hiding. While in the shelter, as part of her recovery program, she began to keep a diary and to write letters to family members as a form of self-expression or self discovery.

March 2, 1990

Dear Elizabeth and James,

I don't know how to tell you that your father was mean to me. I still want you to care about him. How do I tell you that your father was always accusing me of sleeping with other men? How are you supposed to know the truth? I don't want you not to trust what your father tells you, but his accusations were not truthful. I know you always heard us arguing, but I don't know if you ever saw him raise his hand to pound my head in. He left bruises once. Elizabeth, you were only a baby. You are nine years old now. My biggest fear has been that since he hurt me physically once, I never knew when he would strike again.

The night I actually left, Elizabeth, you were aware of what was happening. That we were arguing. When your father brought out the guns and threatened to kill me I had already sent you to your room. But James, you are only five years old. You slept through the whole thing. All you know is you were awakened and taken to the police station and then brought to a shelter to keep us safe. How do I tell you, James, that Daddy wanted to kill your mommy? Who will you hate? I don't want you hating him; he loves you. I don't want you hating me. I love you. I don't want you growing up treating women as violently as your father treated me.

Elizabeth, since you are more aware than your brother of what's happening, and I know you feel better being away from Daddy, I pray for you: I pray that when you're ready for a relationship you're not afraid of loving because love can be beautiful. A healthy relationship must be a two-way street.

I love you always, Mommy

■ ■ ■

March 26, 1990

Dear Mom,

You protected me from being hurt when I was young. You still don't want me to feel pain—pain that I have to feel to get on with my life. I know when I hurt you hurt, and now the tables have turned. I protect you from knowing my pain because I don't want you to be hurt.

I love you, Mom. You have cried with me. You have laughed with me, and you felt my anger with me. Mom, be proud of me now because I have the courage to go on by myself. Without your encouragement I wouldn't have been able to make it. You taught me to be self-sufficient at a very young age, something I had forgotten until now. I know things were tough for you raising me by yourself after Dad died. You taught me that being a single parent is possible. I was angry at you for making me a "latch-key kid," though of course there was no such term back then. Now I realize that was the only way you could make ends meet.

When you remarried I was jealous, but it turned out to be great because you gave me the best stepfather anyone could ask for. He treated me just like one of his own. In my heart, he is my father. The man that died was the "Daddy" I never really knew. Your life gives me hope—hope that I can get through these hard times as you got through yours.

(unsigned)

■■■

April 8, 1990

*From a letter to the editor and to readers of this book.*

My children are adapting well. My daughter, the oldest, I think would disown me if I ever went back to her father. She has seen a lot and doesn't want him to treat me that way ever again. My son is only five years old and thinks that some day his mommy and his daddy will be together again. I just keep telling them both that their father and I both love them, but we just can't live in the same house. The children do spend every other weekend with their father. He is good with them. He has been sober since I left, which is great for him and the kids, but it's too late for me. At one point, I thought that would be enough, but that is not his only problem.

I am safe. He does not try to bother us. He knows where we live, but he is not allowed past the front door. As long as he is sober, I do not feel physically threatened.

Sincerely,

Brenda C.

■■■

*Editor's Note:*

April 7, 1990

Brenda wrote in her diary that she had a date, the first since her separation, with Paul, a man who seemed like a "nice guy" she had not met but had spoken with for five hours on the phone. She felt nervous about meeting him—would he like her, she was not "thin"?—and about going on a date. Subsequent entries describe a blossoming of love and trust and the formation of a "normal," non-violent relationship. The following letter Brenda writes to her daughter compliments the themes in the letter she wrote her mother.

■■■

May 2, 1990

Dear Elizabeth,

I want to tell you how important you are to me. You will always be my first child, my baby. I love you! No matter what happens. I know you feel that Paul is taking your place, but no one and no thing could ever replace you in the space of my heart that is reserved for you only.

You have been a great support to me when everything was so bad. I thank you, but I should never have depended on you like I did. You are only ten years old. This is the time for your childhood. Years that can never be replaced. Now is the time for me to give you back the greatest gift of all: your childhood.

(unsigned) ■

## The Abuse of Forgiveness: The Spiritual Doctrine That Keeps Women Down

Nina Silver

"Forgive and forget" is a phrase that sticks in my throat. In 1979, when I began divulging my history of childhood sexual abuse, I was challenging two widely touted myths: this sort of thing didn't happen in "nice" homes; and even if it did, I should "live and let live," "move on," "forgive and forget." Except for my father who abused me, no one infuriated me more than the people who told me to forgive him. This included my therapist. The day he told me that I needed to forgive the old man already, I knew it was time to move on—to a new therapist.

Such "love your enemies" adages not only push my buttons, they are dangerous to women. Despite what our Judeo-Christian ethic and its well-meaning but pedantic proponents would have us believe, it is not only difficult to forgive, but sometimes it's not even advisable.

Why not? Doesn't forgiveness make us better people? Not necessarily.

The following conversation is typical. I meet someone I haven't seen for awhile, and before I know it I'm getting advice whether I want it or not.

"Forgive your father."

"For what?" I demand. "For being unconscious and not considering my feelings? For being cruel?"

"No, but it's time to let go of the past. After all this time you're pulling skeletons out of the closet? Surely you've dwelled on this for too long already."

"Too long for whom?" I retort.

"Well, you do have a life."

"Yes, I have a life but it's not going to be very fulfilling unless I address the conditions that turned my father into a psychopath. You think men—or anyone—should be allowed to run around molesting little girls?"

My prototypic adversary shifts about uneasily, trying to get into a comfortable position.

"In other words," I continue hotly, "you think I should ignore it now that a certain number of years have passed. What you're really telling me is not to be angry."

People have a hard time dealing with pain—both their own and that of others. Of the many directives in our culture that run our emotional lives, two of the most notorious ones are: Don't get angry, especially if you're a woman; and don't express your pain to others, especially if it is acute. Both of these prohibitions fall under the catchall phrase, "making a big deal out of nothing."

As someone who has worked intensively for ten years to deal with my sexual abuse background and to exorcise the fear, hatred, anger, rage and despair from my system, being told that I should "move on" because I'm making too big a deal out of my experience, hurts. These misplaced platitudes cut even more deeply into the wounds I have just finished nursing. Hearing them is not only unproductive, but it makes things worse.

But I can understand why someone would be tempted to give me that kind of advice. The more incredible the abuse, the greater the tendency is to want to deny both the degree of the trauma and the magnitude of care needed to recover. It can be frightening to witness the depth and intensity of anger that survivors of abuse, once they access their pain, inevitably express. To the extent that some people cannot handle the repercussions in their own lives of experiencing this all-too-real slice of someone else's, they shut down. Like the ancient Greeks who killed the messenger for bringing bad news, they wish that these blabbermouth survivors would leave them alone and go away. But if they can't make a survivor leave, at least they can silence her.

The easiest way to silence an ill-fated messenger/survivor (short of murder) is to make her feel guilty for her feelings. They can shame her by calling her feelings un-Christian or otherwise spiritually un-evolved, socially inappropriate, unladylike, or emotionally unsophisticated—but the effect is the same. The sufferer, without support or a context for feeling her deep anguish, keeps quiet and withdraws, hiding not only from others but from her own self. In a society that endorses and protects male privilege, women's anger is especially threatening.

I remember when I decided to confront my father about his abuse. I was an adult, having officially moved from my parents' house some time before. This separation nourished the growth and autonomy I needed to put the fragments of my life together and understand myself in an entirely new way. I began to realize why I'd grown up terrified of sex. I faced the reasons I hated my father and had felt so utterly alone and unsupported all my life. These realizations gave my life a meaning it never had before. Sometimes, the separation between the ancient trauma and the present awakening helps us remember. It's part of the healing, a way of assessing experience from a safe place. Once I was out of my parents' house, they couldn't really hurt me.

My father denied the abuse. My mother and half-sister called me a liar, brat, evil, and insensitive, accusing me of trying to break up the family. I would come home from work—when I was able to work—and cry my heart out. Those ten years were very hard.

Fortunately, I was able to process a substantial portion of my past with the help of body-oriented (Reichian) therapy. Then the major concerns in my life shifted from the trauma itself to issues raised by having dealt with the abuse: fears that people wouldn't want to know the "real" me, that they might misperceive me or refuse to appreciate what it's like to heal from a past so horrifying that most people would still rather not hear about it. Or—and this was equally distasteful—I dreaded that others would only regard me as a survivor of torment, someone with a dark history. My struggle to be at home in the world continued, going through different stages.

Not surprisingly, among my other professions, I became a therapist. Initially, to my astonishment and then consternation, I discovered that many of my clients had sexual abuse backgrounds. I did everything in my power to help them trust what their bodies and hearts were trying to tell them even while their minds could not believe that such shocking events had happened. Those clients who could accept that they had been abused were bewildered as to why they somehow weren't able to be good sports about the whole thing. After all, they were being offered the same "advice" that had been given to me—advice that taught them to distrust their feelings and doubt the validity of their own perceptions and experiences. How could it be, then, that they were right and everyone else was wrong?

But the only advisor that [we] victims of sexual and other abuse can dare to trust is our own feelings. Each time we are blamed—however covertly with platitudes—for self-indulgence or for refusing to cooperate, we learn that the outside world, like our families, cannot be trusted. This lack of understanding and betrayal of trust, which began with our families and is subsequently reinforced, can be devastating—especially if the abused person is a woman who is being punished for naming and exposing male violence. When sexual abuse survivors need compassionate support and don't get it, it becomes easy to feel unforgiving toward a hostile and unfeeling world that mirrors our family background.

Forgiveness is also flung at victims of trauma in the form of a bromide stating that in addition to forgiving our aggressors, we must forgive ourselves. But forgive ourselves for what? People exhorting self-forgiveness imply that I am guilty, somehow responsible for the abuse I suffered—that as a child I should have "known better" and done something to forestall the abuse. Such assumptions carry the notion that a child has the ability to take charge of her or his own life in the same way an adult can. When I hear accusations that in effect blame me for instigating my own abuse, I become livid. In weighing the balance of power between a child and an adult, there is no contest.

Instead of forgiving, what women really need to do is hate—an emotion considered unacceptable in general and "unwomanly" in particular. According to forgiveness buffs, "polite" society and some spiritual traditions designed to keep us in our place, we are not supposed to hate. But hating can provide a powerful and inspiring release. It's part of the healing process. I have found that once we give ourselves permission to freely hate those who have hurt us, we are then able to take those very important steps toward anger—an emotion even those who were not sexually abused normally don't allow themselves to experience. If I allow myself to feel outrage at having been mistreated, it means that somewhere inside me I must feel self-worth and believe that I deserve to be treated better, with dignity and respect. Accessing and expressing hatred is a way of strengthening self-esteem. The last thing anyone, much less a woman and a victim of trauma, needs is to feel guilty for not being magnanimous enough to "forgive and forget."

But there is one application of forgiveness that I believe is crucial for survivors of incest: that is the true, not the proverbial, meaning of forgiving ourselves. Forgiving myself means that I do not blame the small child I once was for not having possessed the skills and self-reliance of an adult. Forgiving myself means accepting the reality that adults are bigger and stronger than children and that I did not have the power either to prevent the abuse or to protect myself from my family's need to deny it. Once I accept the reality that children are not miniature adults—and therefore need not, cannot be perfect—I can be tolerant of myself as an adult for having human frailties, for making mistakes and errors of judgment. However, a child (in whatever age body) who blames herself for being imperfect will become an intolerant adult.

I'm glad I chose not to heed all those people who tried to tell me how to live my life—for if I had listened to how inadequate, over-emotional, and unforgiving I was, there would not have been a scrap of me left. Loving myself is the most important step I can take, for in loving myself, I can then love others and accept their humanity, allowing for every emotion: hurt, joy, anger, grief, sexual desire, ecstasy.

Eventually in the healing process, we do let go of pain and sorrow; we do "move on." But our moving on is not because someone has decreed that it is not appropriate, spiritual, or nice to hate or be angry. We move on with our lives because, having received support to feel our feelings—no matter how negatively they might be perceived—there is now enough space to experience pleasure and joy as well. I don't need or want to forgive anyone for anything. Forgiving is really "giving for" myself whatever it takes to recover. And the giving—whether to myself or others—is for me and my own satisfaction, not for someone else who thinks that it's noble or virtuous to make sacrifices ("forgive").

A victim of sexual abuse will always remember the past. But she becomes a survivor when she maintains her right to her feelings, her life—her Self. ■

**Stepfather: A Catharsis**

Shirley W. Jones

I'll tell you about him, that asshole.

The other day at my sister's house he told my son, age six: "I told you to keep your goddamned feet off the bed. The next time I catch them up there I'll cut the mother fuckers off and shove them up your butt!"

I expressed how I didn't want my son talked to in that sick perverted manner and my sister said, "He lives here and that's how he talks. You know that!"

Feeling as though I was beating myself in the face, I went to tell him how I felt and my sister jumped all over me for trying to start trouble in her home.

He told me, "I tell someone once, twice and then it gets violent."

In a fit of anger, I pointed my finger at him and said, "Violent. That's the word. Violence. Well I've had enough violence in my life." I left. I took my son and left, never to return again. I will never return to a home that when I walk through the door I am stripped of my rights as a mother.■

**Sanctuary**
Edith Riley

I lock my door upon myself
Christina Rossetti

I build a sanctuary to myself
of granite walls.
Dark simple colors
surround the center
the well guarded secrets
throb.
Embedded in crystal
fragile
a brown velvet cloak surrounds them.
They shine in warmth and softness
    glowing
    steady
    enclosed
    inviolate
the sanctuary stands
protecting peace inside. ■

## Section Seven

## *She Said NO!*

There are men who believe
That when a woman says no, she means yes,
That every woman wants
His cock in her mouth.
I am learning the no of my knee,
My palm heel, the persuasion of an
Axe kick to the head.
Every blow is thrown full force.
I am fighting for my life.
The worst opponent is my father's voice.

Once I punched my partner
In no-contact Kempō class.
My eyes watered. I could not look at anyone
Knowing part of me had
Loved the feel of fist on skin.

Now I wake up to find a man standing over me,
Huge from his protection and my fear.
He strokes my hair.
"I'm gonna fuck your brains out, cunt!"
My no comes from the goddess
Deep inside the dark cave of my body,
From my blood and bones and womb,
For once my father is silent.

I uncoil, strike wholeheartedly as death
Women yell a list of moves and body parts
Like stops along a map,
"Bite, elbow, eyes, groin, snap!"

I kick with the rage of a child told
"No you can't, you're a girl,"
Pound him for the men who yelled out their opinions of my body
The men who stood too close on subways,
The men who grabbed my crotch at concerts,
The man who said, "You have to, I'm your boyfriend,"
The man who jumped me in Boston,
The man who choked me in London,
The man who held a gun against my head
The man who tied my arms and
Raped me in my bed, then stabbed me anyway.

I stand over this man and hurl one final NO
Toward women waiting for their turn to win.
This time I shout for all of us, the mugger almost forgotten.
I yell for our strength and for the space around our bodies
I yell for the banishment of fear.
What I mean is YES !

Alison Stone

In some ways, this whole collection is written "toward women waiting" by women no longer waiting but acting. Action is the password for this section; it is time for all of us to stop waiting for firm solutions and to adopt a spirit of adventure to explore new avenues of change. This book ends as it begins: with a call that we take back the fight against crimes against women and adopt a policy of "zero tolerance" among women and among institutions. Change begins with dreams for change—imagination creates new possibilities.

Gina Bergamino's "Inside a Dream" celebrates feminine strength and sensuality. "Riding Shotgun" reflects the hard work and keen sense of humor it takes to transform dreams into reality and to establish a women-centered program in a male-centered world. M. P.'s journal is edited to obscure the locations her program services. Names of towns, counties, hospitals, sheriffs, and other law enforcement personnel have been altered or omitted. (If any of these sheriffs and district attorneys knew she was recording their sexism and resistance to change, the program would fold.)

"Two Headed Stories" blends the form of short story with memoir to trace one night's work in crisis intervention at a public hospital, highlighting both the possibilities and the limitations of such programs. Set in an institution where Margaret Robison taught writing classes, "What the Heart Knows" poses the question: "Where do we begin?" Here in this "cage of bone/Woman alone" unlocks the prison of her personal and political history through claiming the stories of her life.

"To Eros," Pat Falk's satire of prior entrapment, tempers defiance with humor. By writing our soul stories into success stories, we open ourselves to a new growth. Suellen Kelly's "Morning" catches us "between the old and the new." Between the ebb and the flow of change and resistance to it lies a cycle of self-transformation through which we discover the challenge of transcendence.

Katharyn Howd Machan's poem, "My Name is Gloria," closes the collection with a song of self-celebration. Birthing herself, she births a new generation of women—*women no longer waiting*. We have come full circle. The landscape of tomorrow is painted on the canvas of our past, Robison's "Rorschach" of women's history. Silent Woman Speaks from yesterday into tomorrow. New Gloria listens and sings. ■

## Inside a Dream

Gina Bergamino

I want to sleep forever
I can't stand being
awake while sisters are raped
babies are beaten
roaches live
in my kitchen.
I want to sleep forever
and dream
of beautiful black women dancing
naked
with lace shawls
hanging from hips
rhythmically circling
each other
as drum keeps
on beating
and they finger
their breasts
mouths open
in the glow
of their music. ■

## Riding Shotgun: Journal of an Outreach Worker

M. P.

*10-23-89*

Came in late, computer was de-programmed, too many volunteers at shelter—we'll have to reschedule. Found March of Dimes Health Assessment Charge for use in presenting to health officials and clinics. It's terrible that most of my old files have disappeared since I last worked here. Will have to keep up on this information.

*10-24-89*

Spoke to 3 homemaking classes. Mixed group. Some are obviously in a bad situation. All in all the response was good by the expressions on their faces. Tried to connect with the Sheriff's dept. and PD in Mudville—they must have been out to lunch. Got frustrated after about four calls.

Left and headed down to Carin' County to the Sheriff's Dept. Was able to get the deputy to give me the stats from October on Family Violence (FV). He is insisting that I speak to him personally. He read the stats from reports. That was the best I could get. Maybe next month will be more effective. He mentioned one case that the woman was mad because her husband was not arrested. I asked why not. He said, "Where do you live? This is the United States. We need warrants to arrest." I said I was sure that under certain circumstances a warrantless arrest was not unconstitutional when associated with FV due to new laws over the past several years. He said "Yes, I teach that course." Obviously the teaching needs to be better and so does the enforcement.

Headed to Silverton, PD. The chief is not in favor of the retrieval system because of privacy rights of individuals. Wants us to get a ruling from the DA and county attny. before he lets us do anything like that. Need to write him a letter explaining in greater detail that all we need to see is the incident reports to get addresses. Material that is provided to the Media. Get so tired of obstacles like this.

*10-30-89*

Did paper work and then to T. County, Mudville, to talk to DA. He rarely gives protective orders and has been evading us for 2 months now for a meeting. He was actually there!!! Mr. Macho—didn't even stand up for us when we came in or left. Got somewhat friendly after he discovered we weren't coming in with daggers in our hands. We cleared the air in a general way and feel that he is responsive to our goals of establishing a group in T. County.

*11-01-89*

Went to dentist today. I'm hitting him up for money for billboards. Had to explain that even though we are a United Way Agency, all of our money is specified and cannot be used for advertising. His bookkeeper will send some kind of check by December 1. Didn't really mention how much money we needed—wouldn't it be great if he sent several hundred dollars. Dream on!!!

Had extra volunteer training this night. We emphasized professionalism and some new information on the Hotline sheets that needs to be obtained.

*11-17-89*

Met with hospitals in T. and J. Counties. They seemed receptive to the idea of inservice and assessments toward all women entering the hospitals. Have set up dates for inservice in J.

Sheriff in J. doesn't know if his men are handing out the required notices to victims of FV. He will check and if not will implement this immediately. Sure!!! Discussed retrieving stats from his office each month. Probably will get that done. He wants the exact law on open records, the notices and warrantless arrests. We will get with him next week or so with the information.

Met with T. County D.A. to see what he thinks about us having an office in the Justice Center in Mudville. He said to talk with the county judge. I know that. I just want D.A. to get used to us dropping in on a casual basis. Have an appointment with the judge next week on 21st of Nov.

*11-22-89*

Went to Mudville on 21st. Somehow arranged for office space one day a week in the Adult Probation Dept. Will have the office on Tuesdays. Will spend time in office 1/2 day and rest out in the field.

Talked with Mudville Police Chief who said that they had only one (1) FV call in the past month. Do I really believe this? NO!!!

Had a hostage situation today at a local motel. Thought it was the husband of one of our clients, maybe her. It wasn't. There were two women involved. One of them has been released and is at the shelter. Can't wait to check the story out. Probably prostitutes. Isn't that terrible to say? The girls are from Georgia. Anyway, some excitement.

*12-14-89*

We will be baking cookies for all the PD's and Sheriff's Depts in our area on Monday the 18th.

*1-3-90*

Things are looking up in small ways in our area. T. County DA's office now has typed up Protective Order forms and applications with their own name on them. They have had the form for over a year from J. County and had not even bothered to change the names. Such small advancement, but it beats nothing.

*1-29-90*

Things have been popping in a lot of ways. The protective order we had a client apply for in W. was cancelled. She did it (cancelled it). Very disappointing but very typical. He has committed himself to a drug/alcohol rehab. She is encouraged by this behavior. It is the first time in 14 years that she has been able to see any sign of effort on his part. Her attitude is understandable.

A support group is being started in T. County on Feb. 19. This is great news. Hopefully, we will get a good turnout and that group will grow. Then we will begin one in Jasper. Need to lay some groundwork first.

The Sheriff in T. County has scheduled a week's worth of inservice for his staff and anyone else that wants to come. Domestic Violence is one of the topics. Unfortunately, we were scheduled to provide the training. He didn't have the courtesy to tell us that he was including us in his training. At least they will be gettin' the information they need. We are just irritated at the inconsideration.

We've had two clients in jail in B. and L. It's a bummer because they could have helped prevent the charges. Doesn't help, though, when your clients are in jail and are calling you. ■

## Two Headed Stories

Miriam Kalman Harris

> The heads speak sometimes singly, sometimes
> together, sometimes alternately within a poem.
> Like all Siamese twins, they dream of separation.
>
> Margaret Atwood, "Two Headed Poems"

### Janus/Anna

Her face. Marvelous, I think: rich brown skin. Skin Alice Walker calls chocolate, milk chocolate. A mole on her right cheekbone enhances like a beauty mark, accentuates the pride and strength she demonstrates with every word and action. Her eye, intelligent, furious, burns bright above the beauty mark. Eye, I say, because I can see only her right one. Her left eye is crushed beneath a bloody wash cloth, once blue, now stained with crusting red, laced with fresh crimson streaks. Ice, I think. She is in pain. I should ask the nurse if the patient can have an ice pack. I often see the women back here in ER Surgery nursing their wounds with ice. But not yet. Not until we get a picture. Evidence, if she wants it, is more important now than mere relief of physical discomfort.

We start the consultation. She wants to whisper, wants me to whisper, doesn't want to sit out in the open. We rarely work with a victim out here in the patient waiting area. But tonight the rooms are full and I haven't been able to find a private place. She is the second case I've spoken with tonight, the third one in two days. All three women have been beaten on the left side of their faces; therefore, all three men were right handed.

We have the area to ourselves, I show her. Just one elderly man huddled over in the other corner, asleep. But the lack of privacy for her is yet another form of emotional abuse. I excuse myself, find an empty space. When I return, a small woman in a bright red sweater is sitting in the chair the man vacated. Her eyes are tearing—not crying, just tearing—as she watches me signal to my "patient." She reaches out and touches my arm; she asks me for my card. I tell her I'll be glad to speak with her when I am free. She shakes her head: no, not tonight. She wants to call us on another day. I write our contact number on a blue information card published by the Dallas Police Department.

My patient and I settle into a quiet examination room. She boosts herself up on the table. I comment on her amazing agility after what must have been an ordeal, tell her that she looks healthy and bright. She answers that she is "always the same no matter what," she was just like this ten minutes after she had each of her babies. I tell her that she has a quality of confidence and control. She answers: "I am saved."

"What?"

"I'm saved. I gave my life to Jesus Christ."

I'm Jewish and don't have a clear idea of what that means but I know one thing for sure: it works for her.

She is a large woman, heavy thighs, strong arms, well proportioned. Handsome is the word I'd use to describe her overall appearance, and the right side of her face. She removes the cloth as I ask questions about the injury: "Here's what he did to me!" she says. The left eye is swollen shut, heavily bruised; blood oozes from a cut next to her nose, which she tells me is broken. She casually removes dry blood from each nostril and wipes it on a tissue I hand her as we speak. She is Janus, I think as I write down her answers without missing a beat. She has two faces: her own and the one he gave her.

"He's going to jail for this. I'll see him in the penitentiary or I'll see him dead."

Dead is better, I think. Dead men can't hit strong, beautiful women and turn their faces to pulp.

"Have you called the police and reported this?"

"I was calling them when he caught me and beat me. That's how he got me, see. I got away. Soon as I could I ran from him before he could hurt me. My mom—I live with my mom—she took the baby and my daughter and ran to a neighbor's but they don't have a phone either. I knew I had to get the police fast."

"Does he beat the children as well?"

"No. But my mom, she don't take any chances."

"Smart woman."

"You bet. She left my father the first time he struck her. We never saw him again."

"Smart woman. And your husband?"

"He's not my husband! I'm not married to him. I never took his name. But the law says we're common law and I have to get a divorce anyway. Is that something? I never would marry him. We don't even live together anymore."

"But you did at one time? For how long?"

"Two years. First time he beat me, I threw him out and never let him move back in with me again. After the baby came, I moved in with my mom."

"How many times has he beat you, in all?"

"Three. First time was when he found out I was pregnant. It was his baby. No matter. I packed his bags and threw him out. He came back when the baby was a month old. Beat me bad. I called the police and they arrested him, but he got out. This is the third time. I almost got away. I ran to the corner phone booth and called the police. But just as I was hanging up he came running toward the booth and crashed through the door with his fists and grabbed me and started sluggin'. Two hundred and fifty pounds of sluggin' on my face. Poundin' away on me, kickin', yellin' until he heard the sirens. Then he ran off, disappeared. He left me for dead; I might've been dead for all he knew."

"How did you get here? Police? Ambulance?"

"My mom. They wanted to call an ambulance but Mom wanted to bring me."

"Where is the baby now?"

"At the neighbor's still. But my little girl—she's six and she was so scared she wouldn't stay with them. She was worried I would die so she came here with us and she's out in the waiting room with Mom."

"I'll go tell her you're doing OK in just a few minutes, soon as we finish this form and get you settled. What will you do now? Do you know what your options are?"

"This time I'm gonna make sure he don't get out. When they catch him I'm gonna press charges and stay on that case 'til I see him in the penitentiary — that's what I'm gonna do. I'm gonna make sure he goes in and stays in." She wants to know more about restraining orders, protective orders. Last time the measures she'd taken were not enough. This time she wants to make sure.

"Do you want me to take a picture of your eye? We'll keep it here on file with this questionnaire I'm filling out and then when your case comes to trial you can call it in for evidence."

"OK. Good."

The doctor comes in to examine her and I leave to get the referral information she needs. I've already given her the usual resource cards, but she needs extra information about legal resources, and I have to get the camera anyway and check on her little girl.

This is a county hospital, a teaching institution. Busy, crowded, chaotic, amazingly efficient. Each time I walk past the ambulances and police cars, through the huge mechanical doors of the emergency entrance, Emma Lazarus' words echo in my mind: "Give me your tired, your poor, . . . your huddled masses yearning to breath free." I wonder why there is no Statue of Liberty out on the front lawn somewhere.

The waiting room is smoky, noisy. There seem to be hundreds of six-year-old daughters. How will I find the right one?

Starched pink dress, milk chocolate skin, beautiful. She sleeps quietly in the arms of a strong, proud woman who sits erect against the back wall, away from the noise and smoke. I recognize them as the mother and daughter of the woman I've spent the last hour talking with. I smile and whisper words of comfort; I'm sure they must sound trite. The mother nods in resignation, does not return the smile. The daughter sleeps.

The doctor has left by the time I get back to the surgery area. She moves the rag away to reveal her Janus face. The bruise, now darker, now bluer. The blood still oozes some but not as bad. The swelling has increased. I want to take the picture so they can bring her ice. The light is good in the exam room. The picture comes out clear and realistic.

She motions to me to let her see it. "That's what I look like? Oh,

Jesus. Oh, Lord. That's what he did to me!" It's as close as she comes to breaking down. But she doesn't. "I'll send him to the penitentiary."

I start to hand her the new resource list I've brought her. She doesn't even notice. She's looking at the picture.

"Will you take another one?" she asks.

"Sure. Why?"

"I want to take one home with me. I want to hang it on my bathroom mirror so I don't ever forget what he can do to me. Every evening when I go to bed, and every morning when I wake up I want to remember what he did to me."

The doctor comes back in and tells her he wants to get some x-rays of her face. He's sure her ribs aren't broken, only bruised. He wants to be sure about her face. She dresses, modestly keeping her body covered as she slips on her warm ups and slips off the hospital gown. She doesn't want me to take pictures of the bruises on her body. She doesn't want pictures of her body to appear in court.

The form is complete and I have a record of her circumstances. I have a record of his name and address, age and work place. ("Work place? None. Who knows what he does. I don't ask him for anything — just to leave me alone.") I gather up my papers and the camera and turn to wish her well.

"You ever been like this?" she asks. "Has any man ever hit you?"

"No," I answer, feeling somehow disqualified.

"It's the most humiliating thing in the world. Just imagine how I feel walking around like this out there with all those people knowing some man beat me up."

"They don't know."

"Sure they do. Of course they know."

"The ones who know, will know because it's happened to them too."

"You mean that little black woman? The one in the red sweater who asked you for your card."

"Yes, her too, I suppose. But she isn't out there anymore. She said she couldn't talk tonight but wants to call us later. So perhaps that's what she wants to talk about. But another woman I talked to earlier. She's sitting out in the waiting area hurting just like you, only her skin doesn't bruise. Her pain is all on the inside." The waiting area is crowded again. I know I'm not betraying anyone's anonymity.

"Why doesn't her skin bruise? How can skin not bruise?"

"It has something to do with her medical condition."

She shrugs, shakes her head. I show her the way to x-ray and then circle back, past the ER waiting area.

My earlier patient, the one who "doesn't bruise," now sits quiet, transfixed, staring into the space in front of her, caught in the whirl of her own thoughts, oblivious to the hectic pace around her. Her skin is pasty white, her hair frazzled. Something about her remains "cute." Even after all she's been through, she looks like she'd be fun to know, fun to have as a friend.

I wonder if the seat she occupies—right in the middle of the section, surrounded by the other patients—was the only one available. I wouldn't be able sit ram-rod straight after all she'd been through. I would need to huddle in the corner, stretch out my legs along some vacant chairs. But there are no vacant chairs now.

I stop by and give her some additional forms that might help her to obtain free legal advice—the same forms I've just given the Janus woman. It occurs to me that she is Janus too; it just doesn't show as starkly. I wonder if they both sat down together, side by side—two Janus faces—would they recognize the source of one another's pain?

It occurs to me that I had seen her "case" as "finished," except for a few notations I still needed to make on her report. I suddenly realize how far from finished her case is.

This woman also is embarking tonight on a new journey, the dangerous process of escaping from a man who has threatened to kill her, who has come very close to carrying out those threats. She too wants to put him in the penitentiary. She too would rather see him dead than free to beat her up again. As she told me earlier,

"He sure had me fooled. I never would've thought he'd ever hurt me." She has a way of laughing between statements as she tells her story.

There is tenderness between her and the two women who drove her to the hospital. They live in a small town about forty miles south. Each had her own complaint. They decided to make the drive together, share their woes and a tank of gas.

"Have all of you been beaten?" I inquired when I first began the consultation. None of them showed any outward signs of injury.

"No, no. Just me. They have their own problems."

"What happened to you?" She didn't mind talking in front of people, didn't care who heard. As soon as we could, however, we moved to a private room and she told her story between the doctor's exam and the nurses entering and leaving. Her story is the same as all the others; and like the others, different and unique.

She's small and delicate. Fragile. I cannot imagine how she lives through the attacks her "husband" puts her through. Not that someone large can endure a beating better; just that it looks like one hard blow to her face would crush it. But she has endured many.

She doesn't bruise, she tells me. She thinks it's because of her disease, multiple sclerosis. She shows me that one side of her face is swollen out. I hadn't noticed it at first. When she turns to show me, I see her face is lopsided. Her left cheekbone protrudes—about an inch.

I ask questions about her relationship with "Him," thinking this "Him" is her husband. I've noticed that the women never say "His" name until I ask them. It's always just "He."

Her throat is sore. It is painful for her to speak but she wants to tell me everything. Periodic choking has changed her voice. I had noticed its odd timbre. Now I understand its cause.

"How long have you been together?"

"Five years. That is, I know him five now. He was business partners with me and my husband. That's what I mean—he had me fooled, this one —he lived with us and we was partners, all three of us." She talks fast, like she wants to get it all said so she can rest her throat. But then she stops to swallow hard and start again.

"You mean this man who beat you tonight . . ."

"No. It wasn't tonight. It was yesterday. He wanted to kill me, almost did. I ran away, over to my friend's—the woman out there with me with long brown hair, her—I ran over to her house and called the police on him."

"Your husband?"

"He's not my husband."

"Who beat you then?"

"Well, the police say he's my husband now, by common law. Cause he's lived in my house for five years, I guess. So to get away from him I have to get a divorce. Can you beat that one? But I don't care what I have to do long as I put him away forever."

She is careful to explain that they were never married. Now, as I recall her story to finish my paper work before I turn it in, I realize that both women I have counseled tonight considered themselves single. The law requires that they file for divorce. It seems to me that strict definition of common law marriage was designed in the seventies as a means of protecting women's rights. I wonder how that changed to work to their disadvantage.

"Where is your first husband now?" I asked, continuing the interview.

"In the pen. I put him there."

"Why?"

"For trying to kill me. That's what I mean. This one sure had me fooled. See, he saved my life."

"What's his name?—just to help me keep all this straight."

"Tim. His name is Tim."

I needed his name and address for the form anyway, so I began to ask her questions about Tim and soon the story began to make sense.

"See, my first husband was always knocking me around. Always beating on me—getting drunk and beating on me. Then Tim come to live with us and things got a little better 'cause he couldn't beat me as often—only when Tim wasn't there. But Tim walked in on us one night and pulled him off me just as he was about to kill me. He had a butcher knife pulled and was about to stab me when Tim come in and heard me screaming and broke down the door to the bedroom and got the knife away. We called the police and with Tim as a witness and all, well, I had that bastard put in the pen. He's still there."

"But Tim stayed on?"

"Yes. He was great. Helped me through the whole ordeal and my divorce. Then, he stayed on with me even after we closed the business. I thought I know'd him inside out."

"What does he do now?"

"He's a chef. Over to Dolly's Diner in town. He cooks. He's a good cook. Everybody loves him. He has everybody fooled. He sure fooled me."

"When did he start beating you?"

"I guess about a year ago. I don't know why. I don't know what ever happened to change him. But I come to find out he beat his first wife. Beat her to death and went to prison for it."

"How'd you find that out? And when?"

"First time he hit me. I called his mother. She's a fine lady—lives over in Mississippi. I went to a pay phone and called her just to ask her what in the world could've come over Tim. He's always been so sweet and kind. That's when she told me. He done time in Huntsville for killing his wife. But I didn't know it before."

"How'd he get out?"

"Beats me," she giggles, catching on to her pun. "My luck I guess. I guess he got out so he could work his way over to me."

"Does he drink? Use drugs?" I asked, returning to my form.

"Drugs. Yeah. He does drugs. But he always did long as I've known him."

"Has he ever been in a mental institution?"

"Yes. I can't exactly remember which one, but it was right after Vietnam. He come back from Nam and went to a mental hospital. Then he come out and got married, had a baby, murdered his wife, went to prison, come out and found me. Just my luck." She giggled at herself.

"But you didn't know any of this when you first met him?"

"Nope. Well, I know'd he been in Nam and I know'd he got treated but they all do that. And that's all I knew 'til after he hit me."

"Why'd he hit you tonight—I mean yesterday."

"Oh, who knows. The house wasn't clean. He said the house wasn't clean and I was a lazy slob and he starts to pounding. He's a strong sucker. When he hits, it hurts."

"Is he big? Is he a large man?" I ask, noticing again how frail and vulnerable she is.

"NAW!! Little bitty guy. But STRONG. Strong as shit. That's how he got my husband off me and saved my life. My husband was big, a great big man, six-four. Tim's small—no bigger than me. But I'm no match for him. If I was, I'd have killed him myself yesterday. Instead I just ran."

We talk about her options: how she could stay away from him, what safety protective orders could and could not offer, what legal services were available in her small community. She already had hired a lawyer, but she was worried about expenses.

We talk about a lot of things. She likes to talk, even though it seems to strain her throat. One of the things we talk about is sex. A question on the form deals with rape. Forced sex within a marriage or intimate relationship is rape.

"No," she answers with a giggle when I ask if he ever raped her. "That sort of thing was always good with us." She shook her head. "Why is that, you suppose?"

"I don't know. Why do you think?"

"I can't figure it out. We always enjoyed that sort of thing. How can a man be so loving and tender one night and then beat the shit out of a woman the next?"

"I don't know."

"And how can I enjoy sex with him after he's hit me—I don't mean the same night, but later, say a week later?"

"I don't know that either. But you aren't the only one who feels that way. Part of the whole cycle I guess." We laugh together, both of us shaking our heads, knowing full well that none of it is funny, but that some things about people are funnier when they aren't funny than when they are and that none of it made much sense in the first place. I like it that we both seem to know that.

I also like the way we end our encounter. It lets me know that she's thinking and that she is ready to take responsibility for herself.

"So, what do I do now?" she asks as we say goodbye. I know she's not talking about phone numbers of community resources. She's holding lists of them in her hands.

"Stay safe. Take care of yourself. Hide. So what if he continues to live in your house? That will work out with the protective order. Until you're sure he's behind bars, don't let him know where you are."

"You can bet on that. But then what? After he goes to Huntsville?"

"Stay away from men for awhile." I'm joking, I think. But I know it's a serious joke.

"That's what I mean," she says, with her usual giggle. "How do I do that? How will I know next time?"

Again, I don't have an answer. What is she supposed to do? She's a young woman, thirty-five, with a fatal disease. She wants to enjoy life while she still can. She likes men. Why shouldn't she? And then again, given her life story, how does she dare? I hope that counseling will help her learn to choose somebody safe next time. But Tim seemed safe. After all, he saved her life. And for three years after that he was safe.

I encourage her to join a support group. Counseling, I advise, will give her some new insights. I know that it sounds like a simple solution to a complex problem—how to choose safe men—but it's all I know to tell her. There are no simple answers to any of the kinds of questions that arise, night after night. But at least, women are starting to ask.

I finish filling out the evening's forms and turn them in. It's late, thirty minutes past my quitting time. But the hospital never quits. I pass through the mechanical doors of the ER entrance, past the ambulances and police cars. There, ahead of me, a couple walks. He holds her by the elbow, steers her toward the parking lot. I recognize her by her red sweater—the woman huddled in the corner—the woman who would call another time.

I know she will. ■

**What the Heart Knows**
Margaret Robison

We begin again here
together in this room,
in this prison. Our way
lit by what the blood itself knows,
not the harsh fluorescent lights
that interrogate each word, each
sentence on the page.
What the heart knows. Not
the knowledge that fences and walls
hold on their stiff, insensitive backs.

We claim our lives
word
by word, this
slow birth, this
becoming.

Catherine's fingers curl around a shell
as if in another time
they might have found a home
on some sea's ancient floor.
We come our different ways
to who we are.

Hands of mine, even cuffed
you were still loved, Catherine writes.
Lisa's large rings click together in the quiet.
Her hands are dark
birds of becoming.

Where do we begin?
Catherine, Christina, Jo Ann,
Ruth and Elaine
together in this room.
Lisa, Zenaieda and Sheryl.
I am here too.   I begin
the poem, the word
the line on the page
that is the lifeline
I lay down before me,
the tightrope I walk.

The sewing machine's plug dangles free.
How many miles of fabric
have been guided under the needle
by the hands of women in factories, women
still with necessity, in their hard
straight chairs.

The ironing board
that stands against the wall
could hold the whole of women's history
in the Rorschach
of scorch marks on its cover.

The only women's history
we'll ever know for sure
is the history we write and live ourselves.

It scares me.
How do you begin again? Zenaida writes.
Sometimes I lie awake at night
while my heart knocks
against its cage of bone.
Woman alone  woman alone.

How do you begin again?
Word by word by word I claim
my life, I claim
the stories of my life
as if they were water
I could scoop up in my hands
to quench a deep thirst,
as if they were bread,
a hearty, rich bread for my hunger,
as if they were earth,
firm ground for my bare feet to stand on
And they are.
They are. ■

## To Eros

Pat Falk

you sly
little pea pod
of a god/sliding into my life
when I open/just a bit
when I slip and
gaze graze or taste/it's you
all sticky on my skin
like sin

this is my scream
a clear scream straight to all
the sky gods
sea gods
book/crook and prickly/yellow
corn gods

you/who think me mortal
flabby/flesh and
subject to
love/lust
a garden of vices/a room
of devices

a woman/and you
willy nilly pea pod
of a man/
will never conquer
me ■

**Morning**
Suellen Kelly

This morning as I look around me and see new growth that has come with the changing season, I wonder about my own new growth each day bringing a new change in my behavior. Yet for me not fast enough. Sometimes I feel caught between the old and the new. Wanting to go back and yet knowing I can never go home again. What is the uncharted journey? How many times will I fail to see changes and opportunities put in front of me, longing to stay put, yet wanting to move ahead to find the complete and whole me? ■

## My Name Is Gloria

Katharyn Howd Machan

1\.

I'm the one with golden
long hair curling, eyes blue
as morning's flowers, mouth a perfect
smile of cherry ripe. Laugh
with me, run to where full summer
stirs the lake, sleek rainbow fish
move over pebbles. Girl-child,
woman within a brightness waiting
for time to pull her singing: I
wear the whitest dress a dream
can offer, catch it up in hands
made strong by climb, swing and swing
across the orchard pathway, reaching
all the way to sky.

2\.

Sky: that's what I thought of
when he touched me wrong
and secret. Place of forgetting,
place without faces to see
my shame. Blue escape: clouds
in shapes I will always remember:
pirate ship, lion's mane, torch.
That shadowed corner of room
or shack out in the woods
opened wide in my aloneness,
fear and love together taking me
high towards the soundless throne
of sun, wind without fingers
touching my deepest dark.

3.
Dark, the words I held
a quarter of a century before
the poems began. My brother lives in a box
of cigars. . . If we lived in the South Sea
long ago, brother, you might have been husband . . .
How many years a family holds
its stories prisoner, walls of silent stone
all the world perceives. Grandma dies:
pink roses. Daddy dies: red roses. Mommy
takes her daughter back to live
with her and daughter's brother: purple
pansies leering from every wall,
evil little blossoms hissing
watch out, watch out, watch out.

4.
Out of childhood, out of chains
of body's helplessness, a lady learns
new ways of silence. She lies
to others—family pattern!—
to herself—did it really happen?—
again and again the subterfuge
allows her to go on.
Then one day a word begins.
Then one day a safe voice reaches
yes to her heart's terror.
She names her pain and finds
it stamping its cold feet, tight
bearded face a shriek of fury
that starts to tear in half and disappear.

5.
Disappear, she thinks. Why, I'm already
near-invisible. Brown hair, not gold.
Gray eyes, crooked teeth, a mouth

that likes the taste of cherries
but frowns a somber pink.
Years and years she sees herself
unworthy, dirty, always trying
to prove her right to exist.
Brother distant as a once-loved god.
Husbands pushed away with flight.
Mirror a steady validation
of self-scorn in harsh light.
Even the poems do not bring redemption
in her journey through sky's night.

6.

Night's center falls around my body full
with dancing child. I'm 35; she is
my first, a cry made flesh to push and pull
my vivid dreams. When he first offered his
dark laughing eyes those seas away in land
of lavender and bay, did I begin
to know her voice, her smile, her reach of hand,
the sharing of a story kept within?
Like Demeter, who ran along the shore
as mare and found Poseidon's stallion good
for morning love, I cherish now my core
of strength as I face single motherhood.
I am the child again who swings and swings —
new Gloria, with woman's mouth, who sings. ■

# End Notes

**Acknowledgments**

[1] Published: "And His Name Was Kalman, Too" *Public Library Quarterly*, Vol. 17, No. 3, 1999

**Introduction**

[1] Although there are now programs that offer batterers and couples counseling, the hope that permanent change can be effected is diminished by Walker's findings that "batterers are violent for their own personal reasons, not because of anything their women do or don't do." The batterer, dependent on the woman as a scapegoat, will "almost always function better with the woman than without her whereas the woman will almost always function better when she is out of the relationship for good." Lenore Walker, *Terrifying Love: Why Battered Women Kill and How Society Responds* (New York, NY: Harper and Row, 1989), p.46. Walker's findings further indicate that "battering relationships rarely change for the better" and that couples therapy seems to have little effect on battering relationships once the pattern of violence has been established.

Kit Frieden, in her article "Battered" in *Dallas Life Magazine* (20 Sept. 1992, pp. 9–22) is more optimistic: "Of an estimated 600 men arrested in Dallas who went through counseling . . . only 7 percent returned to their violent ways" as compared to 20 to 30 percent of those convicted who did not receive counseling and returned to violence.

[2] Statistics vary on this figure. Other studies report figures as high as 35 and even 45 percent. Note that injuries and symptoms related to ongoing abuse vary from the obvious to the subtle: "If one looks only for trauma, however, a vast majority of battered women will be overlooked. Violence in the home often manifests itself in anxiety, depression, chemical dependency, chronic headaches, abdominal pains, joint pains, muscle aches, complaints of sexual dysfunction, sleeping and eating disorders, and suicide attempts." *Journal of the American Medical Association*, 266. No. 9 (4 Sept. 1991). See also websites

http://www.cybergrrl.com and http:// femina.cybergrrl.com

[3] "Violence by Intimates," *Bureau of Justice Statistics Handbook*, 1998, Document #158837, and "Women in Prison: Punishing Victims as Penal Policy," 1994, Document #158904. See data from the National Clearinghouse for the Defense of Battered Women, available at http://femina.cybergrrl.com; http://members.aol.com/NCMDR/index.html.

[4] For feminist theories on the heroic journey see: Kim Chernin, *Reinventing Eve: Modern Woman in Search of Herself* (NY: Harper & Row, 1987); Jean Shinoda Bolen, *Goddesses In Everywoman: A New Psychology of Women* (New York, NY: Harper & Row, 1985); Penelope Washbourn, *Becoming Woman: The Quest for Wholeness in Female Experience* (San Francisco: Harper & Row, 1977); and Carol S. Pearson, *The Hero Within: Six Archetypes We Live By* (New York, NY: Harper & Row, 1989).

### Section Two: Thoughts after Rape

[1] Information gathered from Violence Against Women Clearinghouse, the Bureau of Justice Statistics, the National Crime Victimization Survery, and the U. S. Department of Justice websites: http://members.aol.com/NCMDR/index.html; www.mcjrs.org; www.ojp.usodj.gov; and www.RAINN.org/stats.html.

### Section Three: Dark Pages

[1] Statistics from Payne, p. 57.

[2] Statistics from Child Help, USA, a resource to provide care for abused children and their families, March 1992, 1997; see also www.childhelpusa.org

[3] Department of Health and Human Services, Administration for Children and Families, Child Maltreatment, 1995; see also www.RAINN.org/stats.html

### Section Four: On the Grinding of Axes

[1] In *Pornography and Silence*, Susan Griffin states: "In the striptease, culture realizes its revenge against nature. The mystery of the female body

is revealed to be nothing more than flesh, and flesh under culture's control" (p. 36). This statement seems in direct contradiction of Jan Barstow's experience. Griffin examines the exploitation of women through the sex industry, cites instances where women humiliate men and argues that ultimately male power will take revenge. Griffin's study is invaluable; however, we must realize that Barstow's perceptions of her own experiences are equally valid and confirm the complexity of the ethical questions at hand.

[2] Proponents for the censorship of pornography argue that "pornography shapes men's behavior toward women" and that "depictions of subordination tend to perpetuate subordination" (Andrea Dworkin and Catherine MacKinnon, respectively, quoted in Strebeigh, pp. 29 ff.) For our purposes, however, censorship is not the issue. Society's attitudes toward the subjection of women are reflected in images of degradation that provoke violence. Opposition to censorship does not indicate support of pornography.

**SECTION FIVE: BEHIND HIS WALLS**

[1] Letter and article, "'Dad has had me like a prisoner,' slain wife wrote," *Dallas Morning News*, 4 Jan. 1988, Sec. 1, p. 1+ -1ff. A follow-up article, on 26 June 1990, in *Dallas Morning News*, reports that R. Gene Simmons, convicted of the sixteen murders, was put to death by lethal injection on Monday, June 25, 1990, at 9:02 P.M. Sentencing was also reported in the *New York Times*, 12 Feb. 1989.

[2] For a more complete discussion on how the law works when women kill their abusers or when abusers kill their women, see Walker; Angela Browne, *When Battered Women Kill* (New York: Free Press, 1987); *Double-Time*, 1, No. 1 (Oct. 1991) and Holly Maguigan, "Battered Women and Self-Defense: Myths and Misconceptions in Current Reform Proposals" in *University of Pennsylvania Law Review*, 140, No. 1 (Dec. 1991). See also www.ncjs.org and www.cybergirl.com

[3] "Battered women who kill their batterers almost never understand that they have actually killed them, until they are informed by the police." (Walker 1989, 73).

[4] Senate Concurrent Resolution 26 (or SCR 26) applies to cases like Whitmire's where the abused woman has been convicted of killing her abuser but was not allowed to use evidence of her abuse as part of her plea of self-defense. In addition, Governor Ann Richards signed into law Senate Bill 275 that allows expert testimony on battered woman syndrome to be introduced at trial. In the future, women like Whitmire will be allowed to use their history of abuse and medical records as evidence. However, both Richards and Governor George Bush refused to grant clemency to any battered women convicted for murder in self-defense, despite regular requests by domestic violence advocates.

[5] Stacey Kabat, remarks from a presentation at Harvard School of Public Health, Center for Health Communication, June 1991, found at http://www.cybergrrl.com/views/dv/stat/statbwkill.html.

[6] "Battered Women and Criminal Justice: The Unjust Treatment of Battered Women in a System Controlled by Men, A Report of the Committee on Domestic Violence and Incarcerated Women," June 1987, pp. 3-4. From "Battered Women Who Kill," http://www.cybergrrl.com/views/dv/state/statbwkill.html.

[7] E-mail messages, Tuesday, March 14, 2000, from Larry Fitzgerald, Texas Department of Criminal Justice.

[8]E-mail message, Monday, March 13, 2000, from Lynn Schultz, Tennessee Department of Criminal Justice.

**Section Six: Regeneration**

[1] Angela Browne's discussion of the intergenerational transmission theory of violence points out that "while some studies of battered women do find a positive relationship between childhood exposure to violence and later victimization . . . other studies have not found this connection" (Browne 1987, 28–29). Browne points out that there is no simple explanation and that the intergenerational explanation fails to take into account the fact that most women abused as children do not become husband batterers or child abusers themselves. ■

# Bibliography

## Books

Breuer, Josef, and Sigmund Freud. *Studies in Hysteria*. Authorized trans. Intro. By A. A. Brill. Boston, MA: Beacon Press, 1950.

Browne, Angela. *When Battered Women Kill*. New York, NY: Free Press, 1987.

Brownmiller, Susan. *Against Our Will: Men, Women, and Rape*. New York, NY: Bantam, 1975.

Daly, Mary. Gyn/Ecology: *The Metaethics of Radical Feminism*. Boston, MA: Beacon Press, 1978.

Faludi, Susan. *Backlash: The Undeclared War against American Women*. New York, NY: Crown, 1991.

Griffin, Susan. *Pornography and Silence*. New York, NY: Harper & Row, 1981; London: Women's Press, 1988.

Heilbrun, Carolyn G. *Hamlet's Mother and Other Women*. New York, NY: Ballantine, 1990.

Hillman, James. *Healing Fiction*. Barrytown, NY: Station Hill Press, 1983.

Hinz, Evelyn J., ed. *Anaïs Nin: A Woman Speaks: The Lectures, Seminars and Interviews of Anaïs Nin*. Chicago, IL: The Swallow Press, 1975.

Jelinek, Estelle C. *Women's Autobiography: Essays in Criticism*. Bloomington: Indiana University Press, 1980.

Jones, Ann. *Women Who Kill*. New York, NY: Fawcett, 1980, 1982.

Kelly, Liz. *Surviving Sexual Violence*. Minneapolis: University of Minnesota Press, 1988.

Russell, Diana. E. H. *Rape in Marriage*. New York, NY: Macmillan, 1982.

Scully, Diana. *Understanding Sexual Violence: A Study of Convicted Rapists*. Cambridge, MA: Unwin Hyman, Inc., 1990.

Spender, Dale. *Man Made Language*. Boston, MA: Routledge & Kegan Paul, 1980.

Walker, Alice. *Horses Make the Landscape Look More Beautiful*. New York, NY: Harcourt Brace Jovanovich, 1985.

Walker, Lenore. *Terrifying Love: Why Battered Women Kill and How Society Responds*. New York, NY: Harper & Row, 1989.

**ARTICLES**

Armstrong, Louise. "The Personal is Apolitical," *Women's Review of Books*, VII, No. 6, March 1990, pp. 1–4.

"'Dad has had me like a prisoner,' slain wife wrote," *Dallas Morning News*, 4 January 1988, Section A, p. 1 ff.

*Double-Time: Newsletter of the National Clearinghouse for the Defense of Battered Women*, (125 S. 9th Street, #3-2, Philadelphia, PA 19107. 215/351-0010) 1, No. 1, Oct. 1991.

Herndl, Diane Price. "The Writing Cure: Charlotte Perkins Gilman, Anna O. and 'Hysterical' Writing,'" *National Women's Studies Association Journal*, 1, No. 1, Autumn 1988.

Simmons, Bill. "Mass killer is executed in Arkansas," *Dallas Morning News*, 26 June 1990, Section A, p. 18.

Strebeigh, Fred. "Defining Law on the Feminist Frontier." *The New York Times Magazine*, 6 October 1991, pp. 29 ff.

Teitelbaum, Ashley. "Shedding Light on the Prevalence of Marital Rape," *Hotlines* (publication of the National Domestic Violence Hotline), ■

# Suggested Readings


Angelou, Maya. *I Know Why The Caged Bird Sings*. New York, NY: Random House, 1969.

Bart, Pauline, and Patricia H. O'Brien. *Stopping Rape: Successful Survival Strategies*. New York, NY: Pergamon Press, 1985.

Bass, Ellen, and Laura Davis. *The Courage to Heal: A Guide for Women Survivors of Child Sexual Abuse*. New York, NY: Harper & Row, 1988.

Beattie, L. Elisabethe and Mary Angela Shaughnessy. *Sisters in Pain: Battered Women Fight Back*. Lexington, KY: University of Kentucky Press, 2000.

Beauvoir, Simone de. *The Second Sex*. Translated by H.M. Parshley. 1953, rpt. New York, NY: Vintage, 1974.

Belenky, Mary F., et al. *Women's Ways of Knowing: The Development of Self, Voice and Mind*. New York, NY: Basic Books, 1986.

Bolen, Jean Shinoda. *Goddesses In Everywoman: A New Psychology of Women*. New York, NY: Harper & Row, 1985)

Chernin, Kim. *Reinventing Eve: Modern Woman in Search of Herself*. New York, NY: Harper & Row, 1987.

Daly, Mary. *Gyn/Ecology: The Metaethics of Radical Feminism*. Boston, MA: Beacon Press, 1978.

Danica, Elly. *Don't: A Woman's Word*. San Francisco, CA: Cleis Press, 1988.

Delacoste, Frédérique, and Felice Newman. *Fight Back: Feminist Resistance to Male Violence*. San Francisco, CA: Cleis Press, 1981.

Deschner, Jeanne P. *The Hitting Habit: Anger Control for Battering Couples*. New York, NY: Free Press, 1984.

Du Bois, Page. *Sowing the Body: Psychoanalysis and Ancient Representation*. Chicago, IL: University of Chicago Press, 1988.

Du Pleiss, Rachel Blau. *Writing Beyond the Ending: Narrative Strategies of Twentieth-Century Women Writers*. Bloomington, IN: Indiana University Press, 1988.

Faludi, Susan. Backlash: *The Undeclared War against American Women*. New York, NY: Crown, 1991.

Fedders, Charlotte. *Shattered Dreams*. New York, NY: Dell, 1987.

Francisco, Patricia Weaver. *Telling: A Memoir of Rape and Recovery*. New York, NY: HarperCollins, 1999.

Fraser, Nancy. *Unruly Practices: Power, Discourse and Gender in Contemporary Social Theory*. Minneapolis, MN: University of Minnesota Press, 1989.

Gondolf, Edward W. and Ellen R. Fisher. *Battered Women as Survivors: An Alternative To Treating Learned Helplessness*. Lexington, MA: Lexington Books, 1988.

Griffin, Susan. *Woman and Nature: The Roaring Inside Her*. New York, NY: Harper & Row, 1978.

Heilbrun, Carolyn G. *Reinventing Womanhood*. New York, NY: W.W. Norton, 1979.

————— *Writing A Woman's Life*. New York: W.W. Norton, 1988.

Howe, Florence, and Ellen Bass. *No More Masks: An Anthology of Poems by Women*. Garden City, New York, NY: Doubleday, 1973.

Jelinek, Estelle C. *The Tradition of Women's Autobiography: From Antiquity to the Present*. Boston, MA: Twayne Publishers (G.K. Hall), 1986.

Kaye/Kantrowitz, Melanie. *My Jewish Face & Other Stories*. San Francisco, CA: Spinsters/Aunt Lute Book Company, 1990.

Klein, Bonnie Sherr, director. *Not A Love Story: A Film about Pornography*. Toronto, Ontario: National Film Board, 1981.

Ledray, Linda E. *Recovering from Rape*. New York, NY: Henry Holt, 1986, rpt. 1994.

Levy, Barrie, M.S.W. Dating Violence: Young Women in Danger. Seattle, WA: Seal Press, 1991.

Lourde, Audre. *From a Land Where Other People Live*. Detroit, MI: Broadside Press, 1973.

Martin, Del. *Battered Wives*. New York, NY: Pocket Books, 1983, 1977.

McNaron, Toni A. H., and Yarrow Morgan, eds. *Voices in the Night: Women Speaking About Incest*. San Francisco, CA: Cleis Press, 1982.

Nicarthy, Ginny. *Getting Free*. Seattle, WA: Seal Press, 1982.

______. The Ones *Who Got Away: Women Who Left Abusive Partners*. Seattle, WA: Seal Press, 1987.

Olsen, Tillie. *Silences*. New York, NY: Delacorte, 1978; Bantam Doubleday Dell, 1989.

Payne, Karen, ed. *Between Ourselves: Letters Between Mothers & Daughters, 1750-1982*. Boston, MA: Houghton Mifflin, 1983.

Pearson, Carol S. *The Hero Within: Six Archetypes We Live By*. New York, NY: Harper & Row, 1989.

Piercy, Marge. *To Be Of Use*. New York, NY: Doubleday, 1973.

Pizzy, Erin. *Scream Quietly or the Neighbors Will Hear*. London, England: Penguin, 1974.

Rubin, Lillian B. *Intimate Strangers: Men and Women Together*. New York, NY: Harper and Row, 1983.

Russell, Diana. *Against Pornography: the Evidence of Harm*. Berkeley, CA: Russell Publications, 1994.

Schechter, Susan. *Women and Male Violence*. Boston, MA: South End Press, 1982.

Scheffler, Judith A., ed. *Wall Tappings: An Anthology of Writings by Women Prisoners*. Boston, MA: Northeastern University Press, 1986.

Sonkin, Daniel Jay, Del Martin, and Lenore Walker. *The Male Batterer: A Treatment Approach*. New York, NY: Springer, 1985.

Spender, Dale. *Man Made Language*. Boston, MA: Routledge & Kegan Paul, 1980.

Stacey, William A., and Anson Shupe. *The Family Secret*. Boston, MA: Beacon, 1983.

Stacey, William A., Anson Shupe and Lonnie R. Hazelwood. *Violent Men, Violent Couples: The Dynamics of Domestic Violence*. Lexington, MA: Lexington Books, 1987.

Walker, Lenore. *The Battered Woman*. New York, NY: Harper and Row, 1979.

______. *The Battered Woman Syndrome*. New York, NY: Springer, 1984.

Walker, Alice. *Horses Make the Landscape Look More Beautiful*. New York, NY: Harcourt Brace Jovanovich, 1985.

Warshaw, Robin. *I Never Called It Rape: The Ms. Report On Recognizing, Fighting and Surviving Date and Acquaintance Rape*. New York, NY: Harper & Row, 1988.

Washbourn, Penelope. *Becoming Woman: The Quest for Wholeness in Female Experiernce.* San Francisco, CA: Harper & Row, 1977.

Yllö, Kersti and Michele Bograd, eds. *Feminist Perspectives on Wife Abuse.* Thousand Oaks, C: Sage Publications, 1988. ■

## About the Editor

Miriam Kalman Harris, Ph.D. is Associate Professor of English at Tarrant County College, South Campus in Fort Worth, Texas. In 1993, Syracuse University Press published Harris' edition of Claire Myers Owens' 1935 fantasy novel, *The Unpredictable Adventure* with her afterword and glossary. She has completed a biography of Owens and is at work on a novel.

Harris lives in Dallas with her family. ■